The Lesbian Index

SUNY series in Feminist Criticism and Theory
Michelle A. Massé, editor

The Lesbian Index

Pragmatism and Lesbian Subjectivity in the Twentieth-Century United States

Kim Emery

State University of New York Press

Published by
State University of New York Press, Albany

Printed in the United States of America

For information, address State University of New York Press,
90 State Street, Suite 700, Albany, NY, 12207

Production by Christine L. Hamel
Marketing by Jennifer Giovani

Library of Congress Cataloging-in-Publication Data

Emery, Kim, 1964-
The lesbian index : pragmatism and lesbian subjectivity in the twentieth-century United States / by Kim Emery.
p. cm. — (SUNY series in feminist criticism and theory)
Includes bibliographical references and index.
ISBN 0791452239 — ISBN 0791452247 (pbk.)
1. Lesbianism—United States—History—20th century. I. Title. II. Series.

HQ75.6.US E47 2002
306.76'63'09730904—dc21 2001041149
CIP

10 9 8 7 6 5 4 3 2 1

Contents

To Kathryn

Acknowledgments

Financial support significant to the completion of this project was provided by the Division of Sponsored Research, the Humanities Scholarship Enhancement Fund, and the English Department of the University of Florida. The primary research that informs chapters 2 and 3 was conducted at the Center for American History and the Harry Ransom Humanities Research Center, both at the University of Texas at Austin. I'm grateful for the permission to cite materials housed there as well as for the assistance provided by staff at both centers.

Many colleagues and friends have provided helpful commentary on parts of this project, including Malini Schueller, Elizabeth Langland, David Leverenz, Maureen Turim, Marsha Bryant, Pat Schmidt, Pat Craddock, Pamela Gilbert, Anne Goodwyn Jones, Manuel Vasquez, Anna Peterson, Hernan Vera, Louise Newman, Alistair Duckworth, and Danaya Wright. Phil Wegner, Susan Hegeman, and Amitava Kumar have offered professional guidance, practical assistance, and personal support, time and again. I am also grateful to those mentors whose insights helped shape the dissertation from which this book was developed, in particular the members of my Ph.D. committee at the University of Texas: co-chairs Evan Carton and Lisa Moore, and readers Ann Cvetkovich, Lora Romero, Keith Walters, and Marjorie Woods.

Deborah Wilson and two anonymous readers for SUNY Press offered careful readings of an earlier draft that helped me make this a much stronger book. I'm also enormously grateful to James Peltz for his consistently kind and consummately professional handling of the project, to Katy Leonard for her assistance at various points along the way, and to Christine Hamel for her expert oversight of the production process.

I wish to thank all of the above, and remain particularly indebted to Lisa Moore, without whom this project would not have begun, and to Pamela Gilbert, without whom it would not have been successfully concluded.

Finally, a few less conventional acknowledgments. I'm grateful to Lillian Faderman (who likely does not remember me) for affirming my faith in feminism: some years ago, she organized a series of MLA panels for which a graduate-school paper of mine was selected, and then recommended my work to the editors of the *Journal of the History of Sexuality*—who solicited the article on which the second chapter of this book is based. I want to recognize her here for her helpful interest in the career of an anonymous grad student. Secondly, I'm grateful to Kathryn Baker for reaffirming my faith in most everything else; it hasn't always been easy, I know. I want to thank Linda S. for taking me to "the bar" for the very first time, and also the women who were there, especially Waggs. I've been lucky to live in a lot of places with strong lesbian communities and am deeply indebted to the women who built them. I'd like to thank, in particular, my friends from Northampton; the Yam Queens, fans, and fellow travelers of Austin, Texas; and the women of Lavender Menace and Wild Iris Books in Gainesville, Florida. And finally, I need to say that for a long time I did not think I would finish this book in time to get tenure. That this outcome was averted reflects the intercession of many people to whom I am very grateful: in particular, I want to thank my parents, Guy and Marilyn Emery, for both the financial assistance that bought me the time to finish the manuscript and the emotional and intellectual support and encouragement that they've always provided. I'm also grateful to my department chair, John Leavey, and my union, United Faculty of Florida. The stress of trying to keep the job for which I had spent most of my adult life preparing underlined the entire process of producing this book—and I almost didn't make it, despite the considerable material and institutional resources at my disposal. I think it's important to note that my difficulty can be attributed only in part to the predictable professional and personal challenges experienced by almost everyone; it also had something to do with the legal and economic discrimination directed against lesbians in a heterosexist society. The thesis of this book—that lesbian subjectivity cannot be adequately theorized in isolation from the material contexts of its production—resonates anew in the context of this experience.

Introduction

Consider this your guide to lesbian pragmatism in the twentieth-century United States. Like *Gaia*, *Damron*, or the *Gay Yellow Pages*, it points you towards specific locations likely to host the sort of scene you're looking for. No guarantees, of course. Everyone knows that a club's clientele can change faster than any publication could hope to keep up with; that queer bars close, move, and change ownership like some grrls change hairstyles; that there's always some chance of meeting up with the stray lesbian-feminist at a men's leather bar. The sites of queer culture are neither homogenous nor stable. Like signs more generally, they are approximate; their meanings are shifting, always under negotiation. Hence the reliable market for updated editions. Hence, too, the big problem with this metaphor: *Gaia's Guide* and others like it are organized around a structuralist conceit—they attend to neither the material specificity nor the temporal dimension of the reality that they purport to describe. The representation of queer cultures that they offer—useful as it is—is an atemporal abstraction, a system of understanding unattached to actual time and actual space. *The Lesbian Index* is not this kind of guide, nor is it only—or even primarily—for or about lesbians.

What it offers instead is an attempt to localize and historicize certain products and processes of knowledge production particular to the twentieth-century United States; in particular, to more fully integrate consideration of context into a theory of performativity. I focus on constructions of lesbian subjectivity both because I'm interested in lesbians and because this focus provides as good a perspective as any for the project, and (as I will argue) perhaps a better perspective than most. So while this book is certainly about lesbians in a crucial sense, it's also about semiotics, historiography, and, especially, twentieth-century U.S. culture. Similarly, I'm not so much interested in making academic theory accessible to a broader lesbian audience than in bringing a lesbian perspective to bear on theoretical discussions within the academy. I'm wary of the "trickle-down" notion of political relevance, the assumption that lesbians outside the academy constitute an acritical community desperately in need of academicians' sophisticated insights. Instead, I want to invert the attribution of authority implicit in this understanding, to see what academic theory might learn from lesbian experience.

The notion of "experience," of course, has been much troubled of late. Joan Scott's 1991 article conclusively deauthorized appeals to "experience" as "incontestable evidence," an "originary point of explanation," or a "foundation on which analysis [may be] based."[1] Such appeals, Scott warned, tend to "take as self-evident the identities of those whose experience is being documented and thus naturalize their difference," with the result that "questions about the constructed nature of experience, about how subjects are constituted as different in the first place, about how one's vision is structured—about language (or discourse) and history—are left aside."[2] Hence, "we now know," says Sue-Ellen Case, that "as constitutive a role as they may play, experience and memory cannot claim much real empirical power."[3] The alternatives, however—for example, the deconstructions of "identity" and "experience" offered in Scott and Judith Butler's edited volume *Feminists Theorize the Political*—left many feminists and lesbians somewhat disconcerted. "There appears to be a belief," Scott and Butler lament, "that without an ontologically grounded feminist subject there can be no politics."[4] Perhaps. Paradoxically, however, Scott turns to Teresa de Lauretis's "redefinition of experience" in *Alice Doesn't* to ground her own critique of history's "foundationalist discourse." De Lauretis "exposes the workings of this ideology," Scott explains, by describing a process whose effect is "to constitute subjects as fixed and autonomous, and who are considered reliable sources of knowledge that comes from access to the real by means of their experience."[5] That process, Scott neglects to mention, is semiosis—"the general process of sign and meaning formation, a process which articulates and enjoins subjectivity to social signification and material reality."[6] And de Lauretis' account of "experience" is less a redefinition than a reclaiming of an understanding that pragmatism has offered all along. Consider the passage that Scott quotes:

> Experience is the process by which, for all social beings, subjectivity is constructed. Through that process one places oneself or is placed in social reality and so perceives or comprehends as subjective (referring to, originating in oneself) those relations—material, economic, and interpersonal—which are in fact social, and, in a larger perspective, historical.[7]

This is to say that pragmatism understands semiosis to constitute subjects—but *not* as "fixed" or (actually) "autonomous." More to the point, pragmatism makes a principle of fallibility, while also recognizing subjects as sources of knowledge; notably, this knowledge is understood to derive from (mediated) access to a real that is itself a constellation of effects sustained by and within ongoing processes of signification. In the end, interestingly, Scott herself concedes that "given the ubiquity of the term [experience]," it seems impractical "to abandon it altogether" and "more useful to work with it, to analyze its operations and to redefine its meaning"; she advocates "focusing on processes of identity production, insisting on the discursive nature of 'experience' and on the politics of its construction."[8] Rather than discount "the evidence of experience," I conclude, we would do well to attend more closely to precisely that sort of "experience" denoted in the conception that de Lauretis derives from semiotician C.S. Peirce.[9]

"Why is Peirce's assertion of the constitutive power of thought better than a similar claim for language by some literary theorists"—and poststructuralist historians? "The answer," says James Hoopes, is that "the literary theorists derive their semiotic from French linguists [like Saussure]," even though "verbal language is far too narrow a field from which to construct a general theory of signs."[10] Indeed, the notion of "discourse" derived from Saussure not only presumes a purely arbitrary relation between signified and signifier, as Hoopes points out, but does so, and can only do so, because it is a specifically *structuralist* conception, analytically detached from time and space; it has no hold on materiality, no connection, and, indeed, no material existence itself. Hence, Scott's quite reasonable concern about "language (or discourse) and history" evokes without addressing the "essential discontinuity" glossed over by her grammatical conjunction of its terms.[11] I suspect that the unease with which such poststructuralist political theorizing has been met has as much to do with its continued entanglements with structuralist and hence ahistorical understandings of "discourse" as with its detractors' philosophical or theoretical naiveté. One way out, as de Lauretis' work has consistently suggested, is to pursue the implications of a more pragmatic semiotic.

In the millennial issue of *GLQ*, David Halperin refines his famous question—"Is There a History of Sexuality?"—to insist that the task now before us is "to inquire more closely into the modalities of historical being that sexuality possesses: to ask exactly—in what terms, by virtue of what temporality, in which of its dimensions or aspects—sexuality does have a history."[12] One answer is implicit, if not in *Alice Doesn't*, then certainly in the pragmatic conception of "sexual structuring"[13] that de Lauretis proposes in 1994's *The Practice of Love*: sexuality understood as an instance of semiosis would be thoroughly historical in the sense that its appearance would be conditioned by signs, themselves contingent on both the historical circumstances of their intelligibility and the material circumstances of their perceptibility.

Whereas structuralist understandings set semantic categories in relation to other concepts of the same order (other identity categories, for example), the semiotic theories drawn from pragmatism also attend to relations across and between orders. They enable consideration not simply of difference, but of processes of differentiation—of continuity, of contingency, of cause and effect. The idea of "indexicality" is at the crux of such considerations. Peirce, the theoretician of pragmatism, suggested that signification is not a uniform and unitary process, but a generic relation that might draw in different degrees on at least three distinct modes; these he termed "iconic," "symbolic," and "indexical." The terms refer to the character of the connection between the sign and the thing that it signifies. Iconicity indicates a relation of resemblance: a traditional portrait, many hieroglyphs, the stick figures (with and without skirt) that adorn restroom doors all draw to a significant degree on this mode. The symbolic mode, in contrast, emphasizes the arbitrary or conventional dimension of sign relations: Arabic numerals, the hexagonal shape of stop signs, the fact that money is green (in this country) are examples in which the symbolic seems pre-eminent. Indexicality, however, turns on an "actual," "dynamical," "real," or "physical" connection between the sign and its object.[14] The classic examples include the use of a weathervane to signal wind direction, the inference of fire from the evidence of smoke, the existence of a footprint indicating the prior presence of a person. But the relation need not be one of cause. "Index" means to locate, as in space and time; it means to situate, relationally.[15] Etymologically, it means *to point* (hence, "index finger"). The gesture of pointing is the classic indexical move, and it's a relation defined by contingency: meaning depends on the temporal, spatial, or even figurative locations of the speaker, the object, and the person or people addressed. In the absence of context, you can't know what I mean by "that chair"; if we were in the same room, you might determine which chair I mean by discerning the direction that I was looking or pointing. "Yesterday," "today," and "tomorrow" are heavily indexical expressions; so are "here" and "there," as well as "we," "they," and "you."

Indexicality marks the intersection of the historical world with the conceptual one. Hence, it's a concept we can't do without if we hope to come to grips with the "making" of a sexual identity or any of the other categories we rely on to organize experience. (It's also an idea that structuralist approaches are utterly incapable of engaging.) So one contribution that *The Lesbian Index* hopes to make is the introduction of this concept of indexicality as a theoretical tool useful in tracing the development of lesbian existence and lesbian experience. But the connection runs both ways. As an identity category that has been insistently, often bitterly, and very publicly contested, "lesbian" may present a more readily accessible example than most of the ways in which meaning may be socially negotiated. It is a "category of analysis" that can hardly be understood as anything other than "contextual, contested, and contingent"—and hence lends itself to the kind of historical examination that Scott advocates: "*not* the reproduction and transmission of knowledge said to be arrived at by experience, but the analysis of the production of that knowledge itself." Reconceiving the work of historians, Scott recommends "denying the fixity and transcendence of anything that appears to operate as a foundation, turning attention instead to the history of foundationalist concepts themselves."[16] Of course, this is precisely the perspective of Peirce's pragmatic semiotic, an antifoundationalist philosophy of meaning that has been with us for over a century, to the profound disinterest of most professional historians.[17] It is also—and not merely coincidentally, I contend—a perspective that implicitly animates much important work in lesbian and gay studies, including much that has sometimes been dismissed in recent years as essentialist, atheoretical, simplistic, or naive.[18]

In an important but increasingly overlooked essay called "To Be and Be Seen," lesbian-feminist philosopher Marilyn Frye develops the allegory of a stage play to illuminate the centrality of questions of attention to the history of foundationalist concepts: the play is called "reality"; men are the actors and women are the stagehands.[19] For the illusion to sustain itself, "all eyes, all attention, all attachment must be focused on the play" and its actors; "any notice of the stagehands must be oblique and filtered through interest in the play." There is no place for lesbians in this schema—not as actors, not as stagehands, not even in the audience; there is no place for anyone "for whom the background is eventful, dramatic, compelling—whose attention focuses on the stagehands and their projects."[20] Frye's point is the conceptual impossibility of lesbians within the dominant ontological schema; my interest here is in her allegorical illumination of those processes that sustain the apparent fixity and transcendence of foundationalist premises, in her reorientation of *our* attention to their operation.

Indeed, Scott's interest in "changing the focus and the philosophy of *our* history" turns on the indexical presumptions of that "our"; Scott's words gesture outward toward the world, but we can also read back the other way, toward what they tell us about the frame from which she speaks. When she says "our history," she means history as an academic discipline; "we" must be professional historians. Lisa Duggan, however, points out that lesbian and gay researchers, many of them independent scholars, had been "historicizing and denaturalizing categories of sexual identity" for more than a decade when Scott's article first appeared. More to the point, Duggan credits Jeffrey Weeks, John D'Emilio, and Jonathan Ned Katz, among others, for advancing an understanding that Scott characterizes as impossible when she writes that "the project of making experience visible *precludes* critical examination of the workings of the ideological system itself, its categories or representation," etc.[21] Their efforts have often been ignored, and other times, mischaracterized, but since at least the late 1970s, queer historians have worked "to make the historical 'experience' of lesbians and gay men 'visible' *at the same time* that categories of identity are presented as historical, contingent and political—as products of changing and contested systems of representation."[22] I will go so far as to suggest that one aspect of the historical experience of queer subjectivity in the United States today is a perspective oriented towards consideration of contingency, complexity, and historicity. Indeed, I'll go further: I suspect that lesbians in particular may be advantageously positioned to perceive "the changing and contested systems of representation" at work in contemporary U.S. culture—not simply the fact of their contingency, but the actual processes of permutation. Frye follows through on the implications of her allegory to suggest that "becoming a lesbian is a reorientation of attention in a kind of ontological conversion"—a conversion, I contend, *from* the dominant perspective implicated in Scott's "our" and *to* precisely the historically visible and yet antifoundationalist perspective that Scott's poststructuralist framework would seem to preclude[23]—a conversion to pragmatism.

The connection is more than coincidental—although it is that, as well. Modern lesbian subjectivity emerged in the late nineteenth-century United States just as the characteristically "American" theory of meaning production called "pragmatism" was coalescing. At the core of the pragmatist project stood Peirce's understanding of semiosis (the making of meaning) as itself local, variable, changing—not an abstract set of principles, but a socially negotiated (and hence always imperfectly coherent) conglomeration of what Peirce would term "habits."[24] His work provided the theoretical underpinnings of the nation's most significant philosophical movement and arguably the only epistemological tendency truly indigenous to the United States. Because the modern lesbian is perhaps the paradigmatic subject of pragmatism, studying Peirce's theories can help us to think more productively about the history and meaning of female homosexuality in this country. Equally, however, a look at the history of lesbian subjectivity reveals a great deal about the nation's semiotic heritage and ideological development. *The Lesbian Index* not only delineates specific ways in which the meaning of lesbianism has (and hasn't) changed over the course of the past century, but also suggests the extent to which the representation of female homosexuality may serve as index to a whole system of meaning-making crucial to the constitution of twentieth-century U.S. culture.

Judith Halberstam concedes that "Foucault's history of sexuality seems far more pertinent for a history of male sexuality than a history of desiring female bodies," only to conclude that "we can certainly borrow liberally from his methodology."[25] For her project—which reaches back to the eighteenth century and over to Britain and Europe to "to produce more specific details about the forms female masculinity has taken"—this makes a certain amount of sense. But for many reasons, pragmatism provides a methodology more pertinent to my project of examining the negotiation of lesbian meanings in the twentieth-century United States. Chapter 1 of this volume, "Fantasies of Origin," advances this argument in more or less conventionally theoretical terms. Drawing on diverse examples of work in lesbian studies, I re-examine the oft-cited conflict between historical—and presumably (therefore?) foundationalist—work, and anti-foundationalist—and presumably (therefore?) ahistorical—work. The sharpness with which this distinction is often drawn relies on reductive readings of works on both sides, and also ignores the productive tension created and sustained by the division itself. In her brief conclusion to *The Practice of Love*, de Lauretis provocatively positions Peirce's notion of the "habit change" as a sort of bridge between Freudian understandings of intrapsychic processes and Foucault's broad sociohistorical insights. Here, however, I put Peirce into conversation with Butler to focus more precisely on the ways in which his semiotic theories mediate not between the individual and the group[26], but between the conceptual and the material.

The very conventionality of this theoretical first chapter, however, threatens to obscure the point I'm trying to make: the concepts "lesbian" and "indexicality" are mutually illuminating because their conjunction is not arbitrary but informed by contingency. Chapter 2 thus returns to the contexts of their coimplication in a particular time and place. Here I describe the concurrent emergence of self-consciously pragmatist philosophies and specifically lesbian subjects in the late nineteenth-century United States, exploring their common genesis in evolutionary theories and their complex engagements with rhetorics of U.S. imperialism and Anglo-American racism. Structured around a reading of the 1895 novel *Norma Trist; or, Pure Carbon: A Story of the Inversion of the Sexes*, this chapter traces the emergence of the essentialist/constructivist controversy in the distinction between "acquired" and "congenital" "inversion" drawn by late nineteenth-century sexologists in both Europe and the United States. Charting the engagements of this novel with specifically "American" investments and ideologies, I argue that *Norma Trist* participated in a larger cultural movement to reinterpret and indeed remake "the lesbian" in peculiarly U.S. terms. Reimagined within a pragmatic semiotic, lesbian subjectivity came to represent a point of resistance to classical philosophies of language and the political ideologies they served to naturalize.

Not surprisingly, this resistant lesbian subject remained a point of contention, and efforts to reinterpret female homosexuality in less unsettling terms continued throughout the twentieth century. Chapter 3 looks at an especially visible and influential instance of this ongoing struggle for control over interpretation—of female homosexuality and of the core American meanings to which the figure of the lesbian came to serve as index. This chapter reads Radclyffe Hall's *The Well of Loneliness* through the context of its introduction to the United States: the history of its publication here, the *New York Times* coverage of the British obscenity trial, and, especially, the novel's successful struggle against censorship in U.S. courts. A pragmatic look at *The Well*'s U.S. reception reveals the extent to which its meaning here was shaped by the litigious circumstances of its introduction, and how, in turn, debates specific to 1920s U.S. jurisprudence left their mark on lesbian politics and personal experience in the latter part of the century.

Reading *The Well* in context, this chapter briefly reviews Pragmatism's influence on legal thinking in the early years of this century; its challenge, in the form of "progressive jurisprudence," to the foundationalist philosophy of Classical Legal Theory; and its quick co-optation by the increasingly positivistic tendencies of "legal realism." I consider the *Well of Loneliness* case in relation to the era's most notorious criminal proceedings, the trials of Sacco and Vanzetti, and conclude that, in tandem, they suggest a sea change in legal reasoning, as the "individual" possessor of "rights" was arbitrarily alienated from the network of semiosic relations that sustains subjectivity. This abstraction had deadly consequences for Sacco and Vanzetti, and has also proven problematic for lesbians. Ironically, the well-meaning judges who saved *The Well* from censorship simultaneously locked the novel into an effectively foundationalist logic. In predicating their protection of free expression on an essentialist understanding of lesbian possibility as an isolable, innate, individual trait fundamentally unrelated to social conditions and historical circumstance, the "progressive" jurists on the Court of Special Sessions conceptually severed lesbian subjectivity from the contexts that shaped its meaning. Hence, *The Well* remains a touchstone text not simply because it resonates with deeply held cultural assumptions (about gender, race, representation, and shame, as well as about female homosexuality *per se*), but because its encounter with the shifting discourses of U.S. jurisprudence actually changed the shape of lesbian possibility. Dynamically involved in that transformation, *The Well* became an enduring index to the deeply bifurcated conception of lesbianism that emerged and persists: the privileged public image of an isolated and obvious "freak of nature," and its shadowy underside—the amorphous threat of more pervasive possibility.

This "radical incoherence" within the logic of lesbian subjectivity thus serves as a particularly salient example of a logical contradiction that Eve Sedgwick sees at the core of modern discourses of (homo)sexuality: a conception which "holds the minoritizing view that there is a distinct population of persons who 'really are' gay," but also "the universalizing views that sexual desire is an unpredictably powerful solvent of stable identities; that apparently heterosexual persons and object choices are strongly marked by same-sex influences and desire."[27] Apparently paranoid about the potential instability of the minoritizing model legitimated by *The Well*'s obscenity trial, mid-century mass culture both relied on and repressed the latter threat. Chapter 4 explores the culture's continuing unease with this logical incoherence through the lens of Mary McCarthy's 1963 bestseller, *The Group*, which I argue both enacts and critiques the obsessive cycle of evocation and disavowal. The centrality of lesbian possibility to the construction and sustenance of normative heterosexual femininity—in the novel and in the surrounding culture—suggests an anxiety attached to the contemporary fascination with buried truths and hidden meanings, an anxiety that McCarthy exposes, I contend, through self-conscious engagement with contemporary semiotic debates. Drawing from sources as diverse as Noam Chomsky and J. Edgar Hoover, I argue that a certain obsession with convoluted but ultimately foundationalist explanations was not an isolated oddity but a central (indeed, a characteristic) element of early 1960s culture. Although the public negotiation of this anxiety can be seen to open unprecedented opportunities for the reconfiguration of lesbian possibility, this promise goes largely unrealized. McCarthy's novel serves as a case in point, indicating the plausibility of a pragmatic alternative, but unable to articulate its particulars. As Biddy Martin contends, efforts to reconceive identity within an anti-essentialist logic are productive "only as long as the body, the material, is conceived as a drag or limit as well as a potential."[28] In the end, McCarthy's project founders on the impossibility of *discursively* reconciling lesbianism's metaphorical and material dimensions. Caught between the essentialist foundationalism of minoritizing models and the formalist foundationalism of universalizing understandings, *The Group* can only document without displacing the operations of the dominant logic.

Chapter 5 discusses some of the ways in which the opportunities for pragmatic intervention identified in Chapter 4 were further constrained. Recognizing *Rubyfruit Jungle* as a feminist rewriting of *The Well*, I argue that Rita Mae Brown's emphasis on her protagonist's illegitimate birth serves as a strategic disavowal of the earlier text's focus on sexual "inversion." Because Brown rejects restrictive sex-role stereotypes, she cannot rely on images of gender transgression to index homosexuality. Unfortunately, her novel exploits the analogical association of lesbianism with racial difference instead, promoting its putatively feminist agenda by evoking the racist evolutionism of nineteenth-century sexology (explored in novels like *Norma Trist*). Perhaps because it cannot afford to recognize such problematic connections, *Rubyfruit* circumscribes a rigidly self-contained context of colorblind disavowal, refusing to recognize its participation in a web of discourses reaching beyond its own covers, beyond its own moment in time.

Despite its author's significant political activism, then, cultural context is effectively erased in *Rubyfruit Jungle*, grafted root and branch onto a lesbian subjectivity forced to stand metonymically for organized efforts to promote social change. If Brown assumed connections between lesbianism and other vectors of political struggle to be organic or simply obvious, her failure to elaborate enabled superficial substitution of the one for the many. As radical feminist analysis was reduced in the public mind to demands for equal rights on the one hand and calls for cultural separatism on the other, *Rubyfruit*'s frame of reference shrank to debilitating dimensions. In retrospect, it is extraordinarily difficult to read Brown's novel as anything other than the essentialist and effectively antifeminist aggrandizement of American individualism that critics like Bonnie Zimmerman claim it to be. Reinscribing relevant historical context, however, this chapter restores *Rubyfruit Jungle* to a wider frame of reference—and reveals its foundationalism as historically structured. Read as an index to the tensions of 1970s feminism, rather than an attempt to resolve them, *Rubyfruit*'s essentialism is exposed as an historical effect, a contingent foundation indexically connected to a matrix of meanings arrayed across time and space.

In simply directing attention to these popular novels, *The Lesbian Index* breaks no new ground. The first known novel with a lesbian protagonist published in the United States, the twentieth century's most famous fictional representation of female homosexuality, a best-selling novel of American womanhood by the nation's foremost female literary figure, lesbian-feminism's breakout crossover success—these are obvious choices to initiate an exploration of the meanings of lesbianism in the United States.[29] But I intend more than a literary history of lesbian possibility, proposing instead that in its engagement with cultural understandings and socio-political contexts each novel can be seen to provide a kind of case study in the efficacy of performativity as intervention. In many of my examples, I contend, its limitations are illuminated. *The Group* and *Rubyfruit Jungle*, for instance, exemplify distinct, but ultimately flawed strategies of engagement with the minoritizing, essentialist conception of lesbian subjectivity that emerged in the course of *The Well*'s obscenity trial: *Rubyfruit Jungle* falls prey to the trap of re-essentializing one set of assumptions in an effort to unseat another, whereas *The Group* cannot finally authorize a lesbian perspective—any claim to material specificity remains subsumed within the lesbian's metaphorical function in the (hetero)normative narrative.

By directing attention to books' actual engagements with historically specific sites and circumstances, *The Lesbian Index* also seeks to examine the explanatory power of a more pragmatic understanding of lesbian subjectivity, and ultimately to argue that restoring performativity to the indexical parameters that condition its exercise may be seen to provide a more descriptively accurate and politically enabling theoretical context. Employing an experimentalist's test of plausibility adapted from Peirce, this study juxtaposes pragmatic interpretations of the novels' encounters with contemporary conceptual contexts against what we presume to already know about shifting conceptions of lesbian identity over the course of the twentieth century in the United States, and concludes that the readings it produces appear more compatible with other knowledge than most other accounts of these books and their influence. It would be a mistake, of course, to think that attending to historical context could erase the indexical weight of our own messy situatedness; my interest, however, is not in some putatively "pure" understanding of particular pasts, but in the inescapably adulterated significance of those pasts in a material present.

To this end, Chapter 6 shifts the focus from the mainstream to the margins, reading Sarah Schulman's liminal *Girls, Visions and Everything* (Seal Press, 1986) as testament to the persistence of a politically progressive lesbian subjectivity conceived within a pragmatic semiotic. As lesbian social realism, Schulman's novel refuses both the paralyzing abstractions of academic queer theory and the isolating particularity of lesbian history, proving that the mediating specification of "lesbian" and "cultural" in Laura Doan's formulation of "postmodern theory" need not narrow the reach of the project, but can in fact enable and extend it.[30] Despite the insistent dichotomization historically directed at lesbian experience, lesbians have persisted in a subtle subcultural understanding that refuses to invalidate our hard-won sense of *lesbian agency* by the negation of either of its terms, insisting instead that it is neither inauthentic (not really lesbian) nor inevitable (not really agency). This is the truth that Schulman's novel affirms, and the perspective from which it is narrated. Fittingly, it is a contingent truth, self-evident only from its own pragmatic perspective.

In this sense, Schulman's novel compares favorably to some recent work in academic queer theory—work which often struggles to reconcile its conceptual recognition of historical contingency with the universalizing abstractions of its own practice. Taking Butler's *Bodies That Matter* as a case in point, this chapter argues that queer theory has tended to rely on a narrow interpretation of performativity as act abstracted from circumstance.[31] Pragmatism, in contrast, situates the relation between referent and sign within a specific material context—and, hence, within history. This is the subcultural legacy that Schulman invokes in her politically astute novel of lesbian life on the Lower East Side. As its protagonist struggles to reconcile freedom and attachment in her personal life, *Girls, Visions and Everything* constructs a realistic fictional universe in which the exercise of agency is reconciled with an understanding of its historically contingent constraints. By revisiting the irreducibly material circumstances of one particular lesbian's experience, the novel reworks contested notions of community, coherence, spatiality, and temporality, reinventing pragmatism in and for a self-consciously multicultural and postmodern United States—and potentially reinvigorating queer theory in the process.

It's toward such reinvention that I turn in the book's more speculative conclusion. On the one hand, the book as a whole points toward a refiguring of historiography through pragmatism. I try to develop a mode of analysis that might satisfy Scott's desire for a new kind of history, one which "would constitute a genuinely nonfoundational approach[;] one which retains its explanatory power and its interest in change but does not stand on or reproduce naturalized categories."[32] On the other hand, I am in the end more interested in what a lesbian pragmatism may have to offer my own desires, which have less to do with the past than with the future, less to do with traditional scholarship than with strategies of social transformation. As a character in Schulman's 1998 novel *Shimmer* laments, "Exposing the injustice didn't change the injustice, it just normalized it."[33] Those of us interested in instigating change need to understand exactly how, when, and where sign relations do and do not intersect material ones. Because the logic of indexicality is a logic of material implication, it engages the potential for "actual" change and holds out the possibility of "normalizing" something new, something other than injustice. The as-yet-unrealized possibilities remain indistinct, but this is the direction in which *The Lesbian Index* intends to point.

Chapter 1

Fantasies of Origin

> [I]n truth, there is only one state of mind from which you can 'set out,' namely the very state of mind in which you find yourself at the time you do 'set out'—a state in which you are laden with an immense mass of cognition already formed, of which you cannot divest yourself if you would; and who knows whether, if you could, you would not have made all knowledge impossible to yourself?
>
> —Charles Sanders Peirce[1]

Where to begin? Were you born a lesbian, or did you choose to become one? Coming from curious "friends," inquisitive acquaintances, disinterested scholars, and, increasingly, presumptuous passersby, the question has become overly familiar in more ways than one. Moreover, it assumes invidious and unwarranted divisions between discovery and invention, between being and becoming, between fate and free will. Were you born a lesbian, or did you choose to become one? This is a stupid question: of course the answer is not yes or no, but both and neither. The opposition assumed by this inquiry frustrates easy answers even as it asks for one; precisely because lesbian existence plays itself out in the space defined by these poles, it can never fully settle on either—and there is a world of possibility between.

So, where to begin? In the middle someplace, evidently. . . .

At seventeen, standing in the one gay bar in town—in Indiana, of all places, almost a thousand miles from Greenwich Village—I was no student of lesbian history, but its sediment saturated my stance, my style, my psyche. I played softball well, billiards passably, carried my billfold in my back pocket, and stood around a lot, too shy to dance. I cupped my cigarette and shifted my weight exactly as Beebo Brinker had in the pages of Ann Bannon's novels twenty-odd years before. I walked like Stephen Gordon. I hadn't read the books.

Today, I wonder why this was, how I knew, how my body knew before my mind. Whatever role biology may play in sexual identity, whatever crucial functions camp and parody have served in queer cultures, neither seemed central to this—my way of being in the world at seventeen (at twenty-five, at thirty-three . . .). I can't bring myself to believe that a tendency to lean with one foot resting flat against the wall is hardwired into my hypothalamus, can't quite convince myself that it amounts only to a mocking appropriation of masculine ease. No, this is something else again: something real and resilient and natural; something subtle, psychological, and culturally specific. Something always already there; something I made myself.

So perhaps Sue-Ellen Case was on the right track when, in the late 1980s, she suggested "replacing the Lacanian slash with a lesbian bar";[2] certainly, critical theory that attends to context, to the contingencies of place and time, seems more promising—more useful—than foundationalist philosophies, which don't. Instead of focusing a more complexly historicized theory, however, the newly chic lesbian subject got caught up in the constructionist-essentialist controversy that enthralled academia at the time—and, as David Halperin insists, remains unresolved today.[3] By the mid-1990s, Case was lamenting that "now more than ever, there is a formidable divide within lesbian critical studies."[4] In her introduction to *The Lesbian Postmodern*, Laura Doan concurs: on the question of "what constitutes a 'lesbian'," she says, "disagreement abounds"[5]—the result of what Lisa Duggan describes as a situation of "strained relations between what is now called 'queer theory,' and lesbian and gay history."[6] "In this atmosphere," Marilyn Farwell writes, "the word 'lesbian' remains an elusive term that, as noted over ten years ago, 'is plagued with the problem of definition' [according to Bonnie Zimmerman] and more recently has been called the 'hub of conflicting intellectual and ideological interpretations' [by Paulina Palmer]."[7]

The shape of these debates is instructive. Suzanna Danuta Walters complains that "queer theory, particularly in its more academic manifestations, is often posed as a response to a certain kind of feminist and lesbian theorizing that is now deemed hopelessly retro, boring, realist, modernist, *about shoring up identity rather than its deconstruction*"; in defense of lesbian-feminism, she insists that "the thorny issues of authenticity, experience, and co-optation are not resolved by an assertion that no identity is real."[8] Nor are they resolved, of course, by ahistorical and ethnocentric projections of culturally dominant contemporary understandings onto other times and places—the counter-charge typically leveled by "queer" scholars against "lesbian historians."[9]

Leaving aside for the time being the charge that queer theory (which Walters recognizes "is by no means a monolithic and unified field") uniformly exposes identity as fictive and simply leaves it at that, let's consider the seriousness of Walters' concern that "without substantive engagement with complex sociopolitical realities," queer theory's celebrations of performativity, play, instability, and ambiguity "appear as entertaining but ultimately depoliticized academic exercises."[10] Clearly, more than a potentially "fascinating discussion" is understood to be at stake in this division between, as Duggan puts it, "queer theorists [who] have generally either ignored lesbian/gay history texts, or treated them with condescension" and "lesbian and gay historians [who], in turn, have largely ignored the implications of queer theory."[11]

Although apparently approaching from the other side of the aisle, Case describes the divide in terms similar to Walters': "On one side stand those who would identify themselves solely as lesbian, writing in a similarly empirical language and performing traditional literary criticism (with a dash of cultural critique): Bonnie Zimmerman, [K]arla Jay, and Marilyn Farwell, for example. On the other side stand queer theoretical critics, writing in the deconstructive, post-Foucauldian tradition."[12] While this characterization might be taken to imply her own "post-Foucauldian" allegiances, Case's identification of ideological opponents also makes clear a broader alliance: apparently, empiricist, essentialist lesbian traditionalists (*born*) and post-Foucauldian, deconstructionist queer theorists (*made*) alike assume and insist upon the existence of this insurmountable "divide."[13]

Perhaps every academic field (especially a young and embattled one) needs a good controversy to sustain it; perhaps something else is at work here. In any case, it seems only fair to acknowledge that if "now more than ever, there is a formidable divide within lesbian critical studies," this is largely because now more than ever there is something *called* "lesbian critical studies." The question of whether lesbians are born or made may seem new within this relatively new academic arena, but it is hardly news to lesbians; versions of this debate—from late nineteenth-century distinctions between "congenital" and "acquired" inversion to late twentieth-century disagreements over the difference between sexual "orientation" and sexual "preference"—have animated popular as well as professional representations of lesbian possibility from the very beginning. Indeed, the crystallization of this structuring division might be said to mark the beginning of what we now understand as "lesbian"—and a closer look at the current critical impasse suggests a sensitivity to this experience that most characterizations of the debate ignore.

In perhaps the most-cited example of lesbian anti-essentialist tendencies, for example, Judith Butler asks,

> What or who is it that is "out," made manifest and fully disclosed, when and if I reveal myself as a lesbian? What is it that is now known, anything? What remains permanently concealed by the very linguistic act that offers up the transparent revelation of sexuality? Can sexuality even remain sexuality once it submits to a criterion of transparency and disclosure, or does it perhaps cease to be sexuality precisely when the semblance of full explicitness is achieved?

And she answers,

> It is always finally unclear what is meant by invoking the lesbian-signifier, since its signification is always to some degree out of one's control, but also because its specificity can only be demarcated by exclusions that return to disrupt its claim to coherence.[14]

From across the divide, Terry Castle flatly rejects the pause-giving potential of such introspective meditations. Proclaiming herself "flagrantly out of step with current thinking," Castle explains that

> especially among younger lesbian and gay scholars trained in Continental philosophy (including a number of the so-called queer theorists) it has recently become popular to contest, along deconstructionist lines, the very meaningfulness of terms such as lesbian or gay or homosexual or coming out. No one knows what these words really signify, the argument goes; they lack linguistic transparency.[15]

Butler's musings don't move her: "Frankly, I disagree: I don't find it 'always finally unclear what is meant by invoking the lesbian-signifier'. . . . I believe we live in a world in which the word lesbian still makes sense."[16]

Which of course it does, because "sense" does not depend on "transparency."

What I mean to point out is that the terms of this debate tend to obscure the otherwise unremarkable fact that productive inquiry into the meaning of 'lesbian' necessarily engages the question *On what* does *"sense" depend*? "Making sense of the matter" demands examination of those processes through which sense is made, those mechanisms by which matter is made *sensible*. This is to say that lesbian theory and lesbian history are inescapably semiotic inquiries: they attend to the effects and/or functioning of signification and hence demand some theory (implicit or otherwise) of how it is that signs engage with the world and our understandings of it. Interestingly, a look at the semiotic assumptions underlying conflicting positions within the field reveals not only telling instances of internal inconsistency, but also a surprising degree of tacit agreement among disparately positioned approaches. The status of the lesbian subject may appear very much up in the air in the late twentieth-century United States (or perhaps out in the vapors, as Castle's text on "the apparitional lesbian" suggests), but the impression of irreconcilable theoretical differences is considerably complicated by unexpected homologies.

In *A Lure of Knowledge* (1991), for example, Judith Roof employs a deconstructive approach to read "configurations of lesbian desire" that have nothing explicitly to do with desires experienced by lesbians. She argues persuasively that by

> revealing or forcing logical inconsistencies, configurations of lesbian sexuality undo discursive claims to mastery and wholeness and occupy positions of penultimateness, immaturity, and incompleteness that exist alongside of, but not in opposition to, neat systemic closure.[17]

Castle describes a remarkably similar sense of "penultimateness" in her tracing of an historical "ghosting of the lesbian"[18] both "by culture itself"[19] and, more self-consciously, within literary texts by and about lesbians:

> [W]ithin the very imagery of negativity lies the possibility of recovery—a way of conjuring up, or bringing back into view, that which has been denied. Take the metaphor far enough, and the invisible will rematerialize; the spirit will become flesh."[20]

The dense textual base of Castle's argument makes a convincing case for the centrality of "apparitional" tropes to the Anglo/American lesbian literary tradition—and points to a provocative although not fully elaborated metaphor for theorizing substantive relations between the "apparitional" and the actual, between an abstract category of "the lesbian" (not unrelated to the heterosexist projections Roof identifies) and lived lesbian reality.

In *Bodies That Matter*, Butler engages the question directly, explaining her interest in reconciling "performativity" with "materiality," and describing an instability around the edges of intelligible discourse "produced by the effort to fix the site of the sexed body" through the regulatory schemas of normative heterosexuality. Ironically, she ends up sounding eerily like Castle as she explains that

> the forming of a subject requires an identification with the normative phantasm of "sex," and this identification takes place through a repudiation without which the subject cannot emerge. This is a repudiation which creates the valence of "abjection" and its status for the subject as a threatening spectre.[21]

Indeed, Castle's tracing of a tradition of "ghosting"—and conjuring up—lesbian possibility in Western (especially English and U.S.) literary texts, Butler's articulation of the mutual imbrication and interdependency of performativity and materiality in the construction of sexed subjects, even Eve Sedgwick's implication of speech act theory and shame in dynamic relation—at once deconstitutional and foundational—to identity formation more generally[22] all suggest the stress finessed by an acceptance of misleading binarisms between, to put it bluntly but reductively, "essentialist" and "post-structuralist" understandings of lesbian existence.

Were you born a lesbian or did you choose to become one? A look at U.S. academic lesbian theory at the close of the twentieth century suggests that the answer is inevitably an agonizing ambivalence. The disjuncture assumed—and reiteratively enacted—between the foundational and the constructed, the material and its hypothetical conditions of possibility mirrors (and is reflected in) similar separations dissociating actual individuals from abstract categories, specific facts from general truths, even, as Roof's *Lure* makes evident, lesbian reality from heterosexist projection.

For all its instructive provocation, the analysis in *Bodies That Matter* remains unhistoricized if not outright ahistorical, failing, in the end, to attend to that which lies, in Laplanche and Pontalis's formulation, "beyond the history of the subject, but nevertheless in history."[23] Just as Sedgwick seems to invoke psychoanalytic eternals in positing disruption and shame at the foundation of (queer) identity formation, Butler falls back on apparent absolutes in positioning repudiation and abjection at the constitutive instant of sexed subjectivity. The essentially structuralist and synchronic approach shared by Butler and, in this instance, Sedgwick flattens and thus distorts the effects of history, of process—ultimately diminishing the role of performativity, ironically enough. In the end, such "deconstructive" theorizing runs the risk of collapsing back into the essentialism it purports to remedy: by focusing so relentlessly on the constructedness of effects, such "deconstruction" can create the illusion that the *mechanism*s of construction (and of deconstruction) are not similarly suspect. Walters quite reasonably raises the question, "Why must we assume that all identities form around the same structural binarisms and with the same inherent rigidities? Is *that* not essentialist?"[24] Or as John J. Stuhr suggests in a rather different context, "Shouldn't philosophy take its own cultural contexts seriously?"[25]

I think that it should, and am convinced in large part by the evident costs of a failure to do so. Although Butler insists that "gender performativity cannot be theorized apart from the forcible and reiterative practice of regulatory sexual regimes,"[26] for example, her relative inattention to the material and hence historically specific dimensions of discursivity has produced a persistent confusion of performativity with performance. Despite their desire to retain the insights of social construction theory, for example, Saskia E. Wieringa and Evelyn Blackwood bluntly assert that "because she ignores the 'materiality of sex,' Butler cannot escape the impression that she sees a person's gender identity as almost an artificial and dispensable phenomenon."[27] The imputation of a willful, humanistic subject who precedes and performs a chosen gender is most certainly a misreading, one that Butler has been at pains to prevent. But I think that its persistence, particularly in the work of Butler's detractors, bespeaks not only a reasonable, if misplaced, concern about the potential evacuation/evisceration of political agency and/or experiential authority, but also a nascent critique of a tacit foundationalism difficult to excise from Butler's philosophical presumptions.

Teresa de Lauretis' study of lesbian desire, *The Practice of Love*, is suggestively more resistant to such reductive interpretation. Although de Lauretis does not actively historicize her analysis, she does insist on the fact of its historicity[28]—arguing that primal fantasies such as the

Oedipus play a "structuring role" in lesbian sexuality, but simultaneously asserting that

> the importance of theorizing fantasy as the semiosic ground of sexuality lies in that fantasy itself, as sociopsychic process, *exceeds its historically contingent foundations*, the Oedipus included.[29]

Following Laplanche and Pontalis, de Lauretis argues "against the structuralist postulate of universal structures" and insists that the "original" fantasies are themselves "historically structured as well as structuring of the subject's history."[30] As a study of perverse *desire* her book remains "concerned more with intrapsychic than with institutional mechanisms"; it attends to the subject's own history much more closely than to the historical structuring of its foundations—and begs the question of what, if anything, exceeds or sustains "fantasy itself." But by pointing out that "in joining subjectivity to the social as a confrontation with material reality" Peirce's pragmatic semiotics "confer[s] upon the subject an historical dimension," de Lauretis also indicates a direction for lesbian theorizing more responsive to the concerns that Walters and others raise.[31] The challenge lies in developing a *practice* more consistent with, as Stuhr says, "the irreducibly temporal, spatial, social, contextual character of human subjects, languages, thoughts, experiences."[32]

In its insistence on the irreducibly indexical aspect of signification, Peirce's pragmatism promises just such a practice, conceiving a semiotics inseverable from materiality and hence inextricable from history. Unfortunately, this dimension of Peirce's thought has been elided in more recent elaborations of pragmatism nearly so thoroughly as in the work in lesbian studies discussed above—the combination, I can only assume, contributing to such bizarre complaints as Case's claim that "body-less transcendence is produced through the process of semiosis" (for which she blames "queer's consort, 'performativity'").[33] Cary Wolfe, for example, laments neopragmatism's inability to live up to its own putative "commitment to radical plurality, contingency, historicity, and difference."[34] Stuhr similarly acknowledges the need "to make explicit the exclusions, oppositionalities, and single-mindedness embedded in pragmatism's own notions of community, inquiry, and pluralism" and goes so far as to suggest that this is one area in which pragmatism might learn from poststructuralist priorities.[35] But whereas Wolfe rightly critiques Richard Rorty's "debilitating liberal humanism" for its reliance on concepts "whose homogenizing connotations mask and submerge the uneveness of power and resources in the social and economic sphere," and not unreasonably ascribes to neopragmatism in general "an identifiably liberal problematic that cannot take account of asymmetries of power," he also contends that "the case against Rorty's ethnocentric liberalism can and must be made in the absence of normative foundationalist assurances—must be made, precisely, *pragmatically*."[36]

Though Wolfe himself turns to systems theory to build this case, I contend that a powerful corrective to Rorty's empty pluralism can be found closer to home: Peirce's more rigorously contextualized semiotic offers the means to attend to materiality, as Butler phrases it, "as that which is bound up with signification from the start."[37] The problem is that although Peirce is "almost always acknowledged as the great originative mind of pragmatism, . . . he is seldom discussed in the context of political and social theory"—perhaps, as James Hoopes suggests, "because [contemporary theorists] assume that Peirce's intense focus on logic, which distinguished him from Dewey and James, also made his philosophy less relevant to political theory."[38] There is evidence to support this idea. In his book *The Two Pragmatisms*, H.O. Mounce describes a more publicized, more Rortyan "neopragmatism" that bears little resemblance to its Peircean roots—and traces the split to James' difference from Peirce, compounded by Dewey, and exploited by Rorty.[39] The editors of Peirce's *Collected Papers*, Charles Hartshorne and Paul Weiss, concur that "Pragmatism, as it developed, followed the pattern of William James' thought and that of John Dewey rather than the conceptions of Peirce." Ironically, their own introduction to this most influential collection of Peirce's work would seem to propagate precisely the error that Hoopes identifies: "Articles on pragmatism represent only one phase of his work," they write. "Some of his best thought was devoted to logical problems[, including] the theory of signs."[40]

This division is nowhere evident, however, in the work itself. Interpreters have persisted in conceiving Peirce's semiotic theory as somehow peripheral to his pragmatism despite the centrality of sign relations to his philosophical system, his insistence that "all thought is in signs," and his contention that, in Hoopes' phrase, "communicative, interpretative, semiotic relations are at the heart of being."[41] Indeed, the central idea of Peirce's pragmatism is that meaning (identity, essence) is an effect of its own (potential) effects. His 1905 essay "What Pragmatism Is" does not equivocate: it is "the theory that a *conception*, that is, the rational purport of a word or other expression, lies exclusively in its conceivable bearing upon the conduct of life." To wit, pragmatism is a philosophy of the science of signs—a thoroughly semiotic (and thus anti-foundationalist) philosophy. Pragmatism is both centrally concerned with how it is that meaning gets made and certain that the making of meaning is intimately caught up with real world interactions.[42]

While Hoopes merely derides as "weak and vulgar" the pragmatism of "recent antifoundationalists who attempt to claim the mantle of James and Dewey," Tom Cohen offers the more interesting insight that "the oddly *nationalist* rhetoric that has set 'neopragmatism' against *theory* . . . misses what might be called most 'American'" in the intervention effected by Peirce. The problem with Rorty and others like him, Cohen argues, is that their attachment to a humanistic interiority "implicitly evades the *materiality* that has always been at stake in the American break."[43] In his recognition of "a more pragmatic pragmatism that is at once American *and* 'theoretical,'" Cohen refocuses our attention on Peirce and gestures provocatively towards "American Literature."[44] I have suggested that the history of mainstream representations of lesbian subjectivity in this country, and the reception of those representations (which, so far as they are accessible, constitute part of the history of representation themselves), indicate that pragmatism has provided to at least this version of lesbian possibility an enabling epistemology. The readings in American literature and in the American contexts of lesbian literature's reception that comprise the next several chapters will elaborate this argument, endeavoring through their engagements to develop evidence consistent with this proposition. At this point in the discussion, however, I wish to emphasize the inverse implication of this claim: lesbian texts, contexts, and perspectives can be seen to provide pragmatism with specific material, subjective, and social realities tethering it to the world in which we live. The indissolubility of "symbolization and context" within pragmatism suggests that historically specific phenomena can only be accounted for by historically specific theories of signification.[45] Theories of signification, I suggest, are rendered historical by their indexical attachment to sociohistorical circumstance. Absent an indexical anchor, in other words, pragmatism cannot be—it loses precisely that which renders philosophy "pragmatic."[46] In examining the development of lesbian subjectivity in the twentieth-century United States from the perspective of pragmatism, then, I am explicitly rejecting the sort of philosophical practice which seems "to set forth views from nowhere and no time," taking seriously Stuhr's warning against the academic abstraction that analytically severs "philosophical temperaments, questions, methods, and positions from the larger cultural contexts in which they arise and function,"[47] and choosing instead to explore the efficacy of a philosophical predilection that emanates from the same place and time as the developments I seek to explain.

This is consistent with the overview provided by Cornel West, who holds that pragmatism is "less a philosophical tradition putting forward solutions to perennial problems in the Western philosophical conversation . . . , and more a continuous cultural commentary or set of interpretations that attempt to explain America to itself at a particular historical moment." He describes it, in fact, as "a distinctly American response to a European discourse that overlooked and ignored transactional relations between the self and nature, communal relations between the self and other selves, and especially the radical contingency and revisability of both relations."[48] What pragmatism offers, in other words, is a rigorously and radically historicized and contextualized intellectual approach. In focusing on transactional relations, pragmatism not only admits the contingency of its formulations, but attempts to elaborate the mechanisms of their inevitable revision—admits, in fact, the contingency of semiosic processes *per se* and begins to imagine possible mechanisms of their revision.

Even this partial definition of pragmatic predispositions may be seen to suggest how Peirce is relevant to lesbian studies here and now. In sum, recourse to a more Peircean pragmatism may help (1) to account for both the surface antagonism and the underlying homologies that currently characterize lesbian critical studies; (2) to identify a theory of semiosis that can account for the complex imbrication of being and becoming in the experience and articulation of lesbian subjectivity; (3) to articulate a mode of inquiry consistent with its own insights, an approach appropriate to the context of its use, without universalizing, foundational, or totalizing pretensions.

To briefly elucidate the substance of these claims, I'd like to quickly revisit the "formidable divide" between Castle and Butler, troubled already by that uncanny resemblance in diction. Castle's charge that Butler's "queer theory" is marked by "Continental" corruption overlooks the extent to which Butler's interest in regulatory schemas, performativity, and the idea of subjectivity as construction remains rooted in the pragmatist tradition of scrutinizing regulative ideals, action, and effects. If Butler's conclusions are Foucauldian, her terms and concerns are largely Peircean—while her (post)structuralist perspective, with its basically synchronic frame, marks a departure from the deeply historical engagements of both influences.

In Butler's instructively titled essay "Contingent Foundations," for example, we find a Foucauldian formulation of power's mobility and mutability alongside a strikingly Peircean formulation of meaning production:

> [I]f the subject is constituted by power, that power does not cease at the moment the subject is constituted, for that subject is never fully constituted, but is subjected and produced time and again. *That subject is neither a ground nor a product, but the permanent possibility of a certain resignifying process*, one which gets detoured and stalled through other mechanisms of power, but is power's own possibility of being reworked. It is not enough to say that the subject is invariably engaged in a political field; that phenomenological phrasing misses the point that *the subject is an accomplishment regulated and produced in advance.*[49] (emphasis added)

This idea of "permanent possibility" certainly recalls Peirce, but Butler's vague reference to the processes of subject formation ("the subject is constituted by power") introduces a misleading inconsistency: if this subject "is . . . *produced* time and again," how can it be accurate to insist that it is "no[t] a *product*" (emphases added)? If the subject serves as the site or circumstance for "power's own possibility of being reworked," how helpful can it be to insist that this subject is not "a ground"? Butler's crucial insights—that this subject cannot be categorically constrained as either simply "product" or simply "ground," that it may usefully be understood as a kind of "permanent possibility" for resignification—are undercut by her own misrecognition of the relation among these possibilities. A more Peircean grammar might reinterpret the relation between site (the subject) and process (semiosis). By recognizing both the web of transactional relations in which subjectivity is caught and thereby constituted and, especially, "the contingency and revisability of those relations," pragmatism allows for an understanding of the subject as *at once* ground, product, *and* what Peirce terms "peculiar positive possibility."[50]

As this example suggests, Peirce conceives of the basic sign relation not as—in the (post)structuralist tradition—binary (Saussure's signifier and signified); but as tripartite. A sign, he says,

> is the First Correlate of a triadic relation, the Second Correlate being termed its Object, and the possible Third Correlate being

> termed its Interpretant, by which triadic relation the possible Interpretant is determined to be the First Correlate of the same triadic relation to the same Object, and for some possible Interpretant.[51]

Or, somewhat more clearly, "A sign, or *representamen*, is something which stands to somebody for something in some respect or capacity":

> It addresses somebody, that is, creates in the mind of that person an equivalent sign, or perhaps a more developed sign. That sign which it creates I call the *interpretant* of the first sign. The sign stands for something, its *object*. It stands for that object, not in all respects, but in reference to a sort of idea, which I have sometimes called the *ground* of the representamen."[52]

For Peirce, the basic sign relation is thus profoundly social and deeply contextualized. On the one hand, as Cohen explains, "what Peirce says, in brief, is that 'consciousness' or the subject is an *effect* of material or *external* signs ('external facts')."[53] On the other, Peirce's pragmatism countenances no *immediate* access to external objects; instead, it presupposes "acquaintance" with objects, presupposes mediation—presupposes, that is, prior signification. Peirce is quite clear on this point, emphasizing that "that is what is meant in this volume by the Object of a sign; namely, that with which it presupposes an acquaintance in order to convey some further information concerning it," and arguing that

> if there be anything that conveys information and yet has absolutely no relation nor reference to anything with which the person to whom it conveys the information has, when he comprehends that information, the slightest acquaintance, direct or indirect—and a very strange sort of information that would be—the vehicle of that information is not, in this volume, called a Sign.[54]

Thus the "object," in this understanding, is not an extra-semiotic entity, since "acquaintance, direct or indirect," can come only via signs. As Cohen contends, "'outside' of this infinite semiosis there is no consciousness, no subject"—but this does not represent a threat to subjective agency, because there *is* no (relevant) "outside" to semiosis.[55]

Peirce's elaboration of the tripartite sign relation thus enriches Saussure's formulation of static, synchronic binarisms and prefigures both Derrida's "endless chain of signifiers"[56] and Butler's insistence that the subject "is never fully constituted, but is subjected and produced time and again." A "sign," Peirce explains, is "anything which determines something else (its *interpretant*) to refer to an object to which itself refers (its *object*) in the same way, the interpretant becoming in turn a sign, and so on *ad infinitum*."[57]

Like Butler, Peirce locates meaning not in some elusive "original" but in the insistent iteration of "copies"; like Butler, he conceives of a semiotic "ground" which is not foundational, but itself the product of semiosis—and thus can constitute only a *contingent* foundation. Unlike Butler to date, however, Peirce locates the production of meaning very clearly within history, in that his theory of semiosis accounts for the impact of material relations at every turn. Whereas Butler insists that the "subject is neither a ground nor a product," acknowledging only that the "resignifying process" for which the subject serves as site sometimes "gets detoured and stalled through other mechanisms of power"; Peirce conceives of such distinctions only in terms of function, recognizing material as well as discursive relations as integral to semiosis—like the subject and other signs, at once ground and product: "power's own possibility of being reworked." What Butler sees as glitches in the resignifying process (detouring and stalling the expression of pure possibility), Peirce recognizes as *part* of the process (the interplay of grounds and effects that constitutes that possibility).

What this means for lesbian studies is that the "divide" between foundationalist and constructionist understandings of subjectivity is theoretically misleading, but semiosically productive. Lesbians are both born and made, at once ground and product in the always already ongoing process of semiosis. We can only "begin," as Judith Roof would have it, *in medias res*.[58] This is not to say, however, that there is no starting place, no mooring, but rather that *place* is indeed the appropriate term. For Peirce, the linchpin of semiosis is not abstract, discrete, and external, but contingent, contextual, and profoundly subjective. Semiosis begins at home.

Replacing the Lacanian slash with a bar in Indiana, this study recognizes the fundamentally contingent nature of lesbian subjectivity and of meaning production more generally. It suggests that semiosis, like language, may be profoundly ego-centric, while insisting that the ego is an effect of semiosis, of culture—and recognizes no contradiction here. Rife with assumptions and rough with its judgments, this study nevertheless attempts to attend carefully to individual texts and specific contexts—beginning with its own situatedness within late twentieth-century U.S. lesbian studies scholarship. Even the relative abstraction of this introductory chapter, however, is at odds with the project's general logic.

Are lesbians born, or made? Butler contends that "the essentialism/constructivism debate founders on a paradox that is not easily or, indeed, not ever, overcome." The difficulty is that "just as no prior materiality is accessible without the means of discourse, so no discourse can ever capture that prior materiality"[59]— if for no other reason than, as Butler argues in *Bodies That Matter*, "there is no reference to a pure body which is not at the same time a further formation of that body."[60] So if essentialists retain their investments in prior materiality and constructivists remain interested only in an always "inadequate" discourse, the paradox would indeed seem to risk paralysis. But even to raise the question in this way reifies the dislocations effected by both positions. The situation appears paradoxical only when expressed in the atemporal abstractions of theoretical absolutes: in practical terms, discourse and materiality are experienced in tandem (although not simply simultaneously); each is conditioned by the other—and to ask what they might be were they not is truly to indulge in academic irrelevance. As Biddy Martin suggests, "The opposition between conventional understandings of gender [or sexuality] (as stable core) and postmodern conceptions of identity (as the effect of discursive practice) needs to be displaced, not decided in one direction or the other."[61] And supposing that some aspect of the world in which we live is the subject at hand, there is fortunately no need to "capture" an *a priori* materiality, nor to abandon discourse. Infinite, semiosis has no end—hence holding out the promise of a future perennially open to intervention—and also no beginning.

We can only take up the question in the middle somewhere.

Chapter 2

Evolutionary Love

> I have heard what the talkers were talking, the talk of the beginning and the end,
> But I do not talk of the beginning or the end. . . .
>
> Always a knit of identity, always distinction, always a breed of life.
>
> —Walt Whitman, *Song of Myself*

"Identities," as Judith Halberstam so aptly puts it, "do not suddenly emerge from some protean slime." Instead, "the possibility of a sexual identity or category is in fact years in the making and depends on all kinds of other factors in the culture at large."[1] Indeed, the first full-length U.S. novel devoted to the representation of female homosexuality is situated by very specific coordinates, which are taken up in particular ways, to particular effect. *Norma Trist; or, Pure Carbon: A Story of the Inversion of the Sexes* is set in Texas, sometime between the end of the U.S. Civil War and the book's 1895 publication. In these early decades of its statehood, Texas suffered from economic depression and ever worsening Anglo/Mexican relations. In Austin, doctor F.E. Daniel was advocating surgical "asexualization" as a "therapeutic measure" for women inclined to indulge "degenerate" homosexual attractions. Meanwhile, back east, C.S. Peirce published a series of articles on semiotics and evolution in the *Monist*; and, in Tennessee, Alice Mitchell slashed Freda "Fred" Ward's throat with a razor because, she said, "I loved her and she refused to marry me." Most notably, as Siobhan Somerville argues, "the formation of notions of heterosexuality and homosexuality emerged in the United States through (and not merely parallel to) a discourse saturated with assumptions about the racialization of bodies."[2] As dime novelist John Wesley Carhart must have recognized, the time was ripe for reimagining the relation of female homosexuality to race and nation, science and law, sex and gender. These "other factors" not only inform the representation of Norma Trist and the nature of the sexual identity she typifies, but are themselves taken up and transformed in the interaction.

Written by a practicing physician, *Norma* is notable for its role in popularizing medical models of female homosexuality, but also for the ways in which it modified them. Women have made love to and fallen in love with each other throughout history, of course, but Carhart's novel points to a pivotal place and moment in the transformation of the female inverts inherited from European sexology into the U.S. lesbians we know today. Turn-of-the-century Texas provides a prime location for dramatizing the American discourse most influential in contemporary understandings of sexual deviance: the popularized versions of evolutionary theory invoked to explain and excuse U.S. expansion and Anglo dominance.

Norma Trist tells the convoluted tale of its eponymous heroine's doomed romance with the widow Marie LaMoreaux, whom Norma stabs in a fit of jealousy; of Marie's subsequent marriage to the genteel Captain Alphonso Rodriquez of the Mexican Army; of Alphonso's search for buried treasure left by a Spanish mule train massacred by Indians; of farmer Frank Artman's plot to secure the treasure for himself; and of Norma's eventual capitulation—while under the influence of hypnotic suggestion—to Frank's persistent proposals of marriage. It's a wild ride, but revealing. *Norma Trist* came out in the context of several crucial social shifts—from a ranching economy to a farming economy and from relatively accommodative arrangements to violent repression of the Chicano population in Texas; from legal to medical authority over homosexuality; from a national obsession with westward expansion to widespread acceptance of Frederick Jackson Turner's 1893 conclusions about "the closing of the American frontier"; from a realist to a naturalist national literature. The most profound change, however, was perhaps the least acknowledged; this was the development of a distinct, self-conscious, and self-consciously "American" philosophical movement that came to be known as "pragmatism." Carhart's wild Western is a far cry from Peirce's academic articles, but *Norma Trist* marks—and is marked by—a sea change in U.S. semiotics: a turning away from a deterministic faith in the integrity of essences and towards a pragmatic understanding of reality and representation as intertwined and historically specific.

Norma Trist makes sense only in the context of a challenge to both U.S. evolutionism and European sexology; it participates in a more general tendency to remake the lesbian in pragmatic terms. Ironically, this challenge, inarticulable within the frame of U.S. naturalisms—literary and scientific—comes close to coherence only in the context of a genre unaccountable to such "high culture" constraints. Obliged only to provide action, entertainment, and a few formula staples ("Western" setting, mystery, guns, maybe a lynching—all of which are offered in *Norma Trist*), the dime novel was, especially by the late 1800s, a fairly flexible form.[3] Carhart's queer appropriation of popular culture thus becomes comprehensible as an effort to escape premises apparently endemic to more respectable genres. Calling into question the essentializing racism of U.S. evolutionisms and confounding the sexological distinction between "congenital" and "acquired" homosexuality, *Norma Trist* suggests the potential of lesbian possibility realized within a pragmatic semiotic; like Peirce's theory of meaning production, it posits a tenuous, temporal reconciliation of essentialist and constructivist logics within specific material circumstances.

The "Uncouthness That Clings to the Clod": Evolution, Eugenics, and Texas Economics

At the time of *Norma Trist*'s publication, Carhart's physician colleagues were already engaged in public discussion of the causes and consequences of homosexual behavior among both women and men. Published primarily in professional journals, their findings were nonetheless widely reported in both serious and sensationalist stories in the popular press, and increasingly reiterated in advice books and moral guides. Promoting a popular paradigm in which inversion was classified as evidence of evolutionary degeneration, Carhart's fellow Texan Dr. Daniel urged castrating (or, in the case of females, "asexualizing") criminals on the assumption that sexual "perversion" and other criminal tendencies were both hereditary and disproportionately prevalent among "the lower classes, particularly negroes." Others advocated treatments ranging from execution to "cold sitz baths."[4] Carhart, in contrast, chose to write this novel, and this unconventional contribution to his profession's ongoing conversation about causes, signs, and treatments of female homosexuality effects a radical recontextualization of key questions.

On trial for the non-fatal stabbing of Marie LaMoreaux, Norma Trist is initially judged insane. Her crime of passion, committed for the love of another woman, is simply incomprehensible under the terms of popular paradigms available to her contemporaries.[5] Norma's consequent confinement in the Austin Insane Asylum, complete with close observation by the institution's director, establishes her sanity—and subjects her to a second trial. This time around, complete confusion ensues as conflicting interpretations compete for epistemological authority. The defense lawyer proposes to show, first, that "there was in certain cases, what was known as a psychosexual condition manifest in falling in love with another of the same sex," and, second, that love "might be sadistic in character. . . whether between those of the opposite sex, or between those of the same sex" (205–6). Although "abnormalities," he argues, such conditions, singly or combined, "did not imply an insane mind" (206). Norma, however, controverts her lawyer's argument by refusing the ignoble association with "psychopathia-sexualis" (205) inherent in this defense and by representing her love as more chivalrous than sadistic. "It was and is a stimulus to my ambition," she says, "prompting me to highest intellectual effort, inspiring me to delightful, unflinching courage, so that by the power of this innate inspiration I am upborne above the sordid affairs of this life." Asked, "Then you love Marie, as you style her, yet, do you Norma?" she responds, appropriately, "I do love her as devotedly as any knight ever loved a lady." In describing her emotional experience of the fateful moment itself, Norma completely inverts her own lawyer's assessment: "I at first thought, in my jealous frenzy, that I was angry with Marie, and wanted to kill her in revenge; and as I try to analyze my feelings, I think there was something of this feeling until I rushed upon her, when I instantly realized that it was the bewilderment of jealousy from the love I bore her, and I would much rather have received this blow in my own breast." Here Norma pauses to "[lift] her eyes heavenward, as the tears [course], in great drops down her beautiful face," and proceeds to make her point clear: "God knows that I could, at that awful moment, have died for her!" (209–10).

When the asylum director takes the stand to confirm Norma's sanity and affirm the implications of her testimony, he describes her character as unassailable, her condition as congenital, and her orientation as unchangeable. She should be held accountable for her acts, he suggests, "to the same degree that any other would be who, in a transport of jealousy for the opposite sex, should commit overt acts" (216). His testimony is complicated, however, by the next witness called, a physician "placed upon the . . . stand as an expert, having devoted special attention to sexual abnormalities." In direct contradiction of the director's testimony, this doctor claims "that many had been cured of the abnormality [at issue], particularly where the condition was an induced and not a congenital one," by hypnosis. Moreover, even in such cases as Norma's, he implies, "he was confident that good could be accomplished in that way" (217–18). Norma is released from custody when, understandably, the jury is unable to achieve consensus. Grappling with conflicting ideas about etiology, intractability, biological imperatives, and individual accountability, Carhart confronts issues at the core of a larger cultural quandary. Are our fates pre-determined? To what extent and in what ways does evolution influence current reality? What role, if any, does human initiative have to play? In addressing these questions, Carhart's convoluted dime novel resists both the literary conventions of "high culture" models (making no pretension of emulating either the established realist tradition or the emergent naturalist school) and the scientific precepts associated with evolutionary theory in the United States.

The doctrines of determinism and degeneration central to this popular understanding of evolution indicate less the influence of specifically Darwinian ideas, however, than a peculiarly American evasion of them.[6] Ironically, although Darwin's theory of species differentiation via natural selection depended on the occurrence of random variation (however slight or occasional), Darwin's pre-eminent American defender, Harvard botanist Asa Gray, thanked the author of *Origin of Species* for having "brought *teleological* considerations back into botany."[7] Gray accurately identified the philosophical problem posed by the theory of natural selection as a conflict between chance and teleology, and rightly recognized the obstacles to U.S. acceptance raised by Darwin's suggestion that random variation comprises the driving force behind species differentiation. Committed to the defense of Darwinism, Gray assumed the unenviable position of insisting on the concordance of Darwinian evolution and teleological direction.[8] Despite his efforts, however, the apparent incompatibility of natural selection and divine design weighed heavily against acceptance of pure Darwinism in evangelical America.

The opposition of celebrated zoologist Louis Agassiz, whose "Essay on Classification" (1857) represented an absolutely incompatible approach, also affected the American response to *Origin of Species*. According to historian of science Thomas Glick, "Agassiz made clear [that] he intended to use American living forms to demonstrate the universal laws of biology stated in the 'Essay on Classification.'" "No wonder," says Glick, "that Americans, conscious of the youth of their culture and institutions, loved Agassiz, who promised the world a true science based upon American specimens."[9] Agassiz's influence helped establish the neo-Lamarckian strains of evolutionism widely popularized by Englishman Herbert Spencer's accessible work. The hallmark of European Lamarckism, belief in the inheritability of acquired characteristics, was counter-balanced in the "American School" by an emphasis on internal direction, reflected in the "recapitulation" by the species itself of the stages of development observable in its individual members. Indeed, in *The Eclipse of Darwinism*, Peter Bowler claims that "the truly distinguishing feature of the American school [is] its vision of evolution advancing step-by-step along a regular pattern of development mirrored by the embryological growth of the individual organism."[10] This orthogenic approach, advanced by Alpheus Hyatt (who drew his conclusions from the study of fossil shellfish) and Edward Drinker Cope, among others, appealed to those anxious to hold on to the idealist philosophy of nature upon which Agassiz's "Essay of Classifications" was based. According to Agassiz's celebrated "classifications," humankind stood at the pinnacle of a hierarchy of species differentiated according to divine design, the most perfect life form yet developed. The teleological direction driving this differentiation could be discerned, presumably, in the parallels between the development of an individual human life and the whole history of life on earth.[11] The "polygenic" position advanced by Agassiz, as Somerville points out, typified "a predominantly American theoretical development" that distinguished what "was widely referred to as the 'American school' of anthropology"—its purest proponents "held that different races were actually different species with distinct biological and geographic origins."[12] Although the accumulating evidence increasingly discredited Agassiz's uncompromising opposition to Darwinism, American science struggled to adapt evolutionary theories to accommodate something like his idealist vision of a natural, implicitly hierarchical order.

Herbert Spencer, the English philosopher whose evolutionism predated Darwin's,[13] offered a neo-Lamarckian world view peculiarly consonant with contemporary American concerns and conceits. As Paul F. Boller explains in *American Thought in Transition: The Impact of Evolutionary Naturalism, 1865–1900*, "Spencer's popularity is not difficult to understand[:] His uncompromising individualism was appealing to

Americans; so was his seeming optimism and faith in progress. His insistence that science and religion could co-exist was reassuring, and his use of evolution to construct a philosophy that was not too technical for laymen to grasp was bound to be popular in a period in which the reading public was fascinated by science, particularly evolutionary science, and its implications for life and thought."[14]

Spencer's theory held both to belief in the inheritance of acquired characteristics (reassuring to the American religion of individual agency and self-improvement) and to an Agassiz-like idealism which insisted on divinely directed progress of the race[15]—most manifest, as Spencer saw it, in the Anglo-Saxon strain. In an age of intense racial antagonisms and Anglo-American xenophobia, Spencer's laissez-faire pseudo-Lamarckism lent itself to the legitimization of Anglo imperialism and oppression of purportedly "less evolved"—or, conversely, already "degenerate"[16]—groups. F.E. Daniel's advocacy of "asexualizing" undesirables is but a short step from Spencer's widely disseminated opinion that "to aid the bad in multiplying, is, in effect, the same as maliciously providing for our descendants a multitude of enemies."[17] As this example suggests, Agassiz's idealist "hierarchy," even in evolutionist guise, was easily adapted to authorize the idea of a natural hierarchy among human beings.[18]

John Fiske's 1885 essay for *Harper's Magazine* made the imperialist implications of Spencerian evolutionism absolutely clear. In his essay "Manifest Destiny," Fiske proposed that the highly evolved Anglo-Saxon race was destined to extend its influence until "every land on the earth's surface that is not already the seat of an old civilization shall become English in its language, in its religion, in its political habits and traditions, and to a predominant extent in the blood of its people." Soon after, Josiah Strong published an extremely popular piece of propaganda called *Our Country: Its Possible Future and Its Present Crisis*, in which he claimed that

> this race of unequaled energy [i.e.: Anglo-Saxons], with all the majesty of numbers and the might of wealth behind it—the representative, let us hope, of the largest liberty, the purest Christianity, the highest civilization—having developed peculiarly aggressive traits calculated to impress its institutions upon mankind, will spread itself over the earth. If I read not amiss, this powerful race will move down upon Mexico, down upon Central and South America, out upon the islands of the sea, over upon Africa and beyond. And can any one doubt that the result of this competition of races will be the "survival of the fittest"?[19]

This "Americanized" Darwinism is clearly at issue in the novel *Norma Trist*. Although subtitled simply "A Story of the Inversion of the Sexes," *Norma Trist* in fact tells three stories: the sympathetic case history of Norma's "inversion"; the romance of Marie and Alphonso's relationship; and the mystery/adventure of the men's search for buried silver. In contrast to the naturalist novel characterized by Mark Seltzer, however, *Norma Trist* successfully resists "the realist premises of genesis and generation."[20] The twists and turns of its three central plots are anything but inevitable. Instead, human agency—especially that exercised by the Anglo male—acts to influence every important turn of events. It is Frank Artman who engineers Alphonso and Marie's courtship, Frank who finds and hides the treasure, Frank who ultimately has Norma hypnotized into marrying him and bearing his children. Carhart might justly be faulted for remaining vague about exactly *how* Artman happens to locate and unearth the treasure for which Rodriquez and his company had searched for months, but he is nothing if not frank about who ultimately controlled events in turn-of-the-century Texas.

In this he touches on yet another explanation for the U.S. discomfort with Darwin's theory of natural selection, one which C.S. Peirce was prescient enough to note in 1891. The more popular Spencerian theory, Peirce writes, holds that the development of species has been informed by "changes [which] have taken place during the lives of the individuals, in consequence of effort and exercise, and that reproduction plays no part in the process except in preserving these modifications. Thus, Spencer's theory only explains the development of characters for which individuals strive, while the Darwinian theory only explains the production of characters really beneficial to the race, *though these may be fatal to individuals*."[21] This observation underscores the cultural unease with which a nation in love with the lessons of Benjamin Franklin's *Autobiography*—among them, that there is no conflict between individual advancement and civic responsibility—greeted the news that *chance* (not effort, not merit, and not providence) might determine the development of species. As for Frank Artman, he adopts a prototypically American evasion of unwelcome implications. As the very embodiment of Anglo-American male prerogative, Frank personalizes the pseudo-Darwinism associated with U.S. evolutionism (and "manifest destiny" jingoism):

> From his earliest recollection he had been impressed with a conviction of "ultimate destiny." He was not particularly supersti-

> tious, but this conviction that there was for his life a special plan; that some divine or superhuman purpose had to be wrought out in his affairs, followed him by day and by night; nay had already become such a thorough conviction that he regarded it as settled, and ceased to reason about it, because it had passed into a demonstration. (111).

Carhart's cultural critique, predictably, does not extend beyond this allusive acknowledgment of the character's ideological impetus. Frank figures as icon of Anglo imperialism, but *Norma Trist* never explains the forces underlying his apparently accidental efficacy. However, by exposing Frank's myriad successes as relatively undeserved (Alphonso is clearly a better person, if not unambiguously the better man), Carhart implicitly questions that quintessentially American equation of reward with merit.

Unfortunately, the sort of analogical excess associated with Josiah Strong and the fictional Frank Artman was not always so easily contained, nor was it limited to such obviously propagandistic tracts. The lingo (jingo?) of evolutionism permeated even the historian's understanding of events. In his famous 1893 address to the American Historical Association, Frederick Jackson Turner identifies as "the peculiarity of American institutions . . . the fact that they have been compelled to adapt themselves to the changes of an expanding people—to the changes involved in crossing a continent, in winning a wilderness, and in developing at each area of this progress out of the primitive economic and political conditions of the frontier into the complexity of city life." Like Alpheus Hyatt's ancient crustaceans, American frontier settlements recapitulate (in miniature form and accelerated fashion) the development of the larger community to which they belong. Crucially, however, "this perennial rebirth, this fluidity of American life, this expansion westward with its new opportunities, its continuous touch with the simplicity of primitive society, furnish the forces dominating American character."[22]

Turner employs his evolutionary analogy as a lesson to historians; like the geologist who "traces patiently the shores of ancient seas, maps their areas, and compares the older and the newer," he says, the historian would do well to "mark [the chronology of] various frontiers and in detail compare one with another." By this method, he suggests, "not only would there result a more adequate conception of the American development and characteristics, but invaluable additions would be made to the history of society."[23] The analogy, however, has a more explicitly political implication, as well—namely that thanks to the continual presence of a regenerative frontier, American Anglo-Saxons had thus far been spared the downward spiral of degeneration already affecting their less fortunate European ancestors.[24] Like Florida's "fountain of youth" in an earlier era, the western frontier held promise of a mystical elixir which would keep the country miraculously young, vibrant, and healthful—and thus protect it, presumably, from degenerative diseases, including sexual inversion.

This myth of the U.S. frontier is perhaps nowhere as evident as in the enormously popular dime novels of the late nineteenth century. Affordable, accessible, and increasingly sensationalistic, these formulaic adventure stories celebrated the character, as well as the exploits, of the quintessentially American individual who, in the words of prolific dime novelist Prentiss Ingraham, "stood as a barrier between civilization and savagery"[25]—thus avoiding excessive contamination from either. *Norma Trist; or, Pure Carbon: A Story of the Inversion of the Sexes* (1895) points back to these hastily produced and poorly plotted mass-culture publications (with titles like *Deadwood Dick of Deadwood; or, The Picked Party. A Romance of Skeleton Bend* [1880], *Mountain Kate; or, Love in the Trapping Grounds. A Tale of the Powder River Country* [1872], and, *The Forest Princess; or, The Kickapoo Captives. A Romance of the Illinois* [1871]), rather than forward to the naturalist novels of Frank Norris or Theodore Dreiser. However, whereas Carhart's Frank Artman admires and emulates "the Mexican" Rodriquez (and cherishes and courts a woman who is not only an invert, but a murderous assailant, as well), the dime novel hero more typically embraces a "professional duty . . . to fight Indians, Mexicans, and outlaws."[26] Carhart's divergence in this particular from his dime-novel models, like his recourse to the genre in the first place, can be traced to the uneasy engagement of his generally sympathetic portrayal of inversion with the increasing influence of naturalist ideologies.

Driven by imperialist anxiety, scientific debates about the inheritability of undesirable characteristics, about the inevitability of "genetic taint," and about professional authority over these areas of concern centered, customarily, on the subject of race. Thus, whether implicitly or explicitly, uneasily or enthusiastically, discussion of sexual abnormality unavoidably referenced the racial politics that informed the age. In the case of *Norma Trist*, Carhart's explicit (if ultimately unconvincing) morality play about ethical treatment of female inversion takes shape within the context of Texas' wholesale economic reorganization and concomitant social upheaval under encroaching U.S. capitalism. Apparently uncertain in its advocacy of hypnosis as a means to control female sexual insubordination, the novel is comparatively unequivocal in its "treatment" of such presumably peripheral aspects of identity as class and race. Although not a native Texan himself, Carhart seems to reject the overt racism associated with recent Anglo arrivals from the eastern United States and to encourage a return to the "peace structure" defined by sociologist and historian David Montejano as "an accommodative arrangement" whereby "the new Anglo elite was generally Mexicanized and frequently intermarried . . . with landowning Mexican families." According to Montejano, this peace structure disintegrated "at the turn of the century, [when] the second-generation American elite initiated an agricultural revolution," and violent, often racialized conflict characterized the process by which "the ranch country . . . was cleared to make room for farmers and a growing army of agricultural wage laborers."[27] Even within the fiction, Norma's ultimate reintegration into the implicitly Anglo dominant order represents only superficial stability, undercut at the outset by its occurrence within a context of complex social renegotiations whose unsettling implications the novel's thin narrative can barely contain. Marie LaMoreaux's marriage to Alphonso Rodriquez is represented in more clearly affirmative terms. From the outset, Marie welcomes Alphonso's advances. When she accepts his proposal, it is of her own accord—hypnotic suggestion is not necessary.[28] Thus, while Carhart's convoluted novel remains somewhat ambivalent on the foregrounded issue of female homosexuality, it offers a consistent if subtle critique of the "Americanization" of Texas' socio-economic organization. Along the way, it offers a useful example of the historical imbrication of different identity categories and of contemporary epistemologies and social investments that sustain them.

Within the novel, the Anglo Frank Artman—a farmer—compares unfavorably to the mestizo Alphonso Rodriquez, who is distinguished by the compelling combination of "manifest features of the high bred Castillian" with a "dusky" complexion and "hair of such inky blackness as to suggest the aboriginal type" (114). Carhart emphasizes Alphonso's nationality to an almost ludicrous extreme:

> He was a Mexican, at the head of a band of Mexicans, representing a wealthy and powerful company in Mexico, organized for the purpose of exploration in the vicinity of La Grange, with a view to finding, if possible, Mexican treasure of vast amounts, which was said to have been buried somewhere in this vicinity, either in a cave in chalk bluff, or in a ravine near Monument Hill, or else on the line

> of what was known as La Bahia Trail, which was a trail leading through from Mexico to Nacogdoches, and was a great thoroughfare for Mexicans when Texas belonged to Mexico. (13–14)

That this character is introduced in the context of a single unwieldy sentence in which Carhart somehow manages to mention Mexico no fewer than seven times only begins to suggest the problematic centrality of national affiliation and racial identification in this insistently convoluted narrative. Consider, for example, the first full description of Frank, an instance in which Carhart's interest in evolutionary eugenics is evident:

> Through the pearly whiteness of his cheeks there shone a roselike flush of superior healthfulness, whilst his lips, though beautiful with healthful redness, were free from sensual prominence. His cranial development was symmetrical, and would have furnished a model for an artist. It was not of the tall, two-story variety that betokens an utter lack of powers of observation, neither was it characterized by a towering forehead and a sloping but massive cerebellum, expressive of some intellect overshadowed by a gross animal nature. His chin and jaw were neither deficient nor too prominent, but symmetrical, harmonizing with the handsome face and well developed head. (17)

Carhart is similarly clear about the sociological implications, past and present, of Frank's physiognomy:

> [Frank] impressed the careful observer of men as having been favored with an honest, vigorous and healthy ancestry, and as embodying in himself a genial, hopeful and affectionate disposition, combined with patience and strong resolution, and determined purpose to carry out to successful completion any enterprise in which he might engage. (17)

Representing the combined results of heredity and hybridity, Alphonso provides an even clearer contrast to freak-of-nature Norma, she of *homo*racial heritage and *homo*sexual inclination. In his flattering portrayal of Rodriquez, Carhart recalls his colleague F.E. Daniel, who, advocating eugenic asexualization in terms well-suited to his Texas audience, suggests that physicians "bring to bear in the breeding of people the principles recognized and utilized by every intelligent stock raiser in the improvement of his cattle."[29] Just as Texas' trademark longhorn cattle began as specially bred hybrids of hardy (but apparently unappetizing) native breeds[30] and tender (but delicate) English ones, "the Mexican" Rodriquez represents "the glorious splendors of a new republic . . ., girt with power from the concentrated wisdom, virtue, and patriotism of uncounted ages" (113)—while farmer Frank, although improved through emulating Alphonso's elegant manner, can never completely shed "that inevitable uncouthness that clings to the clod" (115).

Alphonso, however, represents hybridity in the sexual sphere, as well. Whereas Frank is insistently described as "manly"—in "form" (72), in "nature" (16), and just in general (115)—Alphonso's "gentle and elegant deportment" (114) bespeaks a more balanced indulgence in gender stereotypes: "He was modest without bashfulness, gentle without foppishness, and delicately punctilious with regard to matters of etiquette" (113). Indeed, he rather resembles Norma's roommate at Maplewood Young Ladies' Seminary; "Miss Daisy" is also "gentle and affectionate in her disposition" while "studious and neat in her habits"—and also "punctilious in matters of etiquette" (48). Although "broad-shouldered and well-developed," Alphonso has hands "small and soft as a woman's" (23). He is, after all, not Frank's rival for Norma's affections, but the romantic rival of Norma herself. If, in his androgynous aspect, Alphonso rather resembles Norma, this makes all the more understandable Marie's apparent indifference as to accepting one's affections in place of the other's.

Norma and Alphonso thus figure as rivals in a double sense: they are equally androgynous romantic rivals competing for Marie's affections; they are exemplars of competing paradigms, with random variation rivaling determinable inheritance for philosophical predominance in a rapidly evolving United States. Carhart's resolution of this conflict—both aspects of it—begins to suggest the complexities of imagining lesbian identity in turn-of-the-century Texas and hints at the significance of his solutions to debate today. Surface appearances within and outside the text suggest that Norma and random variation lose out in the end to the attractive Alphonso and the seductive Spencerian assurance that U.S. imperialism, individual advancement, and Anglo dominance are God-given imperatives, driven by the laws of nature and sanctified by science. But the novel's superficial reassertion of the dominant order rests on shaky foundations. By refusing the association of female homosexuality with degeneration and confounding clear division between "acquired" and "congenital" homosexuality, *Norma Trist* calls into question not just European sexology, but also American evolutionary ideologies characterized by determinism, optimism about human progress, racist premises, and imperialist objectives.

"Pure Carbon": The Literature of Lesbian Identity[31]

Although the early 1890s abounded with speculative and sensationalistic discussion of female "erotopathia,"[32] previous to this period, as Carhart (exaggerating only slightly) notes in *Norma Trist*, "American literature was entirely barren, whether it regarded philosophy, science or fiction, of anything to throw light on the [subject of lesbianism]" (56). Although "French and German literature abounded with fiction to which sexual abnormalities had given rise[,] it was almost universally of so gross a nature as to render it unfit for translation into English for the American reader" (57).

Within the novel, the supposed lack of information available in the United States leaves even the most educated of Norma's acquaintances at a loss to understand her. The president of her school, for example, "flattered himself, as do many educators of youth, that he knew much of human nature, when in reality he had scarcely mastered the simplest elements of science" (70). Limited by unscientific superstitions about sin and depravity, he is unable to reconcile his impressions of the noble Norma with any image of sexual abnormality. Inevitably, under the circumstances, "the beautiful blending of the sensuous—not to say sensual—and the truly sublimely religious and poetic in Norma's nature, was an unsolved enigma to President Spencer" (69).[33] Such "lustful mysteries," the text suggests, are beyond the comprehension of all except scientists specializing in the study of "psycho-pathological states" (70).

The 1893 U.S. publication of Richard von Krafft-Ebing's monumental *Psychopathia Sexualis* marks an effort to change all that. The availability—in English—of this extensive collection of case histories and "expert" analysis of all variety of sexual anomalies instigated, among other things, a popularization of debates about the meaning and nature of homosexual identity and, ultimately, a profound shift in public perception of homosexual behavior.[34] Krafft-Ebing, moreover, was among the very first to examine *female* homosexuality explicitly and extensively. While lamenting that "science in its present stage has but few data to fall back on, so far as the occurrence of homosexual instinct in woman is concerned as compared with man," Krafft-Ebing remains convinced that "inverted sexuality occurs in women as frequently as in men"—a conviction consistent with his belief that such "anomaly is really a manifestation of functional degeneration."[35]

Arguing that, logically, "degenerative influences will [necessarily] prevail alike in women as well as men,"[36] Krafft-Ebing amasses an impressive collection of case histories to prove the point. From the "psychical hermaphroditism" of "Mrs. X" (possessed of "a passionate liking of her own sex," although "there was nothing in the behavior or the manners or the external appearance of this lady which in the least betrayed her anomaly")[37] to the "gynandry" of the "man-woman" Sandor,[38] Krafft-Ebing divides his examples into four distinct "grades" of "antipathic sexual instinct" and attempts to distinguish between "acquired" and "congenital" cases. "In general," he says, "the acquired cases are characterized in that":

> 1. The homosexual instinct appears as a secondary factor, and always may be referred to influences (masturbatic neurasthenia, mental) which disturbed normal sexual satisfaction. It is, however, probable that here, in spite of powerful sensual libido, the feeling and inclination for the opposite sex are weak originally, especially in a spiritual and aesthetic sense.
> 2. The homosexual instinct, so long as sexual inversion has not yet taken place, is looked upon, by the individual affected, as vicious and abnormal, and yielded to only as a makeshift.
> 3. The heterosexual instinct long remains predominant, and the impossibility to satisfy it gives pain. It weakens in proportion as the homosexual feeling gains in strength.

In "congenital" cases, in contrast,

> (a) The homosexual instinct is the one that occurs primarily, and becomes dominant in the *vita sexualis*. It appears as the natural manner of satisfaction, and also dominates the dream-life of the individual.
> (b) The heterosexual instinct fails completely, or, if it should make its appearance in the history of the individual (psychosexual hermaphroditism), it is still but an episodical phenomenon which has no root in the mental constitution, and it is essentially but a means to satisfaction of sexual desire.

The difference here involves both etiology and intractability; "the prognosis of the cases of acquired antipathic sexual instinct is, at all events, much more favorable than that of the congenital cases."[39]

Our heroine Norma Trist "could *not* have inherited her unfortunate abnormality, as nothing of the kind was ever known in the history of [the] family, on either side, so far as we can trace their histories" (244, emphasis added). On the other hand, oddly enough, Norma also exhibits many characteristics consistent with the most extreme grade of congenital lesbianism (what Krafft-Ebing calls "gynandry"). In the case of the aforementioned "Sandor," for example, the experts conclude that, however "abnormal," the subject's sexual inclinations were nonetheless natural *for her*: "S.'s characteristic expressions—'God put love in my heart. If He created me so, and not otherwise, am I, then, guilty; or is it the eternal, incomprehensible way of fate?'—are really justified."[40]

Norma not only shares this understanding of lesbian identity, she influences those around her to adopt it, as well. When Frank suggests that she consent to "treatment for the abnormal condition of [her] mind and heart," her indignant response is effective and an instructive exchange ensues:

> "Oh, Frank! you surprise me. You shock me! I must correct and inform you that my love for Marie is as natural to me as your love for me is natural to you."
>
> "I know, I know!" said Frank with evident embarrassment, "I meant abnormal, as people generally view such things."
>
> "Yes," said Norma, "it is abnormal in the eyes of the community."
>
> "That was all that I meant," said Frank. (228)

Indeed, Norma's insistence echoes Krafft-Ebing's assertion that "the development of the *vita sexualis*" in a congenital lesbian "may proceed with the same harmony and satisfying influence as in the normally disposed"—and accords with his interpretation of this fact as "further argument in favor of the assumption that antipathic sexual instinct is an equivalent for heterosexuality."[41]

Recalling Krafft-Ebing's definition of "congenital cases," however, makes Norma's experience seem even more mysterious. Although not inherited, "the homosexual instinct [incongruously] appears as the natural manner of satisfaction" to her. As evidenced by her letters to Marie, it also "is the one that occur[ed] primarily" and the one that "dominates [her] dream-life." "From my earliest years," Norma writes, "my inclinations have been for the female sex. In my thirteenth year I first felt a trace of sexual feeling. At that time, and ever since, feminine forms have exclusively appeared in my dream-pictures" (62).

As to the question of whether "the heterosexual instinct fail[ed] completely" in her case, Norma is equally clear: "I have no love or desire for the opposite sex—indeed the thought of intimacy with them is abhorrent to all the finer, better feelings of my nature. Such a thing would be impossible" (61).

Under the terms established by Krafft-Ebing, and even according to those scattered alternatives which emerged as *Psychopathia Sexualis* was discussed and debated among alienists in the United States, the existence of an individual like Norma Trist was impossible. Alice Mitchell, the young woman from Tennessee whose story apparently inspired parts of *Norma Trist*, was accordingly assumed to be congenitally inverted. "Expert testimony" offered during her trial for the murder of Freda Ward not only assumed her insanity, but attributed it to an innate instability presumably inherited along the maternal line. Mitchell was duly incarcerated in an insane asylum, where she reportedly committed suicide.[42] Clearly, the stakes surrounding association of heredity with inversion were high. For example, Dr. C.H. Hughes, editor of the journal *Alienist and Neurologist*, echoed Daniel's call for surgical "asexualization" of sex offenders. Both doctors referenced the Alice Mitchell case in calling for increased medical authority over questions concerning sexual abnormalities. Distressed that the "law ignored psychiatry," Hughes insisted that only "medical science" was qualified to "determine for society and for the State, what is restrainable and vicious, and what are the morbid and resistless organic impulsions of these *bizarre* eroto-sexual states." Dr. Irving Rosse stated plainly that "medical men are clearly the only persons qualified to give trustworthy information in regard to sexual matters."[43]

This anxiety over authority in cases of "inversion" remains at the crux of current conflicts and is only partially resolved even in the controlled context of Carhart's novel. Predictably, physician Carhart emphasizes the limits of legal understanding and argues for increased reliance on medical models and scientific approaches. On the other hand, he undercuts the authority of medical experts by (1) juxtaposing contradictory conclusions drawn by different members of the medical establishment, and (2) centering his story on a case—Norma's—which cannot finally be contained or satisfactorily explained within the context of any one of the several theories of female inversion in circulation among his contemporaries. Apparently an "unaccountable freak of nature" (215),[44] Norma can only be explained by a theory—random variation—incompatible with the ethnocentrism of U.S. evolutionary theory and unamenable to medical intervention.

A "Peculiar Positive Possibility": Lesbian Identity in 20th-Century U.S. Thought

As Carhart tells his readers, "should you choose to pursue your investigations further in the direction suggested" in this novel, "we doubt not but what you will find the subject, as we have done, one of scientific and social interest, involving far more in its scope than you would at first be led to suppose" (254). Sex, race, wealth, violence—*Norma Trist* engages the nation's obsessions. Situated *in medias res* of several significant social shifts, the novel is forced to negotiate a series of semiosic crises—the disruptions of meaning effected by shifting contexts and assumptions. Crucially, however, such changes in the "meaning" of material particulars were accompanied (and increasingly informed) by shifting assumptions about the meaning of "meaning" itself, as naturalist philosophies began to give way to pragmatist ideas.

In contrast to the "religious naturalism" of the once intellectually influential Unitarian Church (which held that divine order might be revealed through scientific investigation of the natural world) and to the "philosophical naturalism" influenced by Darwin and Mill (which held that scientific inquiry could expose eternal truths without reference to a supernatural order),[45] the philosophical movement known as "American pragmatism" placed its emphasis not on the invisible (unknowable? nonexistent?) essences of "things-in-themselves," but on their tangible effects in the observable world. Peirce's work on semiosis offers the most in-depth and comprehensive theory of epistemology attempted in the United States to that time (arguably, to date). Although it's difficult to determine the extent to which Peirce's important but somewhat obscure publications actually influenced the ways in which the U.S. public interpreted experience (although Peirce *did* influence more popular philosophers, including William James and John Dewey), it seems plausible that Peirce's articulation of a constructive interrelation between thought and reality may be taken as an index to changing currents in U.S. thought.

As I argued in Chapter 1, the involvement of experience and interpretation in the making of meaning is everywhere evident in Peirce's sign theory, most centrally, perhaps, in his conception of the basic sign relation as inherently triadic. Now I want to briefly revisit that formulation in order to clarify the kind of involvement implied. Peirce suggests that every sign "creates in the mind of [a] person an equivalent sign, or perhaps a more developed sign" *not* through a mechanistic and invariable relation to its object, but in reference to a third term, "a sort of idea" which Peirce calls the *ground*. In Peirce's account, the "laws" of any semiotic system are both imperfect and continually evolving—based upon general, but always incomplete, agreement among disparately positioned participants. The ground on which they build is itself the tenuous achievement of previous significations. Each sign points to another—"equivalent" or "more developed"—sign, which points to another, etc., with each standing in turn for an evolving object "not in all respects, but in reference to a sort of idea" that shifts with each turn of the cycle. Peirce thus attaches the meaning of any isolated sign to an infinite spiral of interrelated, culturally mediated terms.

A second tripartite schema organizes "the ideas that belong to ordinary experience or that naturally arise in connection with ordinary life":

> Firstness is the mode of being of that which is such as it is, positively and without reference to anything else.
>
> Secondness is the mode of being of that which is such as it is, with respect to a second, but regardless of any third.
>
> Thirdness is the mode of being of that which is such as it is, in bringing a second and third into relation to each other.[46]

Elements belonging to the category of "firstness" might be understood as roughly analogous to those syntactic abstractions commonly assigned to the category of "deep structures." Just as an inarticulate deep *syntactic* structure underlies any actual utterance (and informs interpretation), an always immaterial "deep subject," a semantic "firstness," underlies any meaningful instantiation of a quality or characteristic. Firstness is thus related to the element identified as "ground" in Peirce's theory of sign relations and to the "permanent possibility" that Butler invokes; the nature of Norma Trist's "inversion," for example, can be made meaningful only "in reference to a sort of idea" of what a female invert must be—in reference, that is, to a "firstness." But here my analogy fails: although some syntacticians still assume that deep structures are universal and unchanging, hard-wired into the human brain, "deep subjects" are clearly contingent constuctions. Their "firstness" is relative; their independence, illusory. Like the subjects they ground, in this sense, they comprise "the permanent possibility of a certain resignifying process."[47]

In his correspondence with English philosopher Victoria Lady Welby, for example, Peirce offers as illustration "the scarlet of your royal liveries," explaining that

> The quality itself, independently of its being perceived or remembered, is an example, by which I do not mean that you are to imagine that you *do not* perceive or remember it, but that you are to drop out of account that which may be attached to it in perceiving or remembering, but which does not belong to the quality. For example, when you remember it, your idea is said to be *dim* and when it is before your eyes, it is *vivid*. But dimness or vividness do not belong to your idea of the quality. . . . The quality of red is not thought of as belonging to you, or as attached to liveries. *It is simply a peculiar positive possibility regardless of anything else.* [48]

Peirce's category of "firstness" is thus comprised of elements understood to exist *only* as *ideas*—possibility realized (meaning made material) ceases to exist as pure possibility (pure *meaning*). Although "not thought of" as contingent upon material particulars, however, deep subjects exist only as abstracted from them.[49] Here again, then, materiality is understood to be the inescapable interface between ground and meaning.

Crucially, this process of abstraction is contingent upon indexicality; it is predicated upon observations accumulated through perspectival and physically constrained means of perception. Recalling that Peirce characterizes sign relations as iconic, indexical, and/or symbolic "according as the relation of the sign to its object consists in the sign having some character in itself [i.e.: iconic resemblance to its object], or in some existential relation to that object [i.e.: indexical causality/contiguity], or in its relation to an interpretant [symbolic rule-governed, arbitrary association]," the relevance of indexicality to twentieth-century lesbian identity becomes immediately evident in the "scientific" practice of reading observable physical phenomena as *signs* of an interior, essential sexual identity. Sexologists such as Krafft-Ebing attributed both physiological and behavioral "aberrations" to the causal influence of an innate "inversion" of the normative sexual instinct. Imperceptible in and of itself (as is any "quality" falling into the category of "firstness"), such inversion conveniently revealed itself on a regular basis in the manifestation of observable externals such as secondary sexual characteristics (e.g.: the "muscular shoulders", "small, compact breasts", and "slender flanks" of the early twentieth-century's most famous lesbian, Radclyffe Hall's Stephen Gordon).[50]

The significance of indexicality to lesbian identity goes beyond any belief in the validity of such causal associations, however.[51] Beyond (or, perhaps, beneath) questions of causality lies the issue of contiguity—i.e.:

of context. The indexical element is dominant in such inferences of homosexuality as discussed above because of the observer's interpretive dependence on knowledge of "a situation relative to the observed, or assumed to be experientially known." Clearly, the significant secondary sexual characteristics do not refer to homosexuality by means of their resemblance to it, in the manner that an icon indicates its object; nor do they denote homosexuality simply through arbitrary intellectual association, as do symbols their interpretants. It's not that "slender flanks," for example, represent "homosexuality" in any straightforward or consistent manner, but that contextual information about the position of the "speaker" within the socially significant matrix of gender allows us "appropriate" interpretation of this otherwise ambiguous sign. Because Norma Trist's "inversion" is not betrayed by the exterior signs of anomalous secondary sexual characteristics, her abnormality must be indexed by behavioral cues. On being abruptly accosted by an anonymous highwayman, for example, Norma proves "equal to the occasion" while Marie (conveniently providing an appropriately feminine contrast) screams, faints, and falls "over Norma's arm in complete helplessness" (13). That the apparent accoster turns out to be an extremely apologetic Alphonso, who becomes Norma's rival for Marie's affections, only underscores the implications of Norma's proving "equal."

Whereas iconicity inheres in "actual" qualities, and symbolic reference is arbitrary and abstract, indexicality inhabits the intersection. Mediating between the material world and the merely semantic, indexicality invests the former with meaning, the latter with relevance, and itself with the peculiar positive possibility of explaining how it is that each may be seen to inform the other—reinventing the "actual" at every turn.

This theory of sign relations, the invisible underpinnings of the Pragmatist revolution, makes manifest an understanding of the meaning of "meaning" indigenous to the turn-of-the-century United States. Moreover, it marks an epistemological shift, as profound as it was partial, which undergirds and helps to explain concurrent (and similarly conflicted) changes in conceptions of lesbianism. Understanding inversion as physiological was consistent with a Naturalist world view: the essence was innate, congenital and unchangeable; inversion was experiential only insofar as signs of that essence (physical or behavioral) manifested themselves in predictable ways in the observable world. The idea that historical circumstance and social negotiation might also be crucially involved in structuring (homo)sexuality demands different assumptions about the relation between observable signs and immaterial meanings—

and this what *Norma Trist* ultimately, if ambivalently, implies.

Although Carhart retains a certain professional investment in physiological determinism, he is clearly intrigued by new notions about the relation of context to meaning. *Norma Trist* is riddled with allusions, borrowings, and instances of outright plagiarism—i.e.: with the removal of linguistic entities from one context and their relocation in another. Norma's love letters to Marie, for example, include almost verbatim excerpts from Krafft-Ebing's case history of a European female invert, the ubiquitous "Sandor." Krafft-Ebing, for example, relates that "S. complained of her heart, that would allow no reason to direct it; she expressed emotions which were such as only could be felt—not simulated" and cites words written to the woman who had been her lover:

> Thy dear sweet voice; the voice whose tone perchance would raise me from the dead; that has been for me like the warm breath of Paradise! Thy presence alone were enough to alleviate my mental and moral anguish. It was a magnetic stream; it was a peculiar power your being exercised over mine, which I cannot quite define; and, therefore, I cling to that ever true definition: I love you because I love you. In the night of sorrow I had but one star—the star of Marie's love.[52]

Norma, on the other hand, writes to *her* lover (also named Marie):

> O, my dearest one, what a strange heart is mine that will not allow reason to guide it. My emotions seem sometimes as though they would rend me—they cannot be simulated. Your dear, sweet voice, the voice whose tone perchance would raise me from the dead—that has been for me like the warm breath of Paradise! Your presence were enough to relieve my mental and moral anguish. Your dear presence was a magnetic stream; it was a peculiar power your being exercised over me, which I can not quite define. In the night of sorrow I had but one star,—the star of your love! (53–4).

More striking yet is Sandor's impassioned plea—

> O God, Thou All-pitying, Almighty One! Thou seest my distress; Thou knowest how I suffer. Incline Thyself to me; extend Thy helping hand to me, deserted by all the world. Only God is just. How beautifully does Victor Hugo describe this in his *Légendes du Siècle*! How sad do Mendelssohn's words sound to me: "Nightly in dreams I see thee![53]

—repeated verbatim (excepting her addition of the phrase "as I am liable to be" between "deserted" and "by all the world") by Norma (62).

In contrast to the feminine Norma, however, Krafft-Ebing's subject is characterized by "a congenitally abnormal inversion of the sexual instinct *which, indeed, expressed itself, anthropologically, in anomalies of development of the body, depending upon great hereditary taint.*"[54] As a representative of "the extreme grade of degenerative homosexuality," moreover, "the woman of this type possesses of the feminine qualities only the genital organs; thought, sentiment, action, even external appearance are those of the man."[55] Nonetheless, Norma's letters express affection in exactly the terms used by this "invert" to address her lover. Perhaps Carhart sought to establish his heroine's similarity to this real-life female lover of women who, like the fictional Norma, ultimately went unpunished for "criminal acts [which] had their foundation in her abnormal and irresistible sexuality." In any case, the *meaning* of these passages is altered entirely by the change in context. Whereas Krafft-Ebing invokes these utterances to indicate the existence of a masculine soul in a female (but not feminine) body, Carhart introduces the possibility that a woman, physically and psychically female, might actually desire another woman.

On the basis of such evidence, Jonathan Katz concludes that "Dr. Carhart's novel is emphatically pro-invert—until its final turnabout."[56] In the end, Frank Artman hires the hypnotist-physician who testified at the second trial to "treat" Norma's "abnormal" condition. Against all evidence, Dr. Jaspar determines that Norma's apparently innate "abnormal sexual impulse" is, incongruously, neither hereditary nor congenital. By means of hypnotic suggestion, he induces Norma to marry Frank and bear his children. Norma's natural and irresistible sexual impulse is thus paradoxically portrayed as *acquired*, insofar as it is alterable (the clearest evidence of congenital sexual instinct, according to Krafft-Ebing, is its intransigence).

The nature of Norma's lesbianism cannot be clearly fixed according to the explicit standards of her day (or ours). Her sexual identity is depicted as innate *and* acquired, integral *and* alterable. She is one man's romantic rival and another's ultimate conquest. Physically female, she is androgynously athletic. She avoids the company of men, but enjoys "masculine" pursuits. Even her erotic expression, the catalyst of all this confusion, is ultimately ambiguous. Discreetly questioned during her second trial as to the degree of sexual satisfaction achieved with her female lover, Norma answers "frankly and freely" (if somewhat abstractly) that her "love for and relations with Marie afforded the highest and profoundest satisfaction of which the entire human being is capable in the realm of human love" (212)—an equally apt description of ennobling, although chaste, romantic love and orgasmic, although crass, erotic consummation. The ambiguity of this answer calls into question not simply the meaning of Norma's own desires, but the meaning and purpose of love *per se.*

Norma remains a peculiar positive provocation, a challenge to the theoretical impasse between essentialism and constructivism seen to structure lesbian possibility at the turn of this century as surely as at the turn of the last. The nature of that challenge, I propose, is pragmatist; in Norma, Carhart posits a tenuous, temporal, situated reconciliation—inconceivable and hence unreadable within more dominant philosophical paradigms—in which lesbian subjectivity is infused with a pragmatic sensibility.

In the last of his *Monist* series, Peirce engages the scientific debates dramatized in the rivalry between Norma and Alphonso. As Peirce puts it, "Evolution by sporting and evolution by mechanical necessity are conceptions warring against one another."[57] But in this essay entitled "Evolutionary Love," Peirce draws on the earlier articles to delineate "a third method, which supersedes their strife."[58] In 1891's "Architecture of Theories," Peirce argued that "the only possible way of accounting for the laws of nature and for uniformity in general is to suppose them results of evolution":

> This supposes them not to be absolute, not to be obeyed precisely. It makes an element of indeterminacy, spontaneity, or absolute chance in nature. Just as, when we attempt to verify any physical law, we find our observations cannot be precisely satisfied by it, and rightly attribute the discrepancy to errors of observation, so we must suppose far more minute discrepancies to exist owing to *the imperfect cogency of the law itself, to a certain swerving of the facts from any definite formula.*

Peirce's approach, so unexpected in a physical scientist, thus eschews the naturalist imperative to ferret out universal and immutable truths. Instead, he attempts to chart the relays by which material facts and semantic understandings inform each other. He extends his matter-of-fact observation that "the old dualistic notion of mind and matter, so prominent in Cartesianism, as two radically different kinds of substance, will hardly find defenders today" to a remarkable conclusion, arguing that "the one intelligible theory of the universe is that . . . matter is effete mind, inveterate habits *becoming physical laws*." Although, as his semiotic theory makes clear, the constitutive relays are endlessly imbricated and never unidirectional, Peirce accounts for the possibility of *psychical* "truths" informing physical law. Indeed, he goes so far as to suggest that it is *physical laws*, and not psychical habits, which are, relatively speaking, "derived and special."[59]

In "Evolutionary Love," Peirce advances an "agapastic theory of evolution" which holds that while both "fortuitous variation" and "mechanical necessity" play central roles in the development of species, "advance takes place by virtue of a positive sympathy among the created springing from continuity of mind."[60] Although Peirce apparently sought to preserve a specifically Christian sense of love at the core of scientific necessity, his rejection of pure Darwinism is also clearly informed by the kind of "cultural critique" that Cornel West identifies with pragmatism. Writing at the end of the 1800s, Peirce caustically characterizes this epoch as "the Economical Century," mocking the nation's embrace of a capitalist logic which held that "intelligence in the service of greed ensures the justest prices, the fairest contracts, the most enlightened conduct of all the dealings between men, and leads to the *summum bonum*, food in plenty and perfect comfort." ("Food for whom?" he asks. "Why for the greedy master of intelligence.") In Peirce's analysis, *Origin of Species* commits the characteristic error of the age: "the great attention paid to economical questions during our century has induced an exaggeration of the beneficial effects of greed and of the unfortunate results of sentiment, until there has resulted a philosophy which comes to this, that greed is the great agent in the elevation of the human race and in the evolution of the universe." In contrast to his transcendentalist contemporaries, however, Peirce evokes not an originary or underlying unity, but an always imperfect urge *towards* sympathy and understanding. In secular terms, this tendency might be interpreted as a predilection towards sense-making—an impulse towards orderliness, predictability, patterns; a desire for meaning. Peirce argues that this inclination is not a human imposition on the natural world, but itself a force of nature.

From this perspective, material variation may be random, but what we make of it is not—and nature is what we make of it, constrained by history, habit, physicality, but evolving nonetheless. *Norma Trist* introduces an idea of lesbian possibility unassimilable to any one of the dominant discourses then available to explain "inversion." Norma's homosexual desire is not a symptom of inherited degeneracy, nor an effect of physiological gender inversion—but it is innate, irresistible, and integral to her personality. The book's conclusion restores the dominant order—Anglo economic dominance, universal heterosexuality—but exposes its flimsy foundations. Frank's wealth is undeserved, the result of luck and theft; Norma Artman's heterosexuality is compelled, imposed instead of natural. Our heroine is no longer identified as *triste*,[61] but her new name implies that all this normalcy is artifice. By challenging the cultural logic that these surface effects can be reliably read as the mimetic representation of an underlying moral order or independent material reality, *Norma Trist* opens the door to an alternative semiotic understanding. The lesbianism that Norma leaves behind points to the possibility of meaning-making not predicated on greed, the racist rationales that serve it, or determinist understandings of material reality as primary and self-evident. Underlying the surface incongruity of Norma's sexual identity is an unrealized but emergent understanding of meaning as at once contingent and natural, a pragmatic perspective which sees signification as part of a process by which the social permeates perception.

Chapter 3

Legal Realism and Lesbian Representation: *The Well of Loneliness* in the United States

As *Norma Trist* suggests, lesbian pragmatism initially resisted a capitalist logic seeking to naturalize its racist rationales through appeals to an extra-semiotic reality. But as *Norma*'s end presages, this threat to the dominant order has been continually constrained, contained, and controlled, often with the acquiescence of lesbians. As female homosexuality attracted increasing attention, the pragmatic promise of its early appearances was sharply curtailed. The twentieth century's most notorious lesbian fiction—Radclyffe Hall's *The Well of Loneliness* (1928)—was especially influential in this development. Prior to its publication, popular conceptions of female homosexuality in the United States were vague and varied, but with *The Well*, "an abrupt locking into place of meaning"[1] circumscribed the developing discourses of female homosexuality within constraints now so pervasive they pass almost unnoticed.

Most readers contend that this influence is a predictable effect of the publicity generated by the novel's indictment on obscenity charges, and assume that the relatively more stable notion of female homosexuality that emerged is an extension of author Radclyffe Hall's established belief in sexological theories of congenital inversion. *The Well* tells the story of a "queer,"[2] sensitive child raised in wealth on nineteenth-century ideals of honor, chivalry, and noblesse oblige; as an adult, the heroine ultimately sacrifices her own happiness to save her beloved from the tragedy of a lesbian life. Teresa de Lauretis voices the overwhelming critical consensus when she describes the book as "drawing its view of homosexuality from the late-nineteenth-century sexology of Krafft-Ebing and Havelock Ellis" and explains that "it was intended, and in the main received, as a plea for social acceptance or toleration of sexual deviance cast in terms of divine compassion and liberal humanism." Because the terms of that toleration seem to require a narrow conception of lesbianism as gender inversion and "the repudiation of lesbianism as such," most critics concur that the novel simply "confirm[s its protagonist's] view of herself as a 'freak,' 'nature's mistake'—a masculine woman."[3] Even those who value this representation more highly agree in its basic assessment. Judith Halberstam, for example, agrees "that *The Well of Loneliness* closely resembles Havelock Ellis's model of female inversion." Indeed, she takes it to be "the most elaborate of all the depictions of early-twentieth-century female masculinity," and suggests that Hall's heroine seems "much more closely related to what we now call a transsexual identity" than to lesbianism.[4] And Esther Newton defends Hall's strategy on the grounds that it made possible the imputation of desire and sexual agency to an upper-class white female protagonist. Others, however, have concluded that the costs were too high. Catharine Stimpson calls the book "a parable of damnation,"[5] while Newton herself acknowledges that even the novel's appeal may lie in the supposedly damning stereotypes it appears to promote:

> *The Well* has continuing meaning to lesbians because it confronts the stigma of lesbianism—as most lesbians have had to live it. . . . As the Bowery bum represents all that is most feared and despised about drunkenness, the mannish lesbian, of whom Stephen Gordon is the most famous prototype, has symbolized the stigma of lesbianism and so continues to move a broad range of lesbians.[6]

And that's the thing: for all its narrowness, negativity, self-pity, and repudiation, *The Well* has indeed continued "to move a broad range of lesbians" *and* to deeply affect the conditions and conceptions of lesbian possibility in twentieth-century Anglo-America.

Clearly, "*The Well of Loneliness* occupies a complicated place in the the history of lesbian fiction"; Halberstam claims Hall's book is "both the best-known novelistic depiction of a lesbian and the most problematic."[7] Canadian novelist Jane Rule simply calls it "*the* lesbian novel, a title familiar to most readers of fiction, either a bible or a horror story for any lesbian who reads at all."[8] U.S. historian Blanche Wiesen Cook acknowledges that "*The Well* was banned in England only to become throughout western civilization the archetype of all things lesbian—the 'butch,' the tears, the despair of it all."[9] So how can a novel so "trite, superficial," "dull," "unduly long," "melodramatic," "inflated and sentimental" have such staying power?[10] Why would its influence be so profound? Although many have attributed the book's impact to its notoriety in a context offering very few public images of lesbianism,[11] and some, like Newton, have suggested that the book's supposed faults actually underlie its success, these accounts don't fully explain how one book can be both "bible" and "horror story"—and don't even attempt to address the discrepancy implied in Cook's observation that the book was banned *only* to become an "archetype." Newton's insight that the novel's impact might somehow be related to its reliance on negative stereotypes, however, may be usefully extended to examine the role Hall's novel has played in *shaping* the particular "stigma of lesbianism" it has come to symbolize.

Ironically, de Lauretis' widely shared assumption that the appeal to liberal humanism must be a quality intrinsic to the text itself is *itself* an assumption "cast in terms" of liberal foundationalism. Not coincidentally, it is also consistent with the reading of Stephen as an unproblematic example of congenital inversion. By this understanding, the book's influence is overt and unidirectional; the novel affects society exactly to the extent that readers accept and adopt the understanding of female homosexuality depicted within (and presumably exemplified by Stephen). "Society" can act on the novel, in contrast, only by suppressing (censoring) or accepting the terms it sets out. This situation parallels exactly the relationship drawn between the congenital invert and the society (fictional or otherwise) in which she appears: others may accept or reject, deny or expose the truth she embodies, but her sexuality is understood to be an integral and incontrovertible quality of the invert herself.

From a more pragmatic perspective, the "abrupt locking into" (congenital) identity of (lesbian) desire appears an effect less of text (Hall's or those that influenced her) than of the particular historical circumstances through which *The Well* was introduced to the United States. Indicted on charges of obscenity, Hall's novel entered this country via a legal system itself in the throes of a paradigm shift. One result, I believe, was that what Leigh Gilmore calls "the mutuality between literary and legal production" of lesbian identity[12] was cemented, ironically, in a legal preference for understanding female homosexuality as congenital inversion—and a cultural tendency to see lesbians' legal standing as rooted in this foundationalist identity. So while Americans continue to argue whether "real" lesbians are necessarily born that way, a more fundamental presumption has settled into the national conviction that there is a meaningful distinction to be drawn between "status" and "conduct." Whether revered or reviled, disdained or desired, Stephen Gordon has been codified as the quintessential congenital butch—and the example of her experience has contributed in this country to a mindset marginally more comfortable with homosexual identity than with homosexual activity (evidenced, for example, in the oddity of increasing civil rights protections enacted against a backdrop of enduring sodomy laws). Interestingly, *The Well*'s journey through the U.S. legal system marks a juncture at which a very different understanding of lesbianism very nearly entered mainstream discourse.

Incident Added to Incident

In August 1928, the *New York Times* reported that a reputable U.S. publisher was "TO PRINT BANNED BOOK HERE." "Alfred Knopf," the subhead elucidated (misleadingly) had obtained the "American rights to 'Well of Loneliness.'" The brief item, datelined London, describes Hall's novel as "the book on sex matters suppressed by its publishers here on the request of the Home Secretary, after a newspaper controversy." Needless to say, the particular publication history of this particular novel positioned it to enter the U.S. "situation" in particular ways.

First published in England by Jonathan Cape, the book had come out on July 27, 1928, to mixed, but generally respectful reviews; the *Saturday Review*, the *Sunday Times*, and the *Nation and Athenaeum* all applauded the book's sincerity and seriousness, but, to varying degrees, also suggested that the novel's polemic at times overpowered its art.[13] Leonard Woolf was among the harsher critics, describing the story as "extremely interesting" and admitting that "it is written with understanding and frankness, with sympathy and feeling," but concluding nevertheless that "the book fails completely as a work of art."

> Miss Hall loses the whole in its parts, and is so intent on the stars that she forgets the heavens. Her book is formless and therefore chaotic. . . . The first 150 pages are good[,] but after the death of Sir Philip the novel becomes a catalogue, almost a ragbag. Incident is added to incident, and character to character, and one sees the relevance which Miss Hall intended each to have to the theme of the book. But their relevance is intellectual, not emotional, and therefore not artistic. They remain discrete patches which never join to form a pattern.[14]

Woolf's criticisms were mild, however, compared to the attack that appeared on August 19 in the *Sunday Express*. Under the banner headline "A Book That Must Be Suppressed," James Douglas' article denounced *The Well* for promoting perversion. "I say deliberately," he wrote, "that this novel is not fit to be sold by any bookseller or to be borrowed from any library. . . . I would rather give a healthy boy or a healthy girl a phial of prussic acid than this novel. Poison kills the body, but moral poison kills the soul."[15]

On August 20, the *Daily Express* printed Cape's rebuttal—and his offer to forward copies of the book to the Home Secretary and the Director of Public Prosecutions for review. Remarkably, he volunteered to discontinue publication and destroy the printing plates at their request. By subjecting the book's future to the discretion of noted reactionary William Joynson-Hicks, the British Home Secretary (a move made, incidentally, without consulting—or even informing—author Radclyffe Hall), Cape virtually ensured *The Well*'s suppression in England.

The publisher attempted to redeem himself by shipping molds of the text to Paris' Pegasus Press before destroying the plates, and by advertising the resultant Paris edition to English booksellers. But it was too late for England. When shipments of the Paris edition were seized by English Customs and declared obscene, Cape's initial acquiesence came back to haunt him. Both the publisher's voluntary withdrawal of the novel and his apparent duplicity in reintroducing the book via this French connection helped to discredit the project—and, hence, Hall's purpose—in the eyes of the law. After a well-publicized and well-attended trial, Bow Street Magistrates Court declared *The Well of Loneliness* officially obscene on November 20, 1928. The perfunctory appeal was lost on December 19, with the court's conclusion that *The Well* was "a disgusting book [and] prejudicial to the morals of the community."[16]

As if anxious to exert influence similar to that exhibited by the English press, the *New York Times* opportunistically (and inaccurately) characterized *The Well* as a "SEX NOVEL" in both the headline and the copy of their second article about the novel's suppression.[17] Although this article also identifies Alfred Knopf as the U.S. publisher of *The Well*, the Knopfs had in fact long since rescinded their offer, on the excuse that Hall had violated her contract by allowing Cape to bring the book out in England well in advance of the planned simultaneous publication date. Apparently, the Knopfs were deterred by the English legal decision, and preferred not to risk similar reprisals in the U.S.

Back in July, Alfred Knopf had written to Hall about his concerns, claiming that he was "rather disturbed" to learn of Cape's plans for early publication. Instead of scrapping the U.S. edition, however, he proposed hurrying the book to press by early fall, and promised that as long as the proofs were returned promptly "all will be well." At this date, Alfred Knopf claimed to "feel very happy indeed that we are to publish [*The Well of Loneliness*]," describing it as "a very fine book indeed" and professing to "have very great hopes for its success."[18] At least as late as September 5, in fact, production seems to have been proceeding apace, as Knopf's secretary wrote to assure Radclyffe Hall that corrections she had sent had been made.[19]

On September 20, however, Blanche Knopf wrote with disturbing news. "Dear John,"[20] she said,

> When I was in London I was inclined to feel as you did, that there would be no difficulty in the way of THE WELL OF LONELINESS over here. Now that I have been back at the office for a week and have got in touch with the situation here I find it much more serious than I had suspected.

According to this letter, the "seriousness" of the situation involved several related factors, including "a lot of very unfortunate publicity in the American press," quantities of orders "not . . . from the better type of book seller but rather from dealers who expect a sensational demand for the book from people who expect something very s[a]lacious," and Cape's irresponsible handling of affairs in England. Blanche Knopf came down especially hard on this lattermost point:

> Our decision not to publish [The Well of Loneliness] will I am sure, come as a great shock to you but you must view the situation from our point of view. We are . . . faced with the hopeless prospect of attempting to defend a book which had not been defended in its author's own country.
>
> I must point out in this connect[ion] that while it would have been difficult to forsee the English fate of THE WELL OF LONELINESS the unfortunate American situation of the book would have been completely avoided had we been protected, as we should have been, by being able to effect simultaneous publication with Cape. When our deal went through it was certainly on the assumption that we would be so protected. . . . [W]e feel we were definitely sacrificed to Cape's convenience and this is the result.

Although she offered to turn her firm's type over to another U.S. publisher at cost, Blanche Knopf implored her friend John "to keep the book entirely out of the American market," claiming that "no American publisher could now handle it except as pornography."[21]

Fortunately for Radclyffe Hall, this warning proved false. The novel was quickly picked up by the progressive new publishing house of Covici-Friede, who brought out the first U.S. edition of *The Well of Loneliness* in December 1928. Forewarned by the English fiasco, Covici-Friede took a proactive approach to the obscenity issue. As soon as the book was selling well, Donald Friede (who in 1925, as a partner in the Boni and Liveright house, had engineered his own arrest in Boston for selling Dreiser's *An American Tragedy*) reportedly telephoned John Sumner of the New York Society for the Suppression of Vice to turn himself in.[22] Not long afterwards, New York police dutifully seized 865 copies of the U.S. edition's sixth printing, and Friede was duly charged with violating section 1141 of the state penal code.

The publishers had prepared for this eventuality by engaging attorney Morris Ernst (who would successfully defend *Ulysses* against similar charges a few years later) to represent *The Well*, should the need arise. Already an established advocate of free expression, Ernst had agreed to defend the book in exchange for a portion of the royalties. This innovative arrangement radically reduced the publisher's financial risk, while also enabling them to obtain credible representation. Covici-Friede had further prepared by including in their sixth printing of the novel a number of laudatory opinions by literary critics and respected authors—thus slipping into the official record "evidence" of the book's respectability which might otherwise have been inadmissable. On February 21, 1929, the case was heard in the City Magistrates Court (Borough of Manhattan, Seventh District), Judge Hyman Bushel presiding.

"The Movement of Pragmatism as a Philosophy of Law"

The Well entered the U.S. courts during a tumultuous time, as a forward-looking progressive jurisprudence tried to consolidate its successes of the early twentieth century and mount a meaningful challenge to classical legal theory. Legal historians describe this move away from precedent-based jurisprudence and towards a results-oriented practice as consistent with the larger Progressive movement and what historian Morton White has termed the "Revolt against Formalism." Roscoe Pound spoke for many of his contemporaries when he identified this change in legal reasoning with a larger cultural shift, writing in 1909 that "jurisprudence is the last in the march of the sciences away from the deduction from predetermined conceptions." Championing a "sociological" jurisprudence that would advance "the adjustment of principles and doctrines to the human conditions they are to govern rather than to assumed first principles," Pound applauded the trend he termed "the movement for pragmatism as a philosophy of law."[23] The description is apt. Like philosopher C.S. Peirce, progressive or sociological jurisprudes (and, after them, in a fashion, the so-called "legal realists") tended to seek meaning in effects instead of sources and saw abstractions as (relatively) derivative, with historical, material foundations. In 1921's *The Nature of the Judicial Process*, Justice Benjamin Cardozo famously observed that law "is not found, but made"—and argued that "its truth is relative, not absolute."[24]

Given its origins in labor law and contracts, such "legal pragmatism" would seem unlikely to figure in the censorship of lesbian literature, but I think there is evidence that its influence registered even in the obscenity trial for *The Well of Loneliness*—and left its mark on subsequent understandings of lesbianism. Ironically, the effect was not salutory. As the pragmatic insights of the progressive movement grew increasingly reified and decontextualized in their expanding application, their effects, in this case and in general, became increasingly reactionary. Divorced from the semiotic theory that animated them and cut off from the material contexts of their creation, putatively progressive approaches assumed a foundationalist arrogance, positioning themselves as "first principles," and betraying the promise of their pragmaticist heritage.[25]

On entering the United States, then, Hall's novel was caught up in a field of contestation in which not simply its own alleged obscenity, but the very logic and nature of legal judgment were open to question. The question directly before the court, in contrast, was simply whether Friede had violated section 1141 of New York state's penal code, which stipulated that "a person who sells * * * or has in his possession with intent to sell, * * * any obscene, lewd, lascivious, filthy, indecent or disgusting book * * * is guilty of a misdemeanor." In this case, interestingly, even the prosecution agreed that the novel under indictment "contains no unclean words"—and Judge Bushel concurred.[26] And in fact, *The Well* is a singularly unsexy book, devoid not only of "lewd" language, but of any direct description of sexual activity. Because the book could not be characterized as lewd, lascivious, filthy, or disgusting, Bushel based his judgment against the publishers not in the novel's language, but in his estimation of its possible effects. From this perspective, it could be considered potentially indecent and obscene. To legitimate this decision, Bushel was reduced to relying on an 1868 English case for precedent. The ruling in *Regina v. Hicklin* held that the test of obscenity should be "whether the tendency of the matter charged as obscenity is to deprave or corrupt those whose minds are open to such immoral influences, and who might come into contact with it." In their memorandum to the court of appeals, Friede's defense lawyers dismissed this rationale as an "ancient test of obscenity" and denounced it as "patently unfair, unreasonable, and unsound," arguing that "it sought to gauge the mental and moral capacity of the community by that of its dullest-witted and most fallible members, and . . . to withhold from society any material which might conceivably injure its lowest and most fatuous element."[27] Bushel, however, would admit only that this test of immoral influence is "not sole and exclusive"—and concluded that it nevertheless "may be accepted as a basis for judicial decision" in the case of *People v. Friede*. In his view, *Hicklin* is a test that *The Well of Loneliness* obviously fails.

This judgment is of course based in Bushel's understanding of the novel, which he summarizes as follows:

> The book here involved is a novel dealing with the childhood and early womanhood of a female invert. In broad outline the story shows how these unnatural tendencies manifested themselves from early childhood; the queer attraction of the child to the maid in the household; her affairs with one Angela Crossby, a normally sexed, but unhappily married woman. . . . The book culminates with an extended elaboration upon her intimate relations with a normal young girl, who becomes a helpless subject of her perverted influence and passion.

That "the author has treated these incidents not without some restraint" is irrelevant to the test applied. What *is* central to the question at hand is that "the unnatural and depraved relationships portrayed are sought to be idealized and extolled." Bushel takes issue, in other words, not with the letter of the text, but with its implications—not with the words used or even the referents they evoke, but with the book's potential to shift the terms of social judgment. What's objectionable, from his perspective, is the way "the characters in the book who indulge in these vices are described in attractive terms," the way in which "it is maintained throughout that they be accepted on the same plane as persons normally constituted, and that their perverse and inverted love is as worthy as the affections between normal beings."[28]

In this, as in general, Bushel might seem to follow Sir Chartres Biron, the English magistrate who also seized on the *Hicklin* test to support his judgement—but although the similarities are striking, Bushel's decision was rendered in a different context, with distinct stakes and implications. The best refuge of literary freedom in early twentieth-century New York, for example, was the established standard of judging works in their entirety instead of on impressions of isolated passages. But, ironically, because *The Well of Loneliness* contained no "unclean words" and no indecent episodes, a judgment of obscenity could not have been placed on *any* of its parts *per se*. Taken as a whole, however, Hall's novel could certainly be held, as Bushel phrased it, "to debauch public morals." In a sense, as the judge recognized, this was the book's basic *raison d'etre*:

> The theme of the novel is not only anti-social and offensive to public morals and decency, but the method in which it is developed, in its highly emotional way attracting and focusing attention upon perverted ideas and unnatural vices and seeking to justify and idealize them, is strongly calculated to corrupt and debase those members of the community who would be susceptible to its immoral influence.[29]

Because U.S. precedent required that the novel be judged "as a whole," a verdict of "obscene" could be returned on a book containing "no unclean parts."

As Leigh Gilmore observes, under *Hicklin*, "obscenity was determined through a 'test' rather than as a quality in the material." Interestingly, this distinction legitimizes precisely the segregation that progressive jurisprudence sought to trouble. In the context of British common law, Gilmore is probably right to insist that "in the absence of a legal definition of what obscenity *is*, obscenity's criminality exists wholly in relation to what it threatens."[30] But her claim is descriptive, not definitive—and in the United States, at this time, pragmatism seemed to promise a different way of thinking about the relationship between what something *is* and the effects that it has. Following the pragmatic insights of Peirce, jurists such as Oliver Wendell Holmes sought out the relations that informed identity, recognizing that the "qualities" identified by legal categories were the effects of interactions rather than essential, inborn traits.

Although Bushel drew on *Hicklin* to frame his objections to *The Well of Loneliness*, his discussion of the novel suggests a somewhat more nuanced sense of the relations between text and context, cause and effect, identity and interaction. His reasoning is not exactly pragmatic (and his conclusions were hardly progressive), but Bushel seems to have hit upon an intersection between conservative condemnation and progressive semiotics—and hence come closer than we might expect to intuiting the cultural significance of *The Well of Loneliness.* As Gilmore explains, *Hicklin* held that "the problem with obscenity lay in its potential—what would obscenity *do*?" Similarly, the founding insight of pragmatism was that meaning could be understood as a function of function; or, as Peirce himself put it: "Consider what effects that might conceivably have practical bearing you conceive the object of your conception to have. Then your conception of those effects is the WHOLE of your conception of the object."[31] Like the *Hicklin* test, pragmatism looked to potential effects; but unlike *Hicklin*, pragmatism did not separate effects from essence.

In the context of U.S. progressive jurisprudence, then, *The Well*'s contested "obscenity" presented an opportunity to reconsider the connections among identity (what it *is*), function (what it *does*), and relation (upon what is it contingent?). And indeed, Bushel's argument appears to turn not on the fear that Hall's novel would directly incite lesbian desire, but on an intuition that the book could contribute to a change in conditions conducive to lesbian existence. As he saw it, *The Well* was not calculated to seduce individual readers into lesbian activity; instead, it threatened to *recast the terms* through which homosexuality was conceived—and historically condemned.

That the pragmatic impulses of progressive jurisprudence could be turned to serve censorship is, unfortunately, typical of "the movement of pragmatism as a philosophy of law" in the late 1920s and early '30s. In the effort to scrutinize and formalize the progressive practice of sitting judges such as Holmes, heirs to this tradition increasingly overlooked the semiotic underpinnings of this approach, and the era saw a diminution and demeaning of radical potential. These legal theorists and their followers came to ally themselves too closely with social and behavioral sciences that grew increasingly positivistic, and to lose sight (so to speak) of the immaterial—to overlook the trace of history, the real if unrealizable existence of particular abstractions. By the early 1930s, Carl Llewellyn, Jerome Frank, and other exemplars of the "realist" movement had dissociated themselves from their Progressive forebears, including Roscoe

Pound, while Pound himself had seemingly abandoned progressivism. In place of Peircean semiotics, a narrow instrumentalism asserted itself as the legal and philosophical alternative to pure idealism. More often than not, this was revealed to be no alternative at all.

"A Tremor of Seismic Proportions"[32]

Several features of the period's shifting legal landscape may be identified in the decade's most notorious criminal trial. The saga of Sacco and Vanzetti shows how competing models of legal reasoning in the 1920s United States colluded to pit individual freedom against the greater social good, to eviscerate the pragmaticist impulses that inspired truly progressive jurisprudence, and to refigure both individual liberty and community interest as consistent with a conservative social agenda. A year after Sacco and Vanzetti were executed, these features of their tragically flawed trial would reappear in *The Well*'s superficially successful battle against censorship.

Arrested in connection with a gang-style payroll heist in which two men were murdered, Bartolomeo Vanzetti and Nicola Sacco were convicted largely on the basis of circumstantial evidence related to their reaction to arrest. Because the men were armed, appeared nervous, and lied under interrogation, they were considered to have exhibited "consciousness of guilt." Pointing out that Sacco and Vanzetti had "tried to conceal their movements on the day of their arrest, the friends they had been to see, the places they had visited," the prosecution argued that innocent men would have no reason to lie. But as Italian immigrants, labor organizers, and anarchists arrested at the height of Red Scare harassment, Sacco and Vanzetti had reason to be wary. Arrested as "suspicious characters," they were questioned extensively about their political beliefs and activities, about their movements and whereabouts on specific dates, before any charges of robbery and murder were mentioned.[33] Certainly the larger political climate could only have contributed to their anxiety. At the time of their arrest (May 1920), the notorious Mitchell-Palmer raids were well under way, and in what Assistant Secretary of Labor Louis Post would later call "The Deportations Delirium of 1920,"[34] thousands of "Reds" were being arrested, jailed, beaten, and harassed by agents who seem to have taken Attorney General Palmer at his word that "each and every adherent of this movement is a potential murderer or a potential thief, and deserves no consideration."[35] The defendants' fear could only have been intensified by Vanzetti's experiences during the days immediately preceding their arrest. On May 2, 1920, Vanzetti had travelled to New York to inquire after an associate named Andrea Salsedo, who was being detained by the Department of Justice; on May 3, Salsedo's crushed body was discovered on the pavement outside the Department's headquarters, where he'd been held on the fourteenth floor. Vanzetti testified that he learned of Salsedo's death the day after it occurred (May 4) and immediately made plans to dispose of radical literature in his possession. Small wonder, then, that Vanzetti and his friend Sacco seemed nervous when apprehended on May 5.

Faced with the reasonableness of the defendants' fears, and the evident plausibility of this explanation for their "suspicious" behavior upon arrest, prosecuting attorney William Katzman was nevertheless able to play the "consciousness of guilt" issue to great advantage. Katzman convinced the jury that Sacco and Vanzetti were indeed "obnoxious radicals," but that this could not explain the lies they told under interrogation. Judge Webster Thayer was similarly persuaded. In his charge to the jury, he emphasized "evidence of consciousness of guilt" to the effective exclusion of the defendants' alibi evidence. After the fact, he held that "the evidence that convicted these defendants was circumstantial and was evidence that is known in the law as consciousness of guilt."[36]

Problems with the case were myriad, and the conviction and eventual execution of Sacco and Vanzetti have been widely denounced as especially egregious examples of Red-baiting and xenophobia. But while the bigotry that condemned these men attached itself to the self-evident facts of their nationality and politics, it seems to have been animated by an essentializing logic that could not encompass "rights" contingent upon social status or understand reactions rooted in context rather than in the (representative) nature of the standard "reasonable man"—and hence could only interpret the defendants' fear as a reliable index of underlying guilt. As believers in the principle of equality under the law, members of the jury were apparently unable to conceive of an innocent man who would nonetheless be compelled by concern for his own safety to lie to the police. The jury could not incorporate the possibility that however "equal" under the law, the defendants might yet be *situated differently* in relation to that law than they. Holmes' landmark opinion in the *Lochner* case had turned on precisely this point: the "right" to "freely" contract one's labor was always already restricted by one's situation relative to capital. By recognizing that history and whole sets of relations inhere in any individual's "situation"—and hence in such concepts as "civil liberties" and "natural rights," progressive jurists like Holmes brought pragmatism into the courtroom. In sacrificing the defendants' civil rights to serve a supposed social good, however, the forces ranged against Sacco and Vanzetti relied on only a narrow instrumentalism—a self-serving and intellectually bankrupt ideology that bears only a superficial resemblance to pragmatism, and, not coincidentally, is largely compatible with the sort of essentialism that holds first principles to be literally fundamental, disallowing any rupture or inconsistency in the formulation of the "individual" with rights. Indeed, the strange combination of bigotry and blindness that condemned Sacco and Vanzetti limns a more general tendency of idealism and instrumentalism to paradoxically collapse back into each other in the end.

The jury's decision was upheld through multiple appeals, all heard by Judge Thayer. Although public outcry eventually forced Governor Alvin Fuller to convene a special committee to review the proceedings, his hand-picked group of advisors also affirmed the guilty verdict, explaining that, "as with the Bertillon measurements or with fingerprints, no one measure or line has by itself much significance, yet together they may produce a perfect identification; so a number of circumstances—no one of them conclusive—may together make a proof beyond reasonable doubt."[37] When it came to considering evidence of possible bias, however, the committee seems to have adopted a different standard. The pragmatist John Dewey, for one, accused them of "splitting the issue up into separate questions and disposing of each without any reference to its connection with the others," studiously ignoring the "cumulative character" of reasonable doubt. "The main issue as it stands before the world," Dewey charges, "[was] not faced. It was not even mentioned. . . . That issue is whether, taking *all considerations together*, there was or was not reasonable ground for doubt as to a miscarriage of justice in case of the men's immediate execution." As Dewey points out, the "segregation" of elements bearing on the question of doubt into "independent and isolated issues" (each of which, "by itself," could be—and was—dismissed as "inconclusive") "flatly contradicts the cumulative principle accepted and proclaimed in pronouncing the accused guilty."[38]

The Well's eventual victory over censorship in the United States shows similar influences, albeit to more favorable short-term effect. In ruling that Hall's novel did not violate New York's penal code, the Court of Special Sessions demonstrated both a commitment to first principles (held to be wholly uninflected by context) and an ancilliary understanding of any whole as exactly equal to the sum of its fundamentally independent parts. In protecting the novel, these judges adopted an instrumentalist approach grounded in the logic of essentialism. Their rejection of the pragmaticist insights associated with progressive jurisprudence colluded with political expedience to reshape lesbian possibility in the aftermath of *The Well*'s obscenity trial.

Stephen Gordon's Consciousness of Guilt

Much has been made of Radclyffe Hall's indebtedness to Havelock Ellis' theories regarding the "true invert"—of which Stephen was presumably the ideal fictional manifestation. Biographer Michael Baker, for example, asserts that "John took on board without qualification Ellis' distinctive definition of the invert's character and appearance" in her creation of Stephen, presumably due to her intense attachment to Ellis' view that "homosexuality was an in-born condition rather than acquired."[39] Hall's correspondence with Ellis confirms this attachment, but the multiple and multivalent images of lesbian identity offered in *The Well of Loneliness* indicate a wider range of influence. The early, guilty crush on a family servant; the crucial scene in the dead father's study, in which the protagonist recognizes herself in the pages of published texts on inversion—both appear in *The Scorpion*, a lesbian novel published in German in 1919.[40] Terry Castle points out the novel's "striking invocation of the Marie Antoinette topos," and insists that Stephen's relationship with Angela echoes *The Bostonians*.[41]

Considered "as a whole," *The Well of Loneliness* also bears striking resemblance to Krafft-Ebing's 1886 case history of "Count Sandor," a female subject who, like Stephen Gordon, "came of an ancient, noble and highly respected family" and whose indulgent father "brought her up as a boy, called her [by a masculine name, and] allowed her to ride, drive, and hunt, admiring her muscular energy." Like Stephen, Sandor "received a careful education," became a writer, "had a passion for masculine sports, and was a skillful fencer."[42] Indeed, the stories are so nearly identical as to suggest that Radclyffe Hall's major innovation may have been in providing her protagonist with a lover named Mary instead of Marie.

So concerned was Hall with the recognizability of her protagonist that she co-opted the language, ideas, and experiences of other visible inverts to make absolutely clear this aspect of Stephen's identity, even overlaying her clear evocation of congenital inversion with a significant accretion of environmental and psychoanalytic influences. Marked at the outset with both an androgynous body and a hermaphroditic name, this "narrow-hipped, wide-shouldered little tadpole of a baby" christened Stephen Mary Olivia Gertrude Gordon seems destined for unconventional sexual expression.[43] From prenatal conditioning to an agonizing Oedipal drama[44] to obvious environmental influences, Stephen is given every reason to realize lesbian possibility. By any understanding available, then, Stephen was unambiguously identifiable as an "invert"; competing—even contradictory—theories of causality coincide in the author's effort to establish her protagonist's inevitable and unmistakable orientation.

By including this excess of explanation, Hall effectively circumvents curiosity about causality and directs her readers' attention instead to the *fact* of homosexuality in Stephen's life. This shift in focus, this positioning of "inversion" as a starting point, contributes, no doubt, to the novel's enduring popularity. The most salient feature of Stephen's sexuality is not, finally, that it is inborn (although Stephen herself seems to conceive of it as such), but that it is incontrovertible. I want to suggest that Stephen's sexuality is so readily recognized as immutable, however, not simply because it resembles what Americans already knew about female homosexuality, but because it resonates with a complex host of cultural assumptions about gender, race, representation, sex, and shame.

As a child, Stephen resembles her father and is oddly estranged from her conventionally feminine and unimaginatively conventional mother. At the age of seven, she develops a guilty, thrilling crush on one of the household's three maids. Because this servant has made Stephen complicit in an insignificant deceit (involving dirty fingernails), the child's ardor is shot through with shame and ambivalence:

> Oh, Collins, Collins, with those pretty blue eyes and that funny alluring smile! Stephen's own eyes grew wide with amazement, then they clouded with sudden and disillusioned tears, for far worse than Collins' poorness of spirit was the dreadful injustice of those lies—yet this very injustice seemed to draw her to Collins, since despising, she could still love her.[45]

Indeed, Hall makes clear that such love as Stephen feels is in fact inseparable from the act of despising: "Stephen brooded darkly over Collins' unworthiness; and yet . . . she still wanted Collins. . . . Thinking about her made Stephen go hot down her spine" (18). In a move calculated, it would seem, to communicate the sensation of sexual desire to her adult audience, Hall plays on the culture's own intense ambivalence about sex. By thus commingling shame and excitement in her description of the child's emotions, Hall imputes a precocious, almost incongruously Freudian, sexuality to her seven-year-old protagonist. Significantly, however, this section, like others less evocative but more explicit, was not singled out by the courts. Like many literary critics, legal judges of the text's obscenity seem to have had fewer problems with the first half of the book than with the second—even though much of the most explicit description of lesbian sexual expression is found early on.[46] Thus the censors tended to overlook such abbreviated but obvious offensives as "Stephen took Angela into her arms, and she kissed her full on the lips, as a lover" (146). Not coincidentally, Stephen's affair with the married and capricious Angela Crossby is also suffused with a sense of shame.

Bushel focuses instead on an incident appearing almost halfway through the book: the scene in which Stephen finally first stands up for herself, defending her life and her love against her mother's charge that she is "unnatural," an "insult" to her father's memory, and "a sin against creation" (200).

> An idea of the moral tone which the book assumes may be gained from the attitude taken by the principal character towards her mother, pictured as a hard, cruel and pitiless woman because of the abhorrence she displays to unnatural lust and to whom, because of that reaction, the former says: "But what I will never forgive is your daring to try and make me ashamed of my love. I'm not ashamed of it, there's no shame in me."[47]

The early imbrication of Stephen's sexual identity with shame, guilt, and ambivalence is consistent with Hall's evident emphasis on creating a readily recognizable lesbian for a protagonist. In this she was prescient: to this day, historians sometimes equate lack of shame in expression of passionate attachment with evidence of an absence of sexual activity between, for example, nineteenth-century "Romantic Friends." By infusing her protagonist's erotic identity with shame and ambivalence, Hall rendered recognizable an actively lesbian orientation. Not coincidentally, contemporary critics including Leonard Woolf and L.P. Hartley applauded "the first 150 pages" of the novel while dismissing the remainder as too "polemic." Michael Baker continues this tradition in his critical biography of Hall, summing up his assessment of *The Well* in a single sentence: "The early promise of the story, with its powerful depiction of a sensitive child's growing years, too quickly deteriorates into an assortment of stereotypes representing the Tragic Invert."[48] What is revealing about this reading is the way it ignores and in effect inverts the actual strategic distribution of stereotypes within Hall's text. The first half of the novel is rife with stereotypical images of gender inversion and sexual shame, creating, in the terms implicit in the critics' judgment and the judge's criticism, a convincing portrait of an acceptable invert. Once her protagonist's sexual identity is effectively established, however, Hall takes a different tone.

The second part of the book documents Stephen's increasingly direct association with other homosexuals. It also frequently places her, literally and metaphorically, in suggestively (homo)sexual milieus—not simply the "garish and tragic" homosexual night life (327), but, in accordance with contemporary cultural stereotypes, the women's ambulance corps, Parisian salons, and the company of African Americans. The intense, single-sex atmosphere of the ambulance corps, together with the implied usurpation by these unconventional women of traditionally male roles, evokes feminist institutions such as the settlement houses and women's colleges—which were increasingly under attack in the United States and increasingly associated, by Havelock Ellis among others, with sexual anomaly.[49] The association of French and African American cultures with licentious sexuality was nothing new; indeed, it partakes of racist nineteenth-century recapitulation theories that linked inversion with evolutionary degeneracy and primitivism. The establishment of visible homosexual subcultures in Paris and Harlem after World War I only affirmed these stereotypes. Hall exploits such associations in her description of a profound sense of connection presumably shared between inverts and the only black characters in the novel. Henry Jones and his brother Lincoln sing spirituals for a small party of white homosexuals, Stephen Gordon among them,

> and all the hope of the utterly hopeless of this world, who must live by their ultimate salvation, all the terrible, aching, homesick hope that is born of the infinite pain of the spirit, seemed to break from [the singer] and shake those who listened, so that they sat with bent heads and clasped hands—they who were also among the hopeless sat with bent heads and clasped hands as they listened. . . . Not one of them all but was stirred to the depths by that queer, half defiant, half supplicating music.

The racist stereotyping in this episode is obvious: the older, lighter brother (Lincoln, of course) has an "intellectual face" and plays the piano with "expert" fingers; the singer is the younger brother, a "coarse-lipped young

Negro" who is "black as coal." It is this younger brother, unsurprisingly, who represents "animal" appetites—"a taste for liquor and a lust for women." He is "a primitive force . . . rendered offensive by civilization." It is he who gives voice to the suffering and hope with which the others identify, he who articulates the "half defiant, half supplicating appeal." Henry's song, like the novel itself, enacts self-affirmation in its negotiation between resistance to and acceptance of the sociocultural context upon which its existence depends. *The Well* documents the process by which its author protagonist transcends the shame which rendered her recognizable in the first place. Similarly, "as [Henry] sang his sins seemed to drop from him, leaving him pure, unashamed, triumphant. He sang to his God, to the God of his soul, Who would some day blot out all the sins of the world, and make vast reparation for every injustice" (362–363).

The associations which identify Henry metaphorically with Stephen and, metatextually, with the author of *The Well* itself (and which allow Stephen to stand, metonymically, for all homosexuals, and, metaphorically, for "all the utterly hopeless of this world") are reasserted in the novel's last lines. Distraught by the sacrifice she has made, Stephen experiences a vision, a sort of visitation: "the room seemed to be thronging with people. . . . Oh, but they were many, these unbidden guests, and they called very softly at first and then louder. They were calling her by name. . . . She could see their marred and reproachful faces with the haunted, melancholy eyes of the invert—eyes that had looked too long on a world that lacked all pity and understanding" (436). Surely Stephen sees herself in this horde, even as readers are encouraged to see her, in some sense, *as* this horde. It is she, clearly, who is "haunted," envisioning in this host the ghosts of dead friends; she who is reproachful; she whose face is "marred" by the scar of her war wound, the "physical, indexical sign of her symbolic castration,"[50] the mark of Cain.[51] In Hall's use of ambiguous modification, Stephen's individual perspective dissolves into the plural as she sees these faces *with the eyes of the invert*. Her final cry recalls Sandor's plea[52] as well as Henry's song: "'God,' she gasped, 'we believe; we have told You we believe. . . . We have not denied You, then rise up and defend us. Acknowledge us, oh God, before the whole world. Give us also the right to our existence!'" (437).

Clearly, Hall's convincing representation of lesbianism as "normal, at least for the lesbian"[53] is crafted within a wealth of interconnected points of reference. Indeed, the ambiguity of this closing scene may be due to the novel's deep ambivalence about its lesbian subject's simultaneous attachment to singularity and situatedness. As Castle argues, the story's climax can be read as a turning point in lesbian literature ("a fierce and liberating movement from denial to acceptance.")[54] On the other hand, Hall's melodramatic conclusion can also be seen to reinscribe that possibility within the transcendental relationship between "one insignificant creature" and "God Who made it" (126). As de Lauretis argues, the scene "occludes the body in favor of spirit,"[55] removing this potentially revolutionary possibility from the physical, political, potentially *consequential* contexts of actual connections among beings materially situated within social relationships.

Like Henry Jones and his brother Lincoln, Stephen, and through her the whole host of forsaken homosexuals, might seem "to be shouting a challenge to the world on behalf of [herself] and of all the afflicted." Although the similarities are substantial, the difference between this scene and Hall's description of the Jones brothers' singing is also significant. In the earlier instance, Hall unmistakably gestures towards an image of collective resistance: "There rang out a kind of challenge; imperious, loud, almost terrifying. They sang it together, those two black brethren, and their voices suggested a multitude shouting" (363). In Stephen's case, in contrast, "there was only one voice, one demand; her own voice into which those millions had entered" (437). In this voice, the novel ends, with Stephen standing in metonymically for hypothetical hordes of homosexuals (rather than standing *with* any *actual* allies). Here there is no multitude shouting, but a multitude silenced (by death, circumstance, incapacity)—and a lone saviour empowered to speak their case.

This is the reading, in any case, made comfortable by the Court of Special Sessions in their binding ruling on the U.S. obscenity charges against *The Well*. Acting within a frame identical to that outlined by Bushel, the three-judge panel nonetheless returned the opposite judgment, concluding "that the book in question is not in violation of the law" only "after a careful reading of the entire book."[56] Defense Attorney Ernst characterizes their ruling as "a timely imposition of perhaps more sophisticated taste and jurisprudence in order to free an important book." But from his perspective, understandably, "The great significance of the *Well of Loneliness* case" is simply "that since the book was allowed open circulation no theme, as a theme, has been banned by [U.S.] courts."[57] I want to suggest that this verdict has been significant for law and for lesbians beyond its immediate application in the context of subsequent censorship cases.

The crux of the Court's interpretation is evident in the opening lines of the opinion:

> The book in question deals with a delicate social problem, which, in itself, cannot be said to be in violation of the law unless it is written in such a manner as to make it obscene * * * and tends to deprave and corrupt minds open to immoral influences.

The vague language of this decision exploits the inherent ambiguity of relevant legal precedent in order to clear semantic space for the existence of a text inoffensive in its manner, but potentially unsettling in its theme. By separating the book's "theme" from its "manner" and isolating a "tendency to corrupt" as yet an *additional* condition of obscenity (as opposed to an effect of theme and manner), the Court was able to uphold the principle of free expression and rule in the publisher's favor. As this ruling makes clear, "careful reading of the entire book" is not the same as evaluating its cumulative character; the brief opinion suggests that the charge to judge the text "as a whole" was here taken to require only thorough evaluation of all of its parts.

Implicit in the higher court's rejection of the *Hicklin* test is a repudiation of the semiotics at the heart of progressive jurisprudence. Disinterested in moral censure, these jurists strategically refuse speculation about what the text might *do* and restrict themselves to an examination of what it *is*. But the Court's contention that the letter of the text can be read without regard to the connections among its parts betrays an atomistic logic—an assumption that meaning is additive, not integrative—and affirms the liberal attachment to identity independent of (inter)action.

That this indisputably essential victory for freedom of expression was achieved at the cost of both intellectual rigor (in the interpretation and rearticulation of the letter of the law) and deeper understanding (of the complex cultural effects of legal and literary interventions) points to tensions fundamental to contemporary U.S. law and culture—and hence to the making and meaning of lesbian subjectivity in the United States. Whatever Hyman Bushel's faults (he may indeed have been more than moderately conservative, moralistic, self-righteous, and homophobic—although the same has been said of Radclyffe Hall[58]), he proves a peculiarly astute reader—and a more attuned interpellant of cultural processes than his colleagues on the higher court. In understanding *The Well* to embody much more than the mimetic representation of a "delicate social problem" or a straightforward plea for compassion towards congenital inverts, Bushel seems to have intuited the pragmatic significance of Stephen Gordon. Considered in isolation, Stephen the congenital butch represents no more threat to the established order than does the unobjectionable language Hall uses in *The Well of Loneliness*. Stephen as a representative manifestation of larger lesbian possibility, however, is another story altogether—and makes *The Well* a different novel. Stephen becomes the spokesperson, the visible index, of a whole host of inarticulate, effectively unrealized others—"the quick, the dead, and *the as yet unborn*" (436, emphasis added).

In predicating their protection of free expression on an essentialist understanding of lesbian possibility as an isolable, innate, individual trait fundamentally unrelated to social conditions and historical circumstance, the "progressive" jurists on the Court of Special Sessions contained this threat, conceptually severing lesbian realization from the conditions of its own possibility. It is unfortunately characteristic of the era that this separation was carried out with such success and so little self-consciousness; as the pragmatic intuitions of progressive jurisprudence hardened into the positivistic technology of legal realism, the "individual" conceived by law was increasingly alienated from the network of semiosic relations that sustains subjectivity. To this day, readers tend to celebrate or criticize Stephen Gordon's congenital masculinity without exploring the complexity of Hall's representation—perhaps because, in the course of its trials, the book's existence came to depend on its narrow interpretation as a prime example of what Eve Sedgwick terms "the minoritizing model" of (homo)sexuality.[59] The connection between civil liberties and foundationalist philosophies is neither necessary nor self-evident, however. As this pragmatic look at *The Well*'s reception history indicates, the relegation of female homosexuality to a logic bounded by firm distinctions between action and essence is clearly a contingent construction.

Chapter 4

Swampier Depths: Deep Structures and Suppressed Desires

"For over forty years," as Bonnie Zimmerman proclaims, "*The Well of Loneliness* and Stephen Gordon virtually defined lesbianism"[1]—although in 1963, a challenge to the minoritizing foundationalist model compelled by *The Well* emerged from an unlikely source. Mary McCarthy's 1963 bestseller *The Group*, I will argue, engaged both contemporary arguments about language theory and popular culture discourses increasingly attentive to lesbian existence to propose a more pragmatic perspective on female homosexuality than her readers were ready to recognize.[2] Although the book was widely read and much discussed, McCarthy's intervention didn't take. The reasons why, I will argue, involve both the discursive contexts in which it was advanced and the insufficient "drag" attached to the novel's alternative perspective. Although McCarthy attends carefully to things and words (not just signifieds and signifiers) in the contexts of her heterosexual characters' lives, she leaves the lesbian largely outside—largely *as* the outside—of the copious material minutiae shaping their existence. As a result, the narrative is recuperable within a foundationalist logic, albeit a complex and contradictory one that more closely resembles the conditions in which we live.

Riddled with references to Freud and Krafft-Ebing, anchored in the structural centrality of a lesbian character, obsessed with the interrelation of identity, repression, and representation—*The Group* is a novel in which the intimate imbrication of lesbian indices with larger cultural assumptions and signifying practices receives remarkably detailed documentation. McCarthy's strategy of representation in *The Group*—in particular, her insistence on attending to the mundane materiality and everyday language of her characters' lives—bespeaks not neglect of deeper meanings, as some critics have charged, but rather concern with the *relations* connecting content and form.

Although buried beneath an overwhelming "accretion of fact"[3] about the seven non-lesbian members of "the group," the book's lesbian subject is always entangled with its surface representations, her deep-seated significance always ever so obvious to the others and repeatedly referenced in myriad ways. By the time the actual lesbian heroine resurfaces on page 373 with a German-born "friend," her presence recalls not just Freudian repression, but both Radclyffe Hall and Stephen Gordon, Magnus Hirschfield and *Maedchen in Uniform*, Natalie Barney and lurid French novels—as well as 1950s pulp paperbacks, inversion theory, butch and femme bar dykes, sexual slavery, drag, and deep secrets. One thing that sets *The Group* apart from *The Well of Loneliness* is that this lesbian character is able to employ inherited images in her own interest. Far from feeling trapped by the sexologists' typologies, for example, she adopts and adapts them. "My friend," she tells the hateful Harald, for instance, "loves American women. . . . She says American women are a *fourth sex*" (394, emphasis added).[4]

Part of what makes this strategy (and this novel) possible, of course, is the existence of a cultural context rich enough in images of lesbian life to sustain repeated reference to lesbian subjects while resisting reification and without risking monotonous redundancy. By 1963, lesbian presence—as an idea and as an actuality—was a firmly entrenched fact of U.S. life, if also a curious and complicated one.[5] As Eve Sedgwick suggests, "the plurality and the cumulative incoherence of modern ways of conceptualizing same-sex desire and, hence, gay identity" make for queer contradictions.[6] In the popular press of the 1950s and 1960s, images of inversion were inflected with new ideas about psychology and old ones about sin. Indeed, although the "invert" model, in various incarnations, has survived throughout the twentieth century, by the 1950s and '60s, a pseudo-Freudian psychoanalytic perspective was increasingly in evidence. Changing stereotypes about class, race, and gender further complicated the question. *The Group*'s representation of lesbian possibility, however, relies on three primary references: (1) the aristocratic expatriot invert associated with the 1920s and '30s; (2) the working-class 1950s bar butches popularized in pulp fiction and tabloid exposés (including a series written by McCarthy herself for the *New York Post* in 1950); and, (3) the "suppressed lesbian" tendencies associated with psychoanalysis and conventionally called up to enforce the boundaries of acceptable female sexuality at the dawn of the decade of "free love." McCarthy's novel—written in the 1950s, about the 1930s, and published in '63—appears uniquely suited to explore these interrelations. Moreover, McCarthy invents an ingenious plot device which enables her to establish an intratextual fourth point of reference: the character Lakey, who serves simply through her coherent yet complexly inflected existence to tie all the rest together.

If these indexical relations have been consistently underread, as I will argue they have, the oversight may be attributable in part to a culture of interpretation peculiar to the times. If mainstream media is any indication, the nation was obsessed with imagining the relations connecting deep truths to surface manifestations, and American readers may have been predisposed to assume the existence of underlying forces both essential and deeply obscured. Within the academy, ideas about the relation of form to meaning were very much in crisis; in popular culture, Cold War conformity sought to secure more stable ontological footing. Of particular significance to McCarthy's achievement are the Cold War culture of secrecy and surveillance, especially as embodied and articulated by J. Edgar Hoover and his FBI; the saturation of mass media with assumptions and approaches borrowed, often piecemeal, from Freudian psychoanalysis; and the remarkable increase in power and prestige accorded the study of linguistics in the United States during the 1940s and '50s, culminating, ironically, in the introduction of a theory—generative grammar—which turned the whole project on its ear. This period also saw formation of the first widespread, public, identifiably lesbian communities in the United States. This visible lesbian presence, reinforced by widely available mass-market paperbacks publicizing its existence,[7] made possible the phenomenon of a normative femininity predicated on lesbian suppression—and ensured the centrality of lesbian possibility to all female identity in the late twentieth-century U.S. That Mary McCarthy, a notoriously heterosexual public figure, was able to document this phenomenon so convincingly is tribute to her powers of observation, if not necessarily her powers of analysis.[8]

"A Remorseless Cliché": Reviewers Read *The Group*

The Group tells the story of eight Vassar graduates, class of 1933.[9] It begins with the marriage of Kay (now "a thin, hard-driving, authoritative young woman"[9], although once simply "a shy, pretty, somewhat heavy Western girl"[8]) to Harald (a "thin, tense," [11] and pretentious playwright "not to the manor born" [18]); it ends with the funeral following Kay's death. These, at least, are the markers most often mentioned by critics. Lakey is, however, clearly identified as the central and defining presence of the fictional "group," its creator and custodian. It was Lakey "who had discovered Kay as a sophomore, when they were both on the Daisy Chain," and "it was Lakey's idea that they should invite Kay and Helena Davidson to join forces with them"—"when they saw that they could get the South Tower for themselves if they had eight in the group instead of six" (18). Nor are the other group members—Libby and Polly, Dottie, Pokey, and Priss—much more secure in their place than these newcomers, nor more central to the circle of friends. No, "the group" is properly Lakey's property, and the others acknowledge this:

> The girls she chose to collect were mystified, usually, by what she saw in them; they humbly perceived that they were very different from her. In private, they often discussed her, like toys discussing their owner, and concluded that she was awfully inhuman. But this increased their respect for her. (21)

Lakey's enigmatic appeal, her "Indian blood,"[10] the "queer dark-blue rim around the iris of her green eyes"—all mark her as separate and special—("they humbly perceived that they were very different from her"). The exact nature of this difference, however, remains elusive (her lesbianism is not revealed until near the novel's end). Certainly, Lakey herself is unforthcoming. Like the author in her descriptions of this character, Lakey "never enlarged on a suggestion" (20). "Intellectual, impeccable, disdainful" (12), Lakey remains remote (emotionally, intellectually, and also geographically) throughout the bulk of the book. Indeed, this mysterious "Mona Lisa of the smoking room" (20) departs for Europe before page 50 and doesn't reappear until the final chapter, some 300 pages later. She is physically present at Kay's wedding and at her funeral, but—despite her centrality to the group's self-concept—only occasionally mentioned in between.

For most of the book, various other characters marry, separate, have sex, seek employment, bear children, buy things, cook, clean, and travel—and talk and talk and talk and talk. The novel is about their talk and *is* their talk, is itself narrated in the voice(s) of "the group." And although the *New Republic*'s Stanley Kauffmann takes McCarthy to task for "uncertainty of viewpoint, lumpiness of style, thickness of factual detail,"[11] contemporary reviewers in general seemed rather to appreciate this unconventional approach. "Partly because of the nature of her subject and partly because of her virtuousity as a writer," surmises Robert Kiely in *The Nation*, "Miss McCarthy has chosen a variety of tones to define her characters":

> Though the narration is in the third person—each girl does not tell her own story—there is a voice heard through every section that echoes the person being described. . . . [Thus,] from the outset we are getting to know her habits of mind through a kind of osmotic linguistic process.

Kiely, however, is not completely congratulatory; "what is gained in quick tonal variation," he tells us, "is lost in dramatic intensity." According to Kiely:

> There is a lack of emotional momentum in *The Group* which prevents the tragic conclusion from having real force. Possibly sensing this, Miss McCarthy has contrived a series of ingenious surprises and reversals in her final chapters which are not worthy of what has gone before.[12]

William Abrahams, in contrast, is consistently laudatory. Writing for the *Partisan Review*, he applauds McCarthy's "ventriloquial and colloquial" style, explaining that "the author's [own] voice is silent throughout, we are meant to get no sense of *her* on the page." What we are meant to get, in Abrahams' opinion, is rather "the chirp, twitter, gasp, and gabble of the group, betraying themselves to us in a remorseless cliché of speech, thought, and circumstance."

"McCarthy's mastery of the intonations and vocabulary of what one might call 'educated-banal' is," Abrahams concludes, "a remarkable *tour de force*, sustained as it is for almost four hundred pages." Abrahams, however, admits that McCarthy does—albeit "rarely"—"falter in her discipline" at times. He identifies as slips those points at which, presumably, "the *author* enters," points identifiable in the evidence of narration too artistic and observation too astute, presumably, to be plausibly attributed to members of the group. "At such moments," he generously concludes, "one is forcibly reminded of what has been sacrificed to obtain the virtuoso style-that-is-no-style of *The Group* ."[13]

Interestingly, Kauffmann's complaints coincide not infrequently with Abrahams' praise. That which Abrahams celebrates as "mastery" of ventriloquism, Kauffmann condemns as an "uncertainty of view . . . evident on the first page." Those few instances which Abrahams sees as regrettable if forgivable slips in which "the author enters," Kauffmann welcomes as much needed "evidences of her wit and niceness of phrase." Finally, the style which for Abrahams makes the novel a "*tour de force*" is to Kauffmann "the radical flaw from which all other flaws derive."[14] Thus, Abrahams celebrates the author's disciplined "silence" while Kauffmann laments it, but both agree—with Kiely, with Granville Hicks in the *Saturday Review*, Norman Mailer in the *New York Review of Books*, and others—that this is a, perhaps *the*, defining element of the novel. Certainly, it is an element central to their evaluation of the novel's achievement. Hicks quotes McCarthy's comment in a *Paris Review* interview, "I have tried to keep myself out of this book," and affirms that in this "she has been remarkably successful."[15] Thus, those who find value in the book laud its accuracy and realism rather than any emotional impact, political relevance, or theoretical insights to be found within: "It is perhaps as a social history that the novel will chiefly be remembered" (Hicks); "it remains essentially what Miss McCarthy apparently wanted it to be: a period piece" (Kiely); "it is enormously successful as sociology" (Mailer). Kauffmann, of course, won't grant even this: "It is not a social history; it does not mine deeply enough." "But," even he concedes, "the surface reproduction of the thirties is vivid."[16] Abrahams is alone, apparently, in his opinion that *The Group* "is *not* a novel about the 1930's, any more than it is *about* the public themes (breast versus bottle feeding, etc.) that concern its characters."[17] He, however, concludes rather reductively that, "as the title emphasizes, it is about the group, nine Vassar girls in the process of becoming Vassar alumnae."[18]

For all his insight and generosity, Abrahams is no different than the others in his unself-conscious acceptance of two arguable assumptions: (1) that the absence of an identifiable authorial voice amounts to an absence of authorial presence; and, (2) that the surface centrality of the character Kay precludes the possibility of other organizing structures. Like the others, he makes no mention of authorial control or comment implicit in the organization of all the "chirp, twitter, gasp, and gabble"; and he takes no notice of the structural centrality of Lakey, the lesbian. That the novel might be *about* voice, structure, subjectivity, and centrality, about the relations informing representation—that the novel's style might *be* its subject—necessarily escapes those readers, including

Abrahams, unable or unwilling to admit such possibilities. Ironically, exactly such resistance to acknowledging potentially disruptive semiotic possibilities seems to me to be a central theme in the novel, the focus of McCarthy's sweeping cultural critique. If these reviews are any indication, *The Group* has, however, been consistently misread (or at least *under*read), and for the mundane reasons of unexamined heterocentrism and sexism. Curiously, the contemporary reviewer who comes closest to recognizing McCarthy's achievement is a writer renowned for his own unabashed expression of sexist and homophobic impulses—Norman Mailer's remarks, however, merit their own separate section, and I will return to them near the close of the chapter. For the most part, reviews simply dismiss McCarthy's multifaceted work as, in Norman Podhoretz's phrase, "a trivial lady-writer's novel"[19] and appear incapable of reading Lakey's lesbianism in any but the most reductive terms. Consider, for example, the set of equivalences assumed by Granville Hicks:

> As we see the girls at first, fresh from college, they are still full of confidence. . . .
>
> At the end of seven years most of them are considerably chastened. One has had a completely unsuccessful marriage. Two have had disastrous affairs. One has turned out to be a lesbian.

Others (Kiely, Abrahams) decline to mention the issue at all.[20]

In any case, Kauffmann's claim that "of any posited theme the book is innocent" makes a curious complaint; presumably he would prefer McCarthy sacrifice her innocence and state her theme baldly. (Elsewhere he encourages her "*to go straight*. To drop pretense. To restore her voice" [emphasis added].) But of what, then, would she be guilty? The logic leading up to Kauffmann's implied indictment suggests an interesting answer:

> [McCarthy] may have changed her mind about depicting the failure of progress, but what theme has she given us instead? What does the book deal with besides facsimile of an era and the passage of time? At the end Libby is where we knew she would be, buzzing along as a literary agent. Nothing at all seems to have happened to Polly or Helena. Dottie has disappeared into a Southwestern marriage. With a swirl of soap-opera suds, Polly is suddenly swept into marriage by a young doctor in her hospital. *And with what may be irony but is a poor substitute for resolution, the last scene is*

> *given to Lakey, the Lesbian returned from abroad, and Harald,* Kay's moderately bereft husband, who consider themselves the "two superior people" in the cast. Of any posited theme the book is innocent.[21]

Overlooking (for the moment) the clearly stated fact of Lakey's utter disgust with Harald, "whom she had never liked" (393) and "had no pity for" (396), consider the assumptions underlying this assessment. This last scene amounts to "poor resolution" only insofar as the book is in fact "about" something unrelated, or, worse, about nothing at all. The possibility of a "theme" posited in these final pages apparently did not occur to Kauffmann—or to his colleagues, neither those who echoed his assessment nor those who defended the book on other grounds. A different reading, however, requires only admitting the possibility that Lakey's reappearance might amount to more than simply the last "gasp" in "a series of ingenious [but "unworthy"] surprises and reversals"[22] that reviewers have taken it to be. Fortunately, the climactic confrontation between Lakey and Kay's ex-husband Harald offers obvious clues to its own significance. It is Harald—and Harald alone within the fiction[23]—who considers himself and Lakey "the two superior people in a cast of fools and supernumeraries" (396); Lakey, for her part, considers Harald "utterly specious, . . . [a] dreadful man" (396).

> Moreover, from her point of view, which [Harald] did not consider, poor normal Kay would not have sinned by being her prey instead of his. Far better for [Kay], in fact, because Lakey, she hoped, would have been kind to her. (397)

By not considering Lakey's point of view, not admitting even the fact of its existence into their analyses, reviewers replicate Harald's mistake. Like him, they get left by the side of the road as possibilities pass them by. From a lesbian perspective, predictably, things look a little different. If we accept that lesbian possibility might be a significant, as opposed to arbitrary, element in this novel, then McCarthy's interest in the "chirp, twitter," etc., of surface representation can be seen as integral to what I contend is the book's ambitious theme: an effort to reconceive relations between content and form. From this perspective, the novel's reliance on Lakey's structuring absence emerges as ironic commentary on both psychoanalytic narratives of normative sexual development *and* philosophically conservative disavowals of the pragmatic sensibility historically imbricated with lesbian subjectivity.

Chirp and Gabble: Theoretical Linguistics and Everyday Talk

McCarthy's attention to the "gasp and gabble" of everyday speech was hardly anomalous. The late '40s and the 1950s marked the establishment of linguistics as a distinct academic enterprise in the United States, and saw unprecedented and unparalleled institutional support offered the ethnographers and theorists who developed the discipline. Cold War diplomacy, after all, demanded access to and insight into diverse cultures the world over. According to Frederick Newmeyer's history of the discipline, "the relationship began in 1939, as a result of ideas proposed by Mortimer Graves, then executive secretary of the American Council of Learned Societies (ACLS)." "Profoundly impressed" with linguists' work on American Indian languages, Graves suggested their methods be applied to "languages likely to be of strategic importance in the world-wide conflict he considered inevitable." The founding in 1941 of the Intensive Language Program put this idea into action, and inaugurated a relationship between U.S. military interests and linguistic research that only intensified after the war had ended. Graves' remarks at the 1951 Roundtable Meeting on Linguistics and Language Teaching make clear the logic underlying this association: "Ideological World War III has started and there is no certainty that it is well won yet. . . . In this war for men's minds, obviously the big guns of our armament is [sic] competence in languages and linguistics."[24] Two roughly concurrent developments harkened the beginning of the end of this intense and exclusive relationship between the U.S. State Department and narrowly empiricist linguistics. By the late '50s, Cold War hysteria began to wane and the stranglehold empiricism had held over the sciences in general began to loosen. Before the effects of these then embryonic changes could be fully felt, however, the course of linguistic scholarship was altered from within by the introduction of Noam Chomsky's theory of transformational grammar.

Just a few years before Mary McCarthy would engage the cultural obsession with linguistic raw data in her effort to reconceive the relation of meaning to form, Chomsky's *Syntactic Structures* (1957) had shaken the foundations of empirical linguistics by disputing the presumption that syntactic structure could be mechanically abstracted from examples of actual speech.[25] The "Chomskyan Revolution" inaugurated a concerted effort "to construct a formalized general theory of linguistic structure and to explore the foundations of such a theory,"[26] and began by rejecting both the empiricist method of extracting syntactic laws mechanistically from reams of raw data and the empiricist objective of simply deriving descriptive grammars of various specific languages. Instead, Chomsky proposed that "the grammar of a given language be constructed in accord with a specific theory of linguistic structure in which such terms as 'phoneme' and 'phrase' are defined independently of any particular language"; the newly ambitious goal of formal linguistics, then, would be to develop the theory of this underlying general structure which some would come to call "universal grammar."[27]

In order to more elegantly account for the capability of natural languages to generate an infinite yet well-defined set of grammatical sentences, and at the same time to somehow capture the connections between related forms (such as active and passive voice), *Syntactic Structures* advanced an idea called *transformational grammar*. This theory proposed the operation of a set of rules, some optional and some obligatory, intervening between the abstract structure that underlies a meaningful utterance (in which the relations among its components exist at their most basic conceptual level) and the linear order of syntactic components directly accessible to those rules that direct their translation into actual speech.[28] Abstract, unconscious, and inutterable, the underlying conceptual arrangements came to be called "deep structures," in contrast to the "surface structures" produced by the transformational rules.

Oddly, the insights that revolutionized linguistic theory might appear to have analogues, even precedents, in the popular culture of the period. Certainly, the idea that relations between surface representations and underlying structures are rule-governed—but inobvious—seems to have characterized both intellectual and popular understandings of meaning in the United States of the 1950s. In an era characterized by official obsession with ferreting out subversive elements and buried truths, the iconography employed in Chomsky's geological metaphor must have felt like familiar ground. To the extent, for example, that communism and homosexuality raised the specter of underground enemies, the institutionalization of linguistics and, to an even greater degree, the popularization of psychoanalytic theory may have offered a certain intellectual cachet to the suspicion that surface manifestations might bear little resemblance to the truths whence they sprung—and to the idea that expert (or at least informed) analysis was a necessary defense. Certainly, "the term 'deep structure,'" as Newmeyer points out, "has had the unfortunate effect of inviting a metaphorical interpretation by the linguistically unsophisticated."[29] J. Edgar Hoover's own *Masters of Deceit: The Story of Commu-*

nism in America and How to Fight It (1958), for example, represents the author's "attempt to explain communism—what it is, how it works, what its aims are, and, most important of all, what we need to know to combat it," on the logic that this sort of exposé is made necessary by the endemic deceits and disguises through which uninformed Americans are apparently easily duped.[30] Hoover devotes an entire chapter to discrediting "the Five False Claims of Communism," explaining that "one of the chief strengths of the Communist Party has been its ability to appeal, by trickery, to many Americans who are sincere, idealistic, and well-meaning"—and this despite the fact that "in truth, communists stand for everything that is abhorred by normal Americans." Here again, the "first step in arming ourselves against communism is to know how those [deceptive] appeals are made and how to see through them."[31]

The long association of (sexual) perversion with (political) subversion in U.S. policy and mythology is difficult to explain and harder yet to escape.[32] Mary McCarthy points to the phenomenon in her 1950 description of Greenwich Village as "a sort of clearing-house for all those curiosities, sexual, artistic, or merely decorative, that are thought of as un-American."[33] As HUAC made apparent in its wide-ranging investigations, "unAmerican" inclinations can be categorized as plain "unAmerican" regardless of the arena in which they find expression—and all the more so if their deviance from patriotic norms is inobvious or underhanded. Domestic communists, according to Hoover, are of "all nationalities, races, and areas of the country. They may live in expensive mansions or tumble-down homes. They are of all ages. Never can a communist be identified simply by his physical appearance, occupation or clothes."[34] Not surprisingly, "the number of concealed communists is high" and represents an especial danger. Concealed communists "are equally as dangerous as the open member, if not more so. They are difficult to identify and, being concealed, can operate freely."[35]

According to a 1964 *Life* magazine exposé on the "secret world" of "Homosexuality in America," queers are similarly stealthy and hence similarly dangerous:

> For every obvious homosexual, there are probably nine nearly impossible to detect. This social disorder, which society tries to suppress, has forced itself into the public eye because it does present a problem. . . . The myth and misconception with which homosexuality has so long been clothed must be cleared away, not to condone it but to cope with it.[36]

Hoover cites identical interests in his introduction to *Masters of Deceit*: "Every citizen has a duty to learn more about the menace that threatens his future, his home, his children, the peace of the world—and that is why I have written this book."[37] Hoover and *Life* magazine might seem to mimic the linguistic mindset in their preoccupation with mapping those relays by which abstract ideas are transformed into potentially misleading surface representations.

Gasp and Twitter: Sex, Subversion, and Psychoanalysis

In *The Group,* McCarthy plays structurally and thematically with this fear of rupture between available evidence and underlying actuality. Not surprisingly, the cultural anxiety surrounding this insecurity about the existing order gets attached to the lesbian character. In *Come As You Are*, Judith Roof argues that narrative itself appears imbued with a heteroideology structurally dependent "upon an unwitting estimation of narrative's proper (re)productive end" and hence inclined to assume "that the narrative middle, as in Freud's narrative of sexuality, provides the scene for doubt, risk, and uncertainty." In this formulation, "the middle, as Freud suggests, becomes the locus of homosexual suggestion, the place where such possibility is made visible on the way to a reproductive end"—and, as a metaphor of this middle, "the lesbian constitutes some threat to the story but also provides the pretext for the heteronarrative's spectacular return." Seeking information "about how to disimbricate sexuality from narrative as a strategy for potentially altering oppressive social conceptions," Roof surveys diverse examples to no avail: "mainstream narratives [that include lesbian characters]; various lesbian narratives, including coming out stories, narratives of lesbian sex, lesbian detective novels, and the experimental narratives of Monique Wittig and Nicole Brossard; and such 'perverse' fictions as Nightwood" all fall prey to "heteronormative recontainment." Indeed, "what these deliberately lesbian stories reveal," Roof concludes, "is how difficult it is to surmount narrative's reproductive ideology as long as the writer aims only at form and content."[38]

In *The Group*, Lakey, and lesbianism—or, not those precisely, but their traces, marked absences—crop up in many unexpected places, throughout the novel (crop up often enough, in fact, that a lesbian critic, Catharine Stimpson, could identify lesbianism as the novel's "subject" and Lakey as its "heroine").[39] And as Roof's analysis would predict, these traces often appear in the midst of McCarthy's most explicit attention to heterosexual activity and identity. In aiming at the question of *relation* between form and content, however, by mocking Freud and evoking debates within theoretical linguistics, McCarthy is able to expose, if not overcome, her narrative's implication in heteroideology.

The notorious chapter in which Dottie loses her virginity, for example, is suggestive in this regard. Throughout the episode, Dottie remains convinced that it is Lakey, and not herself, whom her lover truly desires. She imagines Kay's opinion—"obviously [he] was using her as a substitute for Lakey, because Lakey was too much of a challenge, *too* beautiful and rich and fascinating"—and agrees (49). Having escaped to the bathroom immediately following intercourse, she finds herself obsessed with the idea:

> Breathing hard, she steadied herself on the washbasin and nervously scratched her jaw. Lakey, she argued, would not have let him do what he had done with *her*; with Lakey, he would not have dared. This line of thought, however, was too unsettling to be pursued. How had he known that *she* would let him? (46)

Intertwined with references to Lakey, an insistent trickle of Freudian imagery intrudes on Dottie's experience of the event *and* McCarthy's representation of it. Indeed, "all sorts of weird, irrelevant ideas floated through Dottie's head *as the key turned in the lock and she found herself, for the first time* . . . alone with a man in his flat" (35, emphasis added). Lest readers overlook the psychoanalytic implications of this passing remark, McCarthy offers another, attributed directly to Dottie this time and marked more explicitly:

> The side of her that wanted to talk was still hoping, probably, to gain a little time, the way, she had noticed, she always started a discussion of current events with the dentist to keep him from turning on the drill. Dottie's dimple twinkled. What an odd comparison! If the group could hear that! (36)

Despite her inexperience, Dottie not only orgasms during intercourse, but experiences "a second climax, which she now recognized from the first one, although it was different" in response to digital stimulation of her clitoris (44).[40] While her vaginal orgasm was satisfying, this other leaves her "jumpy and disconcerted"; "she could not deny that it had been exciting but it seemed to her almost perverted" (44). More basically, "it was something less thrilling and more like being tickled relentlessly or having to go to the bathroom" (44). Dick (yes, McCarthy names him Dick)[41] approves of Dottie's disappointment: "A nice normal girl," he concludes. (And, lest any reader miss the implications of all this, McCarthy also has him ask, "Have you ever done it with a girl, Boston?" She hasn't.)[42]

On the contrary, lesbianism is for Dottie the unthinkable underside of her own anxious heterosexuality. For Dottie as for Freud, homosexual inclination represents regression or arrested attachment to pre-Oedipal influences. In a stunning combination of snobbishness, sexism, psychoanalytic suggestiveness, and lesbian suppression, she concludes that sex is

> just a matter of following the man, as in dancing—Kay was a frightful dancer and always tried to lead. [Hence, "five times . . . before she was penetrated and so much blood and pain."] Mother was quite right, she said to herself comfily, as she drifted off to sleep: it was a great mistake to let girls dance together as they did in so many boarding schools of the second rank. (51)[43]

This layering of mutually illuminating perspectives is everywhere evident in the novel—and in its engagement with external discourses. The image of lesbianism embodied by Lakey, for example, is at once familiar and completely original, a complexly inflected challenge to contemporary stereotypes. Predictably, in this "period piece," she is a sort of anachronism, a 1930s stereotype necessarily read through the refractions of an additional three decades' accreted insights and assumptions. She is an insistently lesbian Mary Llewellyn[44] reasserting her reality in a new era that would deny her, although in oddly familiar terms. In the midst of almost unprecedented butch visibility, and in the face of close to complete conflation of "masculinity" and lesbian identity in the popular press (and, perhaps, again, in the public mind), the fictional Elinor Eastlake recalls an outdated image and thus complicates a contemporary identity. No Stephen Gordon, the feminine Lakey is just enough like her to evoke association—and thus make believable her similar sexual orientation. Like Radclyffe Hall's Stephen, McCarthy's Lakey is not only wealthy and aristocratic, but "intelligent and morbidly sensitive" (12). Significantly, the milieu into which she emerged, extra-textually, was anything but. Indeed, McCarthy's invocation of the 1920s sapphic stereotype may have been informed by precisely this dissonance between the "positive" portrayal of

Lakey necessary to her plot and the overwhelmingly "negative" associations attached to lesbianism in the contemporary culture. By playing off an outdated image, McCarthy subverts contemporary stereotypes without risking—as a less complexly inflected portrayal would require—that the attractive and admirable character would not be recognized as a lesbian.[45]

McCarthy's own 1950s series "Greenwich Village at Night," which ran in the *New York Post*,[46] participated in the popularization of the lesbian image which would come to predominate in the late '50s and early 1960s: the working-class, "rough, tough, streetwise bar butch."[47] Indeed, the class prejudice and heterosexist bias of McCarthy's conclusion to her February 22 installment, about a comfortably collegiate coffee house, could hardly be less subtle:

> Wherever the village is alive, as here in the San Remo, the presence of the university is felt, just in the offing. The Greenwich Village of tonight has already, very plainly, the mark of a student quarter.
>
> But we pass on, though reluctantly, to sound lower and swampier depths.

A boldtype teaser concludes the column, "TOMORROW: An Evening in a Lesbian Hangout."[48]

As promised, the February 23 installment describes a few false starts and, then, finally, the accidental discovery by McCarthy and her straight companions of an actual lesbian bar: "This is it," McCarthy exults, "at the bar, a few odd sailors are talking to a fat-faced girl in a man's haircut, wearing a man's suit and vest." McCarthy professes to be tentative about testing these waters ("I instantly have the feeling that we ought not to be here; our curiosity stands out like a sore thumb, but we begin to watch, nevertheless")—which soon prove to be turgid indeed. The general ambiance, according to our author, is one "of squalor, the adolescent crush, girls' camps, the misery of being fat, ungainly, unwanted, of friendlessness and rebuffed overtures." The material implications of all this barely tethered metaphor are finally made manifest in the arresting image of "vomit . . . running from the ladies room onto the dance floor." In the end, McCarthy says,

> The mechanical bravado and the lameness of the courtships we have just been witnessing, the spark of half-hearted defiance, the cheap boy's clothes and pocked complexions, the girlish breasts and womanly hips, awaken a feeling of despair.

"TOMORROW:" the teaser promises, "A More Cheerful Evening"; Friday's column begins, "To cheer ourselves up, we decide to go back to the San Remo."[49]

On the surface, such squalor appears entirely antithetical to the elegance associated with *The Group*'s Lakey, but the chapter describing Dottie's sexual initiation is clearly structured around an essential connection. When Dottie drops mention of Krafft-Ebing into the swirl of pseudo-Freudian allusion (40, 42), for example, the competing discourses symbolized by those names parallel the curious contrast (and underlying identity) connecting the enigmatic individual Lakey and the amorphous lesbian threat which underlies the other girls' self-conscious construction of themselves as safely straight. Just as McCarthy's 1950 description of "adolescent" infatuation, awkwardness, insecurity, and "girlish" underdevelopment participates in the Freudian fantasy of lesbian possibility as an immature stage of normative (heterosexual) female development, Dottie's obsessive evocation of lesbian possibility becomes a reflex on which her heterosexual identity depends.

In this way, the narrative tends to conflate Lakey with her lesbianism, and also to reduce the latter to an abstract, abject otherness insistently evoked and disavowed in the assertion of normative heterosexuality. The exiled Lakey also figures prominently, however, in a stunning confrontation between Norine and Helena that more explicitly addresses the semiotic concerns suggested by McCarthy's attention to speech. In this example, the novel's ironic distance from the heterologic's structuring divisions is more readily evident. As an outsider, Norine offers a slightly different perspective on "the group"; however, like Dottie, she is influenced, albeit erratically, by psychoanalytic theories of sexuality. Explaining to Helena the psychogenesis of her affair with Kay's husband Harald, Norine blames everything from her own husband's functional impotence ("I'm a good woman; that's why he can't make it with me. He feels he's fornicating with his mother" [138]) to her intense attraction to Harald ("A better bridge player than [her own husband], Harald had come to figure in Norine's mind as an 'erect phallus' just out of her reach" [141])[50] to the trauma of a sophomore-year confrontation with Lakey. This incident, central to Norine's development, to her clash with Helena over sexual mores, and to the novel's suggestive recapitulation of Lakey's significance to "the group" *and* to its own larger designs, is worth examining in detail:

> "The 'spirit of the apples,'" [Helena] quoted, "versus 'significant

> form.'" She could not remember, exactly, what mushy thoughts Norine, sprawled on a sofa, had been expressing about the Cézannes to the smoking room at large, but she could see Lakey now, on whom she and Kay had had a distant crush, look up suddenly from her solitaire as she said coldly and distinctly that the point of the Cézannes was the formal arrangement of shapes. Norine had begun repeating that it was "the *spirit* of the apples" that counted; whereupon Kay, laying down her bridge hand and glancing toward Lakey for approval, had charged in with "significant form," which she had learned about in Freshman English with Miss Kitchel, who had had them read Clive Bell and Croce and Tolstoy's *What is Art?*. "You're denying the spirit of the apples," Norine had insisted, and Helena, laying down *her* bridge hand, had mildly cited T.S. Eliot: "The spirit killeth, and the letter giveth life." (135)

In the end, "Norine, yielding the field, had lumbered out of the smoking room, sobbing, and Lakey, uttering the single word 'oaf,' had gone back to her solitaire" (135). For Norine, the incident represents a turning point at which she "reacted against Lakey's empty formalism" (136). She terms Lakey's group "aesthetes," identifying her own circle as "the politicals"; "You're hipped on forms," Norine criticizes, "while I'm concerned with meanings" (151). Norine, however, is ultimately a comic figure, and a hypocrite; her characterization of Lakey and her group is, in the end, unconvincing. "Glancing about the room," Helena is struck by the realization "that Norine's apartment was all too populous with 'significant form.'" "Every item in it seemed to be saying something, asserting something, pontificating; Norine [was] surrounded by articles of belief, down to the last can of evaporated milk and the single, monastic pillow on the double bed" (137). Norine offers her convoluted psychoanalytic explanation of her attraction to Harald as evidence that, although "Helena had found the two of them kissing in the kitchen[,] it did not 'mean anything'" (141). Norine is both inconsistent (when Helena says "I'm sorry" in response to Norine's revelation of her husband's impotence, Norine responds, "It's not your fault," responding to the form rather than the intent of Helena's remark) and excessive (she describes Harald's childish gesture of burning a play he's written as "a sort of immolation rite, to propitiate [Kay]; he was making a burnt offering of his seed, the offspring of his mind and balls. . . ." To which Helena responds, "Oh, Norine! . . . Do come down to brass tacks!" [142]).

Linguistic Wars: Content, Context, and the Deep Structure Debates

Although Norine is revealed as a fool, her distinction between "the politicals" and the formalists can be seen to recall and illuminate Eve Sedgwick's characterization of minoritizing and universalizing models of homosexuality as staging a "confrontation or nonconfrontation between politics and theory." Certainly, the charge that Lakey represents an "empty formalism" resonates against the novel's metaphorization of "the lesbian" as titillating interlude in the normative narrative of heterosexual identification. And the fact that Lakey as an embodied individual resists this role recalls the "potent incoherence" that Sedgwick contends "has prevailed for at least three-quarters of a century." Although "it has been the project of many, many writers and thinkers of many different kinds to adjudicate between the minoritizing and universalizing views of sexual definition and to resolve this conceptual incoherence," this productive disjuncture appears as resilient as the "heteronarrative" logic that Roof wishes to transform:

> With whatever success, on their own terms, [theories that attempt resolution] have accomplished this project, none of them has budged in one direction or the other the absolute hold of this yoking of contradictory views on modern discourse. A higher *valuation* on the transformative and labile play of desire, a higher *valuation* on gay identity and community: neither of these nor their opposite, often far more potent depreciations, seems to get any purchase on the stranglehold of the available and ruling paradigm-clash.[51]

If this suggests that the novel somehow presages queer theory, I may as well propose that in staging this confrontation between Norine and Helena, McCarthy seems also peculiarly prescient about more immediate developments within linguistic scholarship. Throughout the 1960s, challenges to Chomsky's insistence on the autonomy of syntactic operations charged that his work remained inappropriately in thrall of "significant form," so to speak. In the preface to the much longer manuscript from which *Syntactic Structures* was drawn, Chomsky stated straightforwardly that "syntax and semantics are distinct fields of investigation"; in the 1957 book he confirmed that he was "forced to conclude that grammar is autonomous and independent of meaning."[52] By the late 1960s, however, a new movement known as "generative semantics" had so thoroughly complicated the concept of "deep structure" as to seriously compromise the theory—at least in the opinion of some. In 1967, for example, generative semanticists George Lakoff and John R. Ross circulated a paper titled "Is Deep Structure Necessary?"—and suggested it was not.

Some thirty years later, disagreement abounds about the actual theoretical differences between generative grammar and generative semantics. Newmeyer contends that the core principles of generative semantics were (1) "the non-existence of a syntactic level of deep structure" and (2) "the idea that all profound syntactic generalizations are semantically based."[53] In abandoning deep structure, he charges, "generative semantics had rejected an assumption that had gone unchallenged since the inception of transformational grammar—that semantic and syntactic processes are fundamentally distinct."[54] In a 1993 article on "The Origin and Development of Generative Semantics," Randy Harris concurs that "the kernel of generative semantics was an obliteration of the syntax-semantics boundary at the deepest level of grammar."[55] In 1995's *Ideology and Linguistic Theory: Noam Chomsky and the Deep Structure Debates*, however, Geoffrey J. Huck and John A. Goldsmith contend that "the two programs were in fact quite complementary, and the tensions between them not only bound each to the other, but also steered them jointly on to a more productive path then either of them individually might have taken." Indeed, they conclude that the theories are sufficiently similar to suggest that "external factors"—personal, political, and institutional—must account for both the drama that characterized these debates and the apparent victory of Chomsky's approach. While Huck and Goldsmith dispute "the standard story" that generative semantics "ultimately failed in consequence of certain inherent inadequacies of theory," Newmeyer, in contrast, stands firm in his conviction that "generative semantics was falsified because its core principles were refuted."[56]

To the "linguistically unsophisticated," suffice to say, it might appear that Chomsky's often acrimonious disagreement with the generative semanticists replicates in a more rarified arena the familiar conflict between (a higher *valuation* on) form and (a higher *valuation* on) spirit or meaning. The complexities of the debate, however, suggest that this would be a reductive reading. Newmeyer, for example, complicates this characterization by contending that the relative autonomy of grammatical operations as theorized in *Syntactic Structures* has been overstated; that whatever Chomsky's statements on the issue, "the independence of grammar in no way followed from his METHODOLOGY"; that the question of relation of grammar and meaning for Chomsky was merely "an empirical one."[57] Huck and Goldsmith, on the other hand, maintain that his challengers actually remained vague on the question of deep structure. "As regards whether or to what extent there might be syntactic conditions on surface structure which might require mechanisms roughly analogous to postulating such a level," they write, "generative semanticists were generally silent."[58] All agree, however, that the debate's eventual resolution must be attributable either to the intrinsic intellectual merit of Chomsky's position or to external institutional factors—and this characterization, even more than the debate itself, may be seen to reify the divide between formalism and empiricism.

Like Sedgwick's analysis, like McCarthy's account of Norine and Helena's debate, this rough overview of "the linguistic wars"[59] suggests the resilience of our attachment to simple logics of buried truths—whether to be found in the distinct descriptive grammars of different natural languages or in an underlying universal formal structure, in the minoritizing model of lesbianism as congenital trait or a more Freudian fear that "sexual desire is an unpredictably powerful solvent of stable identities."[60] That *The Group*'s Lakey can represent either, or both, indicates the paradoxical ease with which these contradictory understandings can collapse back into each other.

In the group's inconsistent logic, Lakey is at once metaphor and an undeniably singular human being. She emerges by the novel's end, in fact, as less "cold" (49) and "more human in many ways" (390) than any of the others had remembered. The aristocratic aesthete turns out to be "a strong anti-Fascist" (390) who is "very practical" and also fond of children (391). The simple fact of her physical presence, however, threatens to disrupt what coherence the others have managed to collude in. Kiely and Kauffmann, no less than Polly and Helena, are confused by her appearance—and here, oddly enough, is where Norman Mailer can be of help. Characterizing "the group" as basically "passionless" and "nearly all finally dull," he laments the fact that "the only character one would not likely flee at a cocktail party, a rich arrogant green-eyed beauty named Eastlake, decides to separate from the book itself." He observes that "there is an atrocious anachronism in the book": "Her characters while engaged in the activities of the thirties have a consciousness whose style derives directly from the fifties." He allows as to how, "if one takes a little stillwater of society and captures it in its proportions, its style, its affairs, its moods, *its very relation to reality* (which is to say the mode by which it attempts to perceive reality) . . . , then a magic is worked" (Mailer's emphasis). Somehow, though, Mailer still manages never to name the connections. Presumably, delicacy does not hold him back—commenting on Kay's death, he says, "clearly, she is a suicide-by-accident before the failure of her love, but she is somehow too horsey, and *all-but-dyke*, to buy a single revolutionary tear" (emphasis added). His description of the novel's materiality is similarly pointed: "The real interplay of the novel exists between the characters and the objects which surround them until the faces are swimming in a cold lava of anality, which becomes the truest part of her group, her glop, her impacted mass." Mailer's lack of sympathy coincides with—and perhaps even enables—a certain circumscribed clarity of perception. "Finally," he concludes, "[McCarthy] suffers from a lack of reach" in that "*she chooses to be not close enough to the horrors in the closet*" (emphasis added). In Mailer's vision,

> Nice girls [like McCarthy's characters] live on the thin juiceless crust of the horror beneath, the screaming incest, the buried diabolicisms of the grand and the would-be grand. One does not have to have that in one's novel, but one has to have a sense of that madness if the book is to be resonant. Yet Mary is too weak to push through the crust and so cannot achieve a view of the world that has root.

His view of human nature aside, Mailer comes perilously close to recognizing the stakes and strategies invested in *The Group*. He even notes that between "the first few chapters" and the last, Lakey "become[s] an open as opposed to—would it be a Closet King?—lesbian." To the extent that lesbianism represents "the horror in [McCarthy's] closet," however, Mailer is mistaken in his assumption that "she chooses to be not close enough."[61] Lakey's structuring absence mimics and mirrors the author's own dislocation; McCarthy's authorial elusiveness plays off both Lakey's inscrutability and those amorphous psychosexual depths underlying Oedipal achievement of superficially seamless sexual identity. When Lakey returns from Europe, she brings it all home; both lesbian threat and authorial agency come disturbingly close to the surface.

In the end, the group's ill-concealed fascination with Lakey's sexuality is revealed as the key, as it were, on which this novel turns.

> They asked themselves, in silence, how long Lakey had been a Lesbian, whether the Baroness had made her one or she had started on her own. This led them to wonder whether she could have been one at college—suppressed, of course. In the light of this terrible discovery, they examined her clothes for tell-tale signs. (389–90)

Although "within a month [of Lakey's return] some of the girls found themselves talking of 'having Lakey and Maria to dinner,' just as they might speak of a normal couple, . . . side by side with this the group felt, with one accord, that what had happened to Lakey was a tragedy" (391).

The ambiguity surrounding the lesbian relationship disturbs those straightforward narratives about depth, surface, and singularity in which the other women's heterosexual identities are grounded. To them, Lakey's relationship with Maria seems impossible to pin down:

> On the one hand, there were Lakey-and-Maria, as you might say Polly-and-Jim, a contented married pair; on the other, there was an exquisite captive of a fierce robber woman, locked up in a Castle Perilous, and woe to the knight who came to release her from the enchantment. *But it was possible to see it the other way around.* Supposing it were Lakey, the inscrutable, intelligent Lakey, who had made poor Maria, who was not very bright, her slave? *The fact that it was possible to reverse the relation like an hourglass was what the girls found so troubling.* (392, emphases added)

This unsettling example implicitly calls into question the neat equations by which the others understand their own relations and possibilities; if connections between surface and depth, representation and meaning are ambiguous or, worse, inconstant in Lakey's case, how sure can the others each be of their own? On the other hand, the actual fact of Lakey's lesbianism is also discomforting; certainly, "they tried not to think of what she and Maria did in bed together" (396).

In the end, the contradictory identity of Lakey the radically distinct and unambiguously embodied individual with the amorphous lesbian possibility that serves to secure heteronormativity complicates, but does not displace, the foundationalist logic on which the group's stability depends. Because the culture of heteronormativity no less than the lesbian subject requires this structuring disjuncture (basically the *born or made?* division recast in a different domain), theories that impose formal coherence are fated to descriptive inadequacy.

This recognition, I suggest, lends a different valence to Roof's frustration with the tendency of narrative—or at least narrative theory—to compel coherence; as she notes, narrative's movement appears no more susceptible to subversion than the relative stasis of classic structuralism, and no less wedded to foundationalist logic. She remarks that "structuralist accounts of narrative illustrate the binary premise of structuralism even as binaries are suspended in sequence or space or dislocated into indirect oppositions."

> While these theorists offer a dynamic rather than a static model for the interaction of the binaries they discern, their hypothetical systems are undercut by an unspecified but omnipresent appeal to an underlying narrative where opposing forces combine. While they are all probably correct in asserting that there is no primal narrative, all employ some primal notion of narrative in their narrative mappings. Although their analyses focus on the narrative middle—on the organization and dynamic that characterizes narrative—the middle is still produced by a knowing reproductive end, by functions that are inextricably intertwined with binaries, which are produced by and that produce deferred oppositions, and that know when to join.

In the "contractual, heterological, reproductive model [that] informs the otherwise unspecified mechanisms by which narrative elements are combined," Roof identifies a "covert heterosexual ideology" arguably inextricable (indistinguishable?) from narrative itself.[62]

While I am less inclined to see narrative's binaries as intransigently gendered, and hence less likely to read joinder and resolution as implicitly heterosexual, I share Roof's concern that the introduction of temporality does not trouble the coherence imposed by either structuralist theories or presumptive heterosexuality—which do tend to appear in tandem, even if their coincidence is ideologically instead of simply logically compelled. Roof's thoughtful overview of narrative theory sketches its developmental debts to the linguistic scholarship from which it derives. Not surprisingly, then, her frustration with the resilience of the dominant heteronarrative is anticipated in McCarthy's rejection of generative grammar as a model inadequate to ground effective resistance to the self-contradictory foundationalist logic that she so assiduously documents.[63]

"In Chomsky's model," as Huck and Goldsmith explain, "representations on the different levels were related by a set of rules that applied sequentially, in such a fashion that the representations on one level could be viewed as the input to such a set of rules, while the output of those rules could be viewed as the representation on the 'next' level."[64] This conception of grammar as generative or transformational thus implicitly narrativized structuralism, deriving its depth metaphor from a logic of sequence. But, like Saussure's structuralism, generative grammar was predicated on a founding dichotomy between the formal abstractions of linguistic theory and the rough approximations of actual speech, which Chomsky would come to call the "competence-performance" distinction.[65] Because the theory's idealization of competence attends to temporality without content or context, generative grammar transcended the stasis of Saussurean structuralism, but remained fundamentally "hipped on forms." Similarly, the narrative (theory) that Roof describes seems impervious to meaningful intervention. "I realize how hegemonic and pessimistic this analysis seems," she writes, "with little room for challenge, subversion, or transgression. . . . I do not believe all is as hopeless as I draw it, but drawing it was necessary to begin to see where hope could lie and to dispel the illusory answers offered by narrative itself." She closes with the suggestion "that by defining what we seem to take for granted, we might find a way to begin to think in a radically different way."[66] *The Group*, then, was prescient also in setting its sights on simply documenting both the theoretical contradiction and the real-life coexistence of minoritizing and universalist models taken to be foundationalist. Not surprisingly, in the novel as in life, the dominant culture is compelled to delegitimate lesbian subjectivity—because to do otherwise would disrupt that narrative logic on which heteronormativity depends.

Hence, when in the end Lakey resolves to "take a revenge for Kay, for women," her challenge to the dominant order is underread, recontained within a foundationalist logic which is exposed as inconsistent in its simultaneous attachment to minoritizing and universalist models of sexual identity, but not finally undermined.

> "Could you or I 'love' Kay?" [Harald muses.] "Of course there was her body." He nodded at the hearse. "To think that I've known it!" He gave a quick side glance at Lakey. "Your 'love' for her, I assume, was purely platonic." Lakey looked straight ahead. (396)

Having "made a little pact with herself to speak only the exact truth and insinuate nothing" (397), Lakey says little and reveals less, while Harald's insecurity compels him to pursue the point:

> "Did she reject you? Is that why you 'dropped' her?" "I was tired of her," said Lakey truthfully. "I used to tire very easily of people." "You haven't answered my question," said Harald. "I don't propose to," said Lakey. "You're impertinent." "*Did you sleep with her?*" said Harald violently. Lakey smiled, like

> a lizard. "You ought to have asked Kay," she said. "She would have told you." (396)

In the end, Harald explodes, exposing his insecurities, his anxieties, and, most embarrassing (to his way of thinking) of all, his ugly *ordinariness*. Only Lakey maintains her mystique; her integrity remains intact, uninterrogated. Of course, it can only be so. Representing the "abject" anxiously expelled in the group's universalizing heteronarrative, Lakey remains an "enigma" precisely to the extent that the fiction (and fact) of straight femininity requires. By delineating this "absence" of insight so sharply, however, McCarthy at least makes clear its conventionality. Unlike her critics, she admits the existence of an alternative perspective, and by implication even hints at its potential.

Within the fiction, only Lakey's "clear intellect" (376), ironically, offers the kind of certainty and coherence reviewers claim to seek. Repeatedly "cut[ting] through indecision" (376), Lakey's insights are also suggestively similar to the author's own. Elusive, incisive, and keenly intelligent, Lakey—in all except her lesbianism—is the very image of McCarthy, the very embodiment of the book itself. Those slips in which William Abrahams imagines he hears the author's own voice could just as well be Lakey talking; the closest we come to an authorial presence is when Lakey takes over at the end, orchestrating a conclusion in which McCarthy's supposedly "themeless" book and "soulless" character confuse critics within and without *and* infuse each other with deep significance. At such moments, one is forcibly reminded of what has been sacrificed to obtain the conclusion-that-offers-no-resolution of *The Group*. Once again, lesbian conceptual authority is delegitimated. Potential recognition of a perspective informed by lesbian pragmatism falls victim once again to pervasive cultural anxieties; comforting epistemological illusions demand its denial. McCarthy, at least, is good enough to notice.[67]

Chapter 5

Rubyfruit Revisited

The Group ably documented the significant cultural anxiety attached to universalist understandings of lesbian possibility at mid-century, and in 1977, Rita Mae Brown's *Rubyfruit Jungle* seemed ready to realize that unsettling potential.[1] This popular novel was destined to become almost a *Well of Loneliness* for my generation—the rare example of a clearly identifiable, widely accessible, nominally respectable, and reasonably realistic lesbian text. Indeed, Brown's book seems also to have been taken as similarly originary: according to Lyndall MacCowan, at least, "Everyone hailed *Rubyfruit Jungle* as 'the first lesbian novel' (*The Well of Loneliness* didn't count)."[2] Like *The Well*, Brown's book promised to inaugurate a new understanding of female homosexuality, a redefinition of lesbian subjectivity so influential and so absolute as to render its predecessors practically unrecognizable as such. To begin with, Brown's protagonist is not anguished, lonely, and self-loathing, but optimistic, independent, and downright cocky with self-confidence—Stephen Gordon's diametrical opposite, in other words, her liberated little sister. Brown's Molly Bolt refuses masochism, martyrdom, and male-identification, and remains determined to succeed on her own—ostensibly feminist—terms.

Instead of pursuing *The Group*'s pragmatic potential, however, *Rubyfruit Jungle* served to solidify an individualist ethic and essentialist logic of lesbian subjectivity largely consistent with the paradigm established in the course of the *Well*'s obscenity trials. If this seems curious, we might consider that *Queering the Color Line* offers an important clue: "Part of the reason that Freud's views did not fully supersede the models of the early sexologists," Somerville suggests, "may be that minoritizing accounts resonated with and reinforced prevailing American models of racialized bodies."[3] *Rubyfruit* remains ambivalent about whether to assume a universalizing or minoritizing model, but is consistent in its evocation of a racist imaginary and apparent reliance on a foundationalist logic of lesbian subjectivity. Its popularity in the context of increasing media attention to feminism, I will argue, both depended on and contributed to the centrality of these qualities to the book's representation of female homosexuality.

Brown's novel sold more than 70,000 copies between 1973 and 1977, *before* getting picked up by a mainstream publisher.[4] Bought and brought out by Bantam in September 1977, the book became a national bestseller; by 1985 more than a million copies had been sold.[5] Its "impish, gutsy" heroine put a cheeky but charming face on the "lesbian menace," while its charismatic author was profiled in the pages of *Publishers Weekly*, the *Washington Post*, and *Ms.*[6] *Rubyfruit Jungle* became—and to large extent remains—the mainstream marker of the new, feminist lesbian.

Ironically, Rita Mae Brown, like many lesbian-feminist thinkers, had been a harsh critic of such celebrity. Suspicious of feminist "stars" selected "by the white, rich, male media establishments" to "represent women the way they want women represented," Brown warned in the mid-1970s that "men are using stars to destroy a women's revolution." She also offered a "simple," if self-incriminating, "rule of thumb" for distinguishing opportunistic "stars" from revolutionary organic leaders: if someone "gets money, approval and status from the white, rich male world," then she's a star and not a leader—whatever her stated intentions, she's *not* helping "to destroy male supremacy."[7] Lesbians, in contrast, are vaunted as the vanguard of the feminist revolution; in Brown's analysis, "woman-identification" constitutes the cornerstone of a revolutionary consciousness antithetical to capitalism, imperialism, racism, and sexism. She argues that "this supposed individual trait" is much more than a simple, personal "choice of sex partner and lifestyle"; instead, Rita Mae Brown's lesbianism is nothing less than "an attack on the Amerikan political structure."[8]

But *Rubyfruit Jungle* is not. Some critics contend that it is not even a feminist novel, noting that "Molly's closest relationships are with men rather than women," and arguing that "there is no genuine affection for women" in the novel. "Molly never truly loves the women with whom she sleeps. Women make good lovers, but they are not portrayed as friends."[9] Leslie Fishbein concludes that Brown's book amounts to "the perfect document of the ME generation,"[10] while Bonnie Zimmerman is quick to remind us "just how conventionally American a novel *Rubyfruit Jungle* is":

> Molly Bolt's journey in *Rubyfruit Jungle* (1973) is one of splendid isolation and her unbounded egoism places her above and beyond everyone in the novel, including all other lesbians. The bars and parties in *Rubyfruit Jungle* are populated by pathetic manipulators or losers. Molly lives in a world with just one inhabitant, rather like a god. She develops no social or communal self, partly, to be sure, because no community exists to which she can belong. But Molly remains separate and alone primarily because her sense of superiority sustains the drive and ambition that allows her to triumph over adversity. She remains a radical individualist, the token woman, the grand exception.

Apparently suspicious of stardom herself, Zimmerman goes so far as to suggest that it was "for this reason, perhaps, [that] *Rubyfruit Jungle* was one of the few lesbian novels originally published by an alternative press to be purchased later by a commercial publishing house."[11] Certainly, the publisher sought to capitalize on this quality: on the Bantam edition's back cover, Molly Bolt is no feminist-socialist lesbian revolutionary, but "a full-blooded, all-American, 100% true-blue gay." Even better, she's both "beautiful" and "funny" to boot.[12]

How did Molly Bolt become the Mary Tyler Moore of lesbian literature? How were Brown's radical impulses transformed into safely liberal assurances? To begin with, I think it's significant that *Rubyfruit Jungle* points to a tension around the governing logic of second-wave feminism, a point of contention characterized by Alice Echols in her history of the movement as an ideological conflict between "radical" and "cultural" feminists.[13] As the preceding chapters suggest, this is a tension with some history; it is both a paradox endemic to lesbian existence in the United States and a specifically situated instance of that more general tendency. Because *Rubyfruit Jungle* is index to both at once, and also to the tension between them, the enigma of its unexpected liberalism must be rethought as a *semiotic* problem. Like the object at once "the same" and continually evolving in Peirce's formulation of sign relations, the ground of *Rubyfruit*'s signification is at once foundational and mutable, and also both generic and specific.[14]

Rubyfruit Jungle's "citation" of sexed and sexualized deep subjects demonstrates the relentless indexicality—and, hence, historicity—of representation, but its potentially progressive attentions to indexical relations get overridden, in the end, by the book's more explicit insistence on a logic organized around analogical associations. Because this approach obscures context, process, and causal connection, the book's insights are limited and its implications are conservative. Of course, it could be read differently, and the reasons that it isn't have everything to do with its function as an index to 1970s feminism and the lesbian(-feminist) deep subject.

"The Self Affirms Herself"[15]

Rubyfruit Jungle is a quick read. Less than half the length of *The Well of Loneliness*, it has none of the older novel's tortured prose, none of its protagonist's anguished self-questioning. Instead, it is direct, funny, accessible, and entertaining. The book opens in Coffee Hollow, Pennsylvania, with seven-year-old Molly charging admission to her friend Brockhurst Detwiler's after-school exhibitions of his uncircumcised penis. Molly is clearly the brains behind this profitable operation, while "Broccoli" is merely the incidental possessor of a resource he never thought to exploit. Thanks to Molly's entrepreneurial ingenuity, however, his "wad of pink wrinkles" is transformed into a short-lived economic bonanza "billed as 'the strangest dick in the world'" (3–5). When Molly's mom, Carrie, catches wind of their activities, however, she mistakes her daughter's pecuniary motives for sexual precocity, and symbolically rejects Molly by revealing to her that she was adopted: "I got news for you, you little shitass, you think you're so smart. You ain't so fine as you think you are, and you ain't mine neither. And I don't want you now that I know what you're about" (7). Carrie resolves to start Molly on a strict program of instruction in more ladylike behavior, thus setting up the mother/daughter conflict that provides the novel's central tension and implying a connection between gender nonconformity and sexual transgression overtly repudiated elsewhere in the novel. As the voice of narrow-minded convention, Carrie fulfills a stereotypically female narrative function, lending credence to Fishbein's concerns while serving as foil to Molly's ostensibly feminist development.

From here, the narrative follows Molly's often sexual and occasionally outrageous adventures over some fifteen years and several states.

Having lost her innocence in the aftermath of the Broccoli episode, she gains sexual experience with her sixth-grade girlfriend, Leota B. Bisland. But again the intervention of adults interferes just when Molly seems to have a good thing going. The girls' love affair is cut short when Molly's working-poor family moves to Florida in search of better economic opportunities. Carrie, her good-hearted husband Carl, and Molly end up living in a "flamingo-pink eyesore next to the railroad tracks" in Fort Lauderdale (82), while Molly's cousins Leroy and Ted and their dad, Ep, find a trailer in Loxahachee (60). As time goes by, Molly fools around with Leroy as well as her high-school football hero boyfriend, but also beds the beautiful head cheerleader—all the while earning stellar grades, excelling in student government, starring in several sports, and charming the entire school.

The pace slows only slightly in the later chapters. Molly receives an academic scholarship to the University of Florida, has an affair with her roommate, and gets kicked out in short order. Rejected by Carrie, she heads to New York to begin again, determined to overcome her humble beginnings in the best Horatio Alger style. There she briefly befriends a homeless gay hustler and bemoans the shallow artificiality of organized gay life before embarking on a series of low-paying jobs and inadequate lovers. Meanwhile, she puts herself through film school at NYU, determined to eventually make "real movies about real people and about the way the shit comes down" (174). As this synopsis suggests, the novel moves quickly. One constant is Molly's disdain for "artificial obstacles and social strictures." Molly believes she should be "able to do whatever she wants" without interference from parents, convention, or society. As Carol Ward suggests, the novel tends to affirm its heroine's opinions and to frame her struggle for self-determination as a conflict between natural truths and cultural artifice.[16]

From the start, *Rubyfruit Jungle* appears to discourage indexical connections, offering instead a lesbian protagonist apparently unencumbered by influence or antecedents—in essentialist terms, an authentic lesbian subject. From the book's first line, the first-person narrator disavows the importance of lineage, history, and heritage implied in the opening lines of *The Well of Loneliness*.[17] "No one remembers her beginnings," she says. "Mothers and aunts tell us about infancy and early childhood, hoping we won't forget about the past when they had total control over our lives and secretly praying that because of it, we'll include them in our future" (3). The implication is clear: what knowledge one has of her own "beginnings" is inevitably inauthentic, a cultural construct imposed on reality by self-interested others. Like Radclyffe Hall, Brown seeks to divert attention from questions of causality. Instead of excessive explanation, however, Brown's text offers none. Molly Bolt's sexual identity seems to exist outside the influence of history and of external agents; it simply *is*—eternal, essential, and inexplicable. Molly is who she is and refuses to narrativize her "beginnings." By marking this refusal on page one, *Rubyfruit Jungle*, like its protagonist, establishes its uniqueness at the outset, asserting its difference from the definitive lesbian text to that time. Having done so, however, it proceeds to tell a story rife with resemblance to its infamous predecessor.

Although it tries to deny the connection, *Rubyfruit Jungle* is clearly anchored in *The Well*.[18] Consider the names. "Stephen Mary Olivia Gertrude Gordon"—the feminine core flanked by a masculine mask might seem to suggest that Stephen's name represents the inverse of her essence. The full burden of this appellation, however, hangs in its juxtaposition of the Christian name of a martyred saint with the family name of Lord Byron, a relation reflected in Stephen's role as the singled-out savior of a degraded class. "Molly Bolt" might seem safely simple by comparison, but it too embodies an interesting duality. A molly bolt is a piece of hardware, a kind of fastener consisting, in effect, of nut and bolt together; it's used when only one side of a surface is accessible. In the jargon of the trade, then, a molly bolt contains both the "male" and "female" parts. Whereas Molly's name is on the surface unambiguously feminine, it unmistakably alludes to an androgynous independence (or hermaphroditic self-sufficiency), as well.

This is the first of many similarities. Both protagonists are the only children of open-minded and indulgent fathers and intolerant, less loving mothers. Both are effectively introduced to us at age seven, and immediately characterized as precocious, perspicacious, tomboyish, and temperamental. Both mature to be athletic, attractive, and intelligent. Both lose their beloved fathers in late adolescence and leave home to develop their talents in larger cities. Each ends up in a more cosmopolitan setting yet, Stephen in Paris and Molly in New York.[19] Both novels end with the protagonist alone and embattled, Molly complaining, "Damn, I wished the world would let me be myself" (246) and Stephen praying, "Acknowledge us, oh God, before the whole world. Give us also the right to our existence."[20]

Bonnie Zimmerman notes an additional connection:

> Stephen feels herself to bear "the mark of Cain," the mark of inversion and damnation. . . . But, reading Genesis more closely,

> we note that God actually marks Cain to protect him from harm, not to punish him. So it is possible to interpret the mark of Cain as a sign of God's protection, as if lesbians are singled out for a unique role in society.

In Zimmerman's analysis, Molly "epitomizes this identification between difference and specialness" established in the story of Stephen's "special gift and responsibility."[21]

Significantly, however, Molly's "difference" is not initially identified with sexual deviance, although, like Stephen, she resists conventional gender-stereotypes. Molly is first set apart not by gender-ambiguous behavior or physical attributes (although she exhibits some), but by her status as a "bastard." It's Molly's "illegitimacy" that places her beyond the pale of social acceptability and leaves her worried (as Stephen worried), "that people will laugh at me and look at me like I'm a freak" (8). This displacement of "freak" status onto social "illegitimacy" is index both to dissimilarities between the sociopolitical contexts in which the two novels were produced and to the continuity of certain racist paradigms providing a sort of shorthand by which shame, martyrdom, and outcast status could be connoted.

On the one hand, *Rubyfruit*'s representational strategy is rooted in the history of racist evolutionary theories that constrained *Norma Trist* as surely as in the atomistic foundationalism legitimated by *The Well*'s obscenity trial. On the other hand, however, *Rubyfruit Jungle*'s frame of reference is distinguished from *The Well*'s by a growing uncertainty about the sources and significance of traditional gender roles—and, especially, by its author's feminist refusal to reaffirm them. In this context, Molly's "androgynous" attributes signify differently than Stephen's substantially similar "masculinity" did a half century earlier. In the words of an early lover, "Molly's pretty and all that but she's a better athlete than most of the boys that go to this school, and besides, she doesn't act like a girl, you know?" (106). Stephen, similarly, possessed "a fine face, very pleasing" (although there is also "something about it that went ill with the hats on which Anna insisted—large hats trimmed with ribbons or roses or daisies, and supposed to be softening to the features"). Like Molly Bolt, Stephen in adolescence is a "graceful, light-footed, proficient young athlete" and a "clever and somewhat opinionated young scholar."[22]

Despite their similarities, Molly and Stephen fare very differently in the different worlds in which they move. While Stephen struggles through awkward social situations in feminine clothes, attempting to approximate gender-appropriate behavior, Hall makes clear that "could [Stephen] have met men on equal terms, [she] would always have chosen them as her companions; she preferred them because of their blunt, open outlook, and with men she had much in common." Men, however, are not prepared to meet Stephen on equal terms: "[They] found her too clever if she ventured to expand, and too dull if she suddenly subsided into shyness. In addition to this, there was something about her that antagonized slightly, an unconscious presumption."[23] Molly, in contrast, appears to have no difficulty meeting men on traditionally masculine terms, whether it's discussing motorcycle mechanics with Leroy or describing to Carl her disinterest in marriage—"It'll never happen. . . . Why should I buy a cow when I can get the milk for free? I can go out and screw anytime I damn well please" (92).

While Stephen is early reduced to tortured confusion ("'What am I in God's name[?]'" she wonders "with a kind of despair . . . 'Why am I as I am—and what am I?'"[24]), Molly never questions her own apparently self-evident femaleness. Accused of adopting a "masculine" approach at one point, she confidently references her female body in arguing an alternative interpretation. An acquaintance protests after an uninvited kiss: "You shouldn't have done that. I don't see that you're any different from a man, coming over here and kissing me like that without asking." And Molly confidently replies, "Here, let me give you another one, so you can be sure to know the difference. I'd hate to have you confuse me with the opposite gender" (200–201).

Within the fiction, appropriate interpretation of the kiss depends indexically on Molly's material body as a paralinguistic point of reference. Similarly, the text invokes an essentialized if unconventional conception of "women," a crucial component of the text's own context of utterance. Within the fiction, Molly's body functions effectively in this example because it is presumed to be unproblematically gendered. Whereas Stephen's androgynous aspects are still sometimes read as indices of an essentially masculine subject,[25] Molly's "masculine" attributes are used in the 1970s to exemplify an expanded understanding of what's proper to women—arguably even offered as a liberated ideal. Thus Molly's gender-style may be understood as insufficiently "queer" *in this context* to serve as marker to her "difference" (or sign of her "specialness").

The advantages of locating Molly's difference somewhere other than in the shifting and politically problematic standards of gender-appropriateness are not hard to see. As Shane Phelan notes, "Being a tomboy is not an indicator of lesbianism except to those who believe that real women do not climb trees."[26] The identification of that foundational difference with "illegitimate" birth, however, raises more complicated questions. On one level, the explanation could be autobiographical; Brown herself was born to an unmarried woman and adopted into a family much like Molly's.[27] This historical fact, however, does nothing to explain how it is that "illegitimacy" and the experience of being "orphaned" can be made to carry the symbolic weight of that specific sense of alienation attached to growing up a lesbian in a homophobic culture.

Here again, however, Somerville's detailed analyses of the "intersecting representational histories of sexuality and race" can be of help.[28] Almost from the outset, she notes, both Havelock Ellis and Edward Carpenter expressed discomfort with the "connotations of illegitimacy" contained in the very term "homosexual"—Ellis railing in *Sexual Inversion* that "'homosexual' is a barbarously hybrid word," then tempering his complaint in a later edition to merely note that "it has, philologically, the awkward disadvantage of being a bastard term compounded of Greek and Latin elements"; Carpenter emphatic that "'homosexual,' generally used in scientific works, is of course a bastard word," and inclined to consider "homogenic" a more appropriate term. In this, Somerville contends, "Ellis and Carpenter expressed pervasive cultural anxieties about questions of racial origins and purity."

> Concerned above all else with legitimacy, they attempted to remove and rewrite the mixed origins of "homosexuality." Ironically, despite their suggestions for alternatives, the "bastard" term took hold among sexologists, thus yoking together, at least rhetorically, two kinds of mixed bodies—the racial "hybrid" and the invert.[29]

This rhetorical association would persist, providing to subsequent generations a ready—if problematic—means of suggesting sexual difference.[30]

And here, also, *The Well of Loneliness* again fleshes out what *Rubyfruit Jungle* has only to evoke through unacknowledged resemblance. Stephen's lineage, of course, is unambiguous; it is she who is an affront to generations of upstanding Anglo-Saxons "whose loves had made children from father to son—from father to son until the advent of Stephen."[31] Her less repressed double, however, is made to stand in once again for that from which racist ideologies demand Stephen's own dissociation. Henry Jones, the African American vocalist who, with his performance, stands in for the author/invert and her book, sings one last song at the end of what has devolved into a depressing evening. As the white homosexual guests stumble drunkenly through their preparations for departure, Henry Jones (engaging in some suggestive gender-bending of his own) begins "to sing at the top of his lungs in a high falsetto."

> *"Oh, my, help, help, ain't I nobody's baby?*
> *Oh, my, what a shame, I ain't nobody's baby."*

The implication of orphanhood in this song of romantic loss—as well as the intimation of impropriety that associates this expression, however subtly, with homosexuality—is immediately reinforced: Henry's older, whiter brother is offended enough by *something* to command "'Shut your noise, you poor mutt!' . . . [B]ut Henry still continued to bawl: 'Oh, my, what a shame, I ain't nobody's baby.'"[32]

Although Henry Jones' projection into the position of an abandoned, bawling "baby" serves specific purposes in *The Well of Loneliness*, the image of African Americans as lost children is nothing new in U.S. literature, to be sure, nor is the idea that black Americans bear the "mark of Cain."[33] Like *The Well of Loneliness*, *Rubyfruit Jungle* relies on images of black Americans to serve as a sort of stigma bearer through which the reality of an implicitly white lesbian subject can be communicated. Hall's novel invokes racist paradigms with a directedness indicative of its era and also explicitly articulates its investment in homosexual identification with the image of African American alienation; Brown's book, in contrast, is more circumspect—and arguably unself-conscious—in its claims. Although *Rubyfruit Jungle* explicitly allies itself with an ideal of "color-blind" impartiality, it simultaneously reflects the extent to which, within a wide array of popular discourses, black American *identity* had come to stand in, by the early 1970s, not only for racial *difference*, but for difference *per se*. Subject to this dynamic, difference, instead of representing an ineffable relation, gets displaced onto a material host—in this case, African Americans.

And in *Rubyfruit Jungle*, it is displaced once more: onto the white lesbian's analogical identification with *difference* figured as *black*. Biddy Martin describes a similar dynamic at work in racially-inflected representations of butch-femme relationships whereby "disidentification from assigned gender is accomplished through darkness, as if whiteness and femmeness could not be differentiated and as if blackness were pure difference."[34] But *Rubyfruit* is less about "making lesbian desire visible as desire, rather than identification," than it is about rendering a recognizable lesbian subjectivity hypothetically available to all (white) women—*within* an economy of identification. Molly disidentifies from her assigned gender, but *not* from her foundational sex. And her disidentification relies not on a "paradigm of visibility" in which this limited understanding of racial difference becomes a privileged signifier,[35] but on the historical entanglement of sexual deviance and racial difference in an evolutionary logic that understands each as a sign of the other because coimplicated in a causal degeneration or primitivism. It is this association, finally, which replaces gender inversion in Brown's reworking of *The Well of Loneliness*, literalizing the larger historical trajectory by which "butch-femme is displaced by racial analogies in white lesbian-feminist writing."[36] Hall's explicit reliance on gender difference to suggest and sustain her lesbian subject is directly displaced in Brown's text by a largely implicit (and often obscured) dependence on white identification with racial "difference" figured as both illegitimate and African American. It bears repeating, I think, that this is a "difference" grounded in racist evolutionary ideologies and a trope more readily accessible to white lesbians than to women of color.

Molly's reaction to her uncle's colloquial use of the epithet "bastard" is suggestive in this regard: "That word made me cringe. How come whenever a person was bad they called him a bastard? My face went hot and I didn't dare look up . . . for fear someone would see my color" (20). In an incident shot through with shame, Molly's bastard status is marked by the color of her face. This relation is reaffirmed in the eleven-year-old Molly's response when her mother yells at her for innocently using a "colored" public restroom in Georgia. "Since I don't know who my real folks are," she reasons, "maybe they're colored. Maybe it's all right for me to go in those bathrooms." Her mother immediately associates this comment with Molly's already evident nonconformity: "My God!" she explodes, "if you ain't enough trouble now you want to go and be a nigger" (59).[37]

This series of displacements by which illegitimacy is identified with racial "otherness" which is figured as African American—and all are associated with homosexuality—comes full circle in the scene where Molly is directly confronted with her best friend's homophobia. "Do you think you're a queer?" she is asked, and Molly's defensive response makes clear her sense of isolation:

> "Oh great, you too. So now I wear this label 'queer' emblazoned across my chest. Or I could always carve a scarlet 'L' on my

> forehead. Why does everyone have to put you in a box and nail the lid on it? I don't know what I am—polymorphous and perverse. Shit. I don't even know if I'm white. I'm me. That's all I am and all I want to be. Do I have to be something?" (107)

Molly's desire to be nothing except her "own self" is reflected in an ambivalence about labeling evident throughout the text. Alternately dismissive and distrustful of identity tags, Molly Bolt paradoxically revels in an uncertainty predicated on the fixity and readability of racist projections onto others. Molly is not socially or culturally black. She is assumed to be white by all with whom she comes into contact; she does not participate in or identify with African American cultures. Her birth mother, she learns, was a poor white American, while her biological father seems to have been a white Frenchman. In functional terms, the text's obsession with racial identity has little to do with Brown's well-documented interest in racial justice, and little relation to actual black persons or cultures. Certainly, it does not involve any interrogation of "whiteness" as a cultural or political construct, but serves primarily to establish a metaphor by which the white lesbian subject can mark her own difference.[38]

Second-wave feminism, of course, was notoriously prone to making similar analogies, beginning with its founding texts. The anonymously authored SNCC position paper on "Women in the Movement," for example, asserts that

> assumptions of male superiority are as widespread and deep-rooted and every [bit as] much as crippling to the woman as the assumptions of white supremacy are to the Negro. . . . The woman in SNCC is often in the same position as that token Negro hired in a corporation. . . . It needs to be known that just as Negroes were the crucial factor in the economy of the cotton South, so too in SNCC, women are the crucial factor that keeps the movement running on a day-to day basis.[39]

The "Sex and Caste" manifesto co-authored by Casey Hayden and Mary King in 1965 is similarly straightforward in its suggestion that "there seem to be many parallels that can be drawn between treatment of Negroes and treatment of women in our society." Among a number of relevant observations, the authors point out that

> Many people who are very hip to the implications of the racial caste system, even people in the movement, don't seem to be able

> to see the sexual caste system and if the question is raised they respond with: 'That's the way it's supposed to be. There are biological differences.' Or with other statements which recall a white segregationist confronted with integration.[40]

Although *Rubyfruit Jungle* is neither original nor anomalous in its invocation of such parallels, its simultaneous dependence on and disavowal of a history of ideas about native difference extends the explicit comparisons of these feminist antecedents. As Roof argues, "The emergence of the model of racial oppression in lesbian-feminist writing in the late 1960s and early 1970s was not only compelled by the need to establish lesbian feminism as a bona fide oppressed group, but appeared specifically as an injunction against the [putatively] self-defeating political impurities imported by such manifestations of masculinity or heterosexuality as butch-femme."[41]

By establishing a lesbian subjectivity based in formal resemblance to a projection of African American identity, rather than actual connection to African American experience, moreover, *Rubyfruit Jungle* not only signals its defining distance from gender-inversion models of homosexuality, but also allies itself with a governing logic that is iconic as opposed to indexical, a logic reliant on analogical instead of actual relations. Judith Butler points out the political limitations of such paradigms in reminding us that it's "crucial to resist the model of power that would set up racism and homophobia and misogyny as parallel or analogical relations" because "the assertion of their abstract or structural equivalence not only misses the specific histories of their construction and elaboration, but also delays the important work of thinking through the ways in which these vectors of power require and deploy each other for the purpose of their own articulation."[42] As Somerville notes, "these analogies have a history and perform specific kinds of cultural work, often with contradictory political effects."[43] Her examples suggest that the sometimes conflicting effects result from diverse circumstances and strategic intents; in the case of *Rubyfruit Jungle*, however, the contradiction is clear and simultaneous: the novel conceives a lesbian subject unbeholden to the logic of binary gender and thus in this sense consistent with feminism, but this conception invokes and hence implies essentialist understandings of sex as distinct from gender, of women as identically sexed, and of lesbians as implicitly white. In this sense, the text does not simply delay, but actively precludes the kind of analysis that Butler advocates. "The comparison benefits [white] lesbian feminists," as Roof argues, "by locating them within the field of identifiable oppression, but it also tends to mask feminism's residual racism which is itself marked by its easy appropriation of race as an analogy."[44]

Nor do the problems abate with the introduction of African American characters to the novel. Once arrived in the big city, Molly befriends Calvin, a gay, black man who has abandoned his wife and baby for a life of homelessness and hustling (148–50), and later Holly, an African American lesbian "with no apparent ambition other than to attract attention" (154), who is a self-described "kept woman" (156). Within the text, Molly's refusal to engage the force of such obvious stereotypes reflects her resistance to self-analysis and reinforces the impression of an originary, ahistorical essence to this lesbian subject. When Molly turns down a wealthy woman's offer of financial assistance, for example, Holly challenges her to interrogate her motives: "You think you're too good to be kept? I'm kept, so what am I, a whore or something? Or maybe it's symptomatic of my race's refusal to be responsible. Is that what you think?" Molly, however, refuses to engage: "No. We're different people and it has nothing to do with whoring or color or any of that shit. I can't do it, that's that" (172). The incident recalls an earlier exchange between Molly and her cousin Leroy, who, unlike Molly, experiences some anxiety about sexual identity. "Do you think I'm a queer?" he asks. "I think you are Leroy Denman," answers Molly, "that's what I think. I don't give a flying fuck what you do, you're still Leroy" (67). In Molly's view, identity is *a priori*, antecedent to action, uninflected by context. Molly's sex and sexuality appear as givens; to the extent (and it's not a large one) that the novel documents process at all, what it describes is discovery, not development. After she sleeps with Leroy, her first experience with heterosexual intercourse, Molly decides on a strictly scientific approach to determining her sexual orientation. "I'm not gonna base my judgment on one little fuck with ole Leroy," she reasons. "We got to do it a lot more and maybe I'll do around twenty or thirty men and twenty or thirty women and then I'll decide" (70). Lesbian identity is depicted as antecedent to the process of experimentation—inobvious perhaps, but fundamentally independent of social influence.

At times, *Rubyfruit* seems to rely on dual strategies, alternating between the exposure of social constructs oppressive to individual liberty and the assertion of an originary truth located within individual bodies. Within this fictional frame, "constructs" are always cultural, always *communal*, regardless of the sway they hold over individuals. Hence,

Molly denaturalizes heterosexist popular media representations for the edification of a supposedly straight lover named Polina, explaining:

> If you want to see blatant propaganda then look at the ads in the subways, magazines, t.v., everywhere. The big pigs use heterosexuality and women's bodies to sell everything in this country—even violence. Damn, you people are so bad off you got to have computers to match you up these days. . . . You don't see ads of women kissing to get you to buy Salem cigarettes, do you? (199)

Similarly, Molly derides the butch-femme bar culture she discovers in New York as "the craziest, dumbass thing I ever heard tell of." "What's the point of being a lesbian," she rails, "if a woman is going to look and act like an imitation man? Hell, if I want a man, I'll get the real thing not one of these chippies" (147). In this, Lyndall MacCowan contends, *Rubyfruit* is typical of a lesbian-feminist literature that presents butch-femme as "a product of false socialization, proof of identity confusion, sexually limiting, artificial, and most likely to be found among 'lower-class [*sic*]' lesbians in bars."[45]

Reality, in contrast, asserts itself in isolation. Its mark is nonconformity: radical individualism equals essential truth. When Molly rejects Polina and her complicated sexual fantasies, and takes her teenaged daughter to bed instead, she's delighted to discover that while "Alice steamed and shook and sighed, . . . she hadn't one sexual quirk in her mind." In contrast to her mother, Alice simply "loved being touched and she loved touching back. . . . She was there, all there with no hang-ups, no stories to tell, just herself. And I was just me" (210). But if Molly's "bastard" status appears a metonym for the novel's own adamant disavowal of influences, antecedents, and significant context, it also signals significant attachments to a world beyond the novel and a history beyond the individual.

The Hand That Cradles the Rock

Rita Mae Brown may have written, in fact, with more complicated assumptions in mind. Although *Rubyfruit Jungle* came out when Brown was still only in her twenties, its writing was informed by her already extensive experience in radical political activism. As a student at NYU, Brown was protesting U.S. involvement in Vietnam as early as 1967, and helped found the first gay student organization in the United States.[46] Soon after, she began working with the young National Organization for Women, quickly becoming editor of its newsletter and administrative coordinator of its national office.[47] Driven from NOW for her unapologetic lesbianism and her outspokenness, Brown joined the Redstockings for a time before turning increasingly to gay liberation and working to generate a specifically lesbian feminist movement. She was a primary force behind the infamous Lavender Menace action at the Second Congress to Unite Women and the collectively authored position paper "The Woman Identified Woman." In 1971, she left New York, relocated to D.C., and helped found the lesbian-separatist Furies collective, a short-lived but influential political force. In New York, Brown had written for the underground paper *Rat*; in D.C., she worked on the Furies' nationally known newspaper and became a founding editor of the feminist publication *Quest*. She also served a stint as a research fellow at the Institute for Policy Studies. By the time *Rubyfruit Jungle* came out, Brown had published two unabashedly polemical collections of poetry—*The Hand That Cradles the Rock* (1971) and *Songs to a Handsome Woman* (1973)—and many of the political essays that would later be collected in *Plain Brown Rapper* (1976).

Indeed, Brown's involvement in politics can be traced all the way back to her high-school days, when, like Molly, she was active in student government. But whereas the fictional Molly is merely elected governor of Girls' State, Brown herself actually served as honorary Governor of Florida for one day during her senior year in high school. Her real political education might reasonably be said to begin at that symbolic juncture, as the man whose office she filled promised that same year to protect academic freedom, while the president of the university she would soon attend reaffirmed his commitment to ridding the campus of homosexuals.[48] Brown's introduction to anti-racist activism occurred soon after she enrolled at the University of Florida in 1962. Inspired by professor David Chalmers, Brown joined efforts to speed desegregation and improve conditions for African Americans in the area.

> I sometimes attended student meetings. There weren't even ten people there, and the group had no name. We uncovered some unsavory facts. For instance, some of the slum housing in Gainesville was owned by university administrators and city fathers. If a Negro family slipped behind in the rent in the winter, the doors would be removed from their home. It doesn't get as cold as in Vermont, but it gets cold enough.

> The facts piled up like dead leaves. We were young, idealistic, and very naive. We started making noises.[49]

Like Molly Bolt, Brown was forced to leave UF under pressure of charges of lesbianism, an event she recounts both in *Plain Brown Rapper* and, twenty years later, in her memoir, *Rita Will*.[50] But Brown was and remains convinced that the university's concern about her sexual orientation was primarily a cover for their efforts to quell unrest by expelling activists—and her interpretation is consistent with the historical record provided in scholarly accounts of the era's activities. At the time, Florida was still intensely embroiled in its own late and local version of McCarthyism. From 1956 until the mid-1960s, the state legislature maintained an ad-hoc watch-dog group under the leadership of Senator Charley Johns, a former acting governor from the small north-central town of Starke.[51] The Florida Legislative Investigation Committee (FLIC) exploited the wide latitude of its enabling legislation to preserve disproportionate representation for northern Florida counties, harass the NAACP, resist federal desegregation orders, inhibit intellectual freedom, and remove homosexuals from public payrolls; its tactics included intimidation, extortion, sting operations, surveillance, and other extra-legal means. Among its achievements was the institution of a state-wide mandatory high-school class called "Americanism versus Communism" and the removal of about 20 University of Florida employees and an unknown number of students suspected of homosexual activity.[52]

In an assiduously researched 1995 M.A. thesis, James Schnur confirms that "the University of Florida continued to suffer from probes into the 1960s," and clarifies differences between the situation of employees (who could be fired under the "moral turpitude" clause in their contracts) and the treatment of students:

> While faculty and staff suffered immediate dismissal if accused of homosexuality, gay students could remain on campus only if they visited the infirmary and submitted to psychiatric treatments throughout their academic career. As Committee members scrutinized the patient records of the University of Florida's clinic, the threat of expulsion continued to haunt those students under orders to receive counseling.[53]

Molly Bolt's misadventures at the University of Florida appear a barely fictionalized account of Brown's own mistreatment, with one crucial difference. Molly's run-ins with a closeted female dean and a prurient school psychiatrist parallel Brown's published memories of her own experiences; UF's president J. Wayne Reitz becomes President Reich in *Rubyfruit*'s retelling. But the campus unrest, the protagonist's civil rights activities, even the actual integration of the undergraduate school in 1962 disappear in the novel's narrow focus on Molly's lesbianism. The FLIC barely registers in *Rubyfruit Jungle*, resonating slyly in the name of the New York restaurant (The Flick[54]) where Molly briefly works after her expulsion—an in-joke surely lost on the national audience introduced to the novel more than a decade after Florida's legislative investigation committee had ceased to exist.

Thirty-odd years after the fact, Brown maintains that she "will always be grateful to the University of Florida for teaching [her] that those in power will do almost anything to stay in power,"[55] but in *Rubyfruit Jungle* political analysis and activism is effectively erased, grafted root and branch onto a lesbian subjectivity forced to serve as a stand-in for organized efforts to promote social change. The logic of liberal selfhood that seems to inform the novel may be a strategic response to the era's egregious violations of civil rights; in this sense, too, *Rubyfruit Jungle* evokes the problematic legacy of *The Well of Loneliness*. But if Brown assumed connections between lesbianism and other sites of political struggle to be organic or simply obvious, her failure to elaborate encouraged superficial substitution of the one for the many. Approached from this angle, sign relations appear only iconic or symbolic, accidental or wholly arbitrary; the governing logic is analogy, and significant intervention appears impossible because the material and the symbolic are rendered separate and entirely self-contained.

In retrospect, *Rubyfruit Jungle*'s reductive substitution of individual nonconformity for collective political action appears simply consistent with the times. According to Alice Echols, the year of *Rubyfruit*'s publication marked a turning point in the process by which an increasingly isolationist cultural feminism eventually overpowered its own radical roots.

> Radical feminism remained the hegemonic tendency within the women's liberation movement until 1973 when cultural feminism began to cohere and challenge its dominance. After 1975, a year of internecine conflicts between radical and cultural feminists, cultural feminism eclipsed radical feminism as the dominant tendency within the women's liberation movement, and, as a consequence, liberal feminism became the recognized voice of the women's movement.[56]

By the time Brown's novel reached the mainstream market in 1977, the struggle between "social constructionists who wanted to render gender irrelevant" and "essentialists who sought to celebrate femaleness" was ostensibly over; the essentialist cultural feminists had won. Their retreat into a separatist women's culture, Echols charges, left liberal feminism alone "to define the political agenda of the women's movement for the public-at-large."[57]

The implication that lesbianism is somehow at fault here appears intentional. Terms such as "separatist" and notions of "celebrat[ing] femaleness"—even the phrase "women's culture"—have become code words for "lesbian," as Echols is clearly aware. Although she takes care to distinguish lesbian-feminism as such from the worst excesses of cultural feminism, lesbians—and, specifically, Rita Mae Brown and her cohorts in the Furies collective—emerge as the narrative link in Echols' storyline of the second wave's derailment and decline. Her guarded observation that "in some respects, the emergence of lesbian-feminism edged the movement closer to cultural feminism" immediately gives way to a more damning interpretation. On the one hand, lesbian-feminism's "emphasis on female counter-culture and its essentialist arguments about female sexuality were quintessential cultural feminism." On the other, "lesbian-feminism was an affront to the cultural feminist idea of a universal female experience"; "in fact, cultural feminism's ascendancy within the movement is in large measure attributable to the turmoil created by lesbianism and class." Apparently, lesbianism is at fault in *all* respects for the exacerbation of feminism's counter-culturalist, essentialist, and universalizing tendencies; in this account, both its sympathies and its philosophical differences with cultural feminism pushed the movement as a whole towards this problematic position.

Elsewhere, Echols makes the connection explicit, arguing that "with the rise of lesbian-feminism, the conflation of the personal with the political, long in the making, was complete and unassailable." As a result, she asserts, "how one lived one's life, not one's commitment to political struggle, became the salient factor."[58] But for lesbian-feminists like Brown, the separation was not so simple: "how one lived one's life" supported and confirmed "one's commitment to political struggle" even as political commitments informed daily life. The essays in *Plain Brown Rapper* document an incomplete but impassioned attempt to "unite the concept of material change with the concept of emotional/spiritual change." That this effort so frequently founders reflects the persistent intrusion of foundationalist ideas from both within and without. Brown, for example, devotes several pages of *Plain Brown Rapper* to the notion of the "self beneath the social self." She calls it "the bedrock self, the root self" and describes it as a self "owned . . . before the moment of comparison[, before] the first moment of self-consciousness." Curiously, however, this flood of foundationalist language appears in an essay arguing *against* the acritical essentialisms associated with cultural feminism. "Recognizing that our collective past was as painful as our individual pasts," Brown explains, "the Movement sought a solution to all that pain and desolation." She characterizes this solution mockingly, however: "Toss away your hateful past and as for a collective past, dip into the mists of matriarchy, at least life was better then. With the help of your sisters you too can build a new and stronger self. When in doubt pray to the Great Mother in the Skies or Isis or Sappho." In Brown's analysis, "here is where we hurt ourselves, intellectually and organizationally." Instead of denying our complicated and often painful histories, she says, "we need to understand our past and use it for the future."[59]

This perspective is missing from the argument Judith Roof advances in her otherwise illuminating reading of *Rubyfruit* as a prototypical lesbian narrative in which "the lure of knowledge"—of certainty, of origin—is sustained by the acknowledged impossibility of its fulfillment. In Roof's account, lesbian being is thus indissociable from lesbian desire. Both are driven by a desire for desire, not fulfillment; both are predicated, in the prototypical story, on the absence from the outset of the biological mother: "Lack of mother means lack of origins and vice versa." The acceptance of this absence, the acknowledgment of the impossibility of return to a past that never was, frustrates conventional narratives—historical and psychological—organized around a drive towards completion, plenitude, mastery, and fulfillment. In contradistinction to the heterosexual convention, "lesbian narrative severs the connection between present and past and eliminates the past—the origin—as any useful explanation for the present."[60]

The confusion stems from this conflation of "the past" with "the origin." As Brown's essay suggests, the rejection of origin as "any useful explanation for the present" does not necessitate a repudiation of history *per se*; indeed, productive attention to temporality would seem to demand something other than the dichotomous collapse of "history" into a single, undifferentiated "past" as distinguished from a similarly synchronous "present." Roof concludes that "lesbian fictional histories thus exist in a paradoxical relation to any notion of history," but her explication suggests otherwise: "Origin denied or useless," she says, "the lesbian novel traces a history with no beginning urged by a desire for a total picture already defined as unfulfillable."[61] Exactly. And this is one sense, I offer, in which lesbian representation in the late twentieth-century United States may tend to be consonant with a pragmatist semiotic. Roof's formulation is not paradoxical unless "a history with no beginning" is assumed to be a contradiction in terms.

As I suggested in Chapter 1, Roof's description of lesbian narratives as "beginning, instead, in media res, after mirror stage differentiation" captures this quality very nicely. This possibility she raises certainly "confound[s] post-mirror stage history itself, by denying the importance of origins," as Roof suggests, but it does much more, as well.[62] It opens up a "notion of history" unassimilable to a psychoanalytical model that is both rooted in notions of origin/return and inclined to confuse the stories it scripts and stages with "history itself."[63]

Whatever exactly Brown's vision entails, the position she stakes out in *Plain Brown Rapper* would seem to resist the simple conflation of history with origin and cannot be reduced to the universalizing essentialism that Echols, for instance, associates with the term "woman-identified." Brown's description is certainly vague, arguably even confused, but it clearly privileges connection over conflation and even seems to suggest that the "root self" may be an effect of sociality:

> By clearly seeing ourselves we can use the jolt of self awareness as an oppressed person to lead us back to our past and simultaneously to our future. By identifying with other women, with ourselves, we gain a definite goal: Freedom. Our self is linked to other selves. . . . Slowly, heightened self-consciousness fades as we connect, understand, love and breathe the lives of our sisters. . . . Within the goal of women's freedom we find our more personal goals.[64]

Elsewhere, Brown excoriates as heterosexist "attempts to smash Lesbianism by treating it as a personal luxury rather than dealing with it as a political ideology." In her analysis, "This sweeping us under the rug as some great apolitical, individualistic freedom" is not a reasoned response to any intrinsic aspect of lesbianism, but an example of "classic heterosexual blindness."[65]

If none of this makes *Rubyfruit Jungle* a better book, necessarily, it does cast Molly's "radical individualism" in a somewhat different light. Read as an index to the tensions of '70s feminism, rather than an attempt to resolve them, Molly's "root self" is exposed as an historical effect, a contingent foundation indexically connected to a matrix of meanings arrayed across time and space. Molly's assertion of self is recast as an act of political will. In *Plain Brown Rapper*, Brown explains "woman-identification" in practical terms, as "process," "self-awareness," "work." "Identification," in this context, is not a single action, a naming of what's already there, but an ongoing activity; and "woman-identification" becomes the persistent enactment of solidarity and selfhood, as opposed to an expression of essence. (Or, as Brown warns us, "Feminism, the root self, isn't one magic moment of understanding then life becomes easy."[66]) We might read this as conflation (the simplistic equation of identity with ideology); we might read it as essentialist (the assumption encoded in the phrase "women's liberation," that the movement would free women to live in accordance with their nature); or we might read it pragmatically, as an historically situated possibility in which the "self" becomes not a premise, but a politics.

I will admit that, despite my best efforts here, I find it difficult to read *Rubyfruit Jungle* as anything other than the simplistic, essentialist, and effectively anti-feminist aggrandizement of American individualism that critics like Bonnie Zimmerman hold it to be. But the irony, of course, is that the novel's essentialism is only a superficial effect, while the deep structures that support its foundationalist implications are themselves thoroughly contingent. The fact of its foundationalism is historically structured. As radical feminist analysis was reduced in the public mind to demands for equal rights on the one hand and calls for cultural separatism on the other, *Rubyfruit*'s frame of reference shrunk to debilitating dimensions; in this context, the paradox it poses can only be resolved in essentialist terms. But by dismissing *Rubyfruit Jungle* as ahistorical without assessing the forces that make it so, we risk repeating the error. The novel's flat prose may work to wall off the complexities of feminist and lesbian history, but behind the book's slick surface, a far-reaching matrix of indices and antecedents offers stronger support for political engagement than the self-contained Molly Bolt could possibly provide.

Chapter 6

Getting Some Perspective: Lesbian Pragmatism

> Somewhere along the line, I knew there'd be girls, visions, everything.
>
> —Jack Kerouac, *On the Road* (1957)

And "somewhere down the line," says Lillian Faderman, "theory needs to move into practice or nothing gets improved."[1] In Sarah Schulman's aptly titled 1986 novel, there are indeed *Girls, Visions and Everything*, as lesbian-feminism meets Jack Kerouac in a pragmatic critique of "American" arrogance, and practice is the implicit condition of a kind of queer theorizing that moves beyond the *born or made?* dichotomy.[2] In Schulman's novel, I contend, we can discern a signifying practice that usefully extends Judith Butler's theory of performativity to more productively integrate context and content; one result is a vision of lesbian agency clearly inflected and enabled, as well as constrained, by history and materiality, as well as discourse.

As Biddy Martin contends, "Butler's climatic challenges to identity politics, to ahistorical assumptions of the shape of the symbolic have done the crucial ground-clearing work of opening the analysis of interiority to its construction in and through relations of power." As a result, she concludes, queer theory is positioned to undertake "renewed and innovative approaches to the entanglement of organism/psyche/sociality." I am concerned, however, that Martin's desire to "pause longer over the differences that materiality and interiority make once we introduce the crucial element of temporality into the equations" is underserved by Butler's formalist interpretation of performativity. As we saw in Chapters 4 and 5, the introduction of a temporal dimension to structuralist theories of sign relations does not of itself bridge the gap between history (or politics) and theory. Reversing the frame, Martin contends that "discourse theory does the work of introducing forms of spatialization into otherwise linear, developmental, teleological narratives of formation." But she rightly worries about its limitations, as well: "When it comes to questions of gender, sexuality, and identity, however, temporality reminds us that inside/outside encounters have the effect again and again of making bodies and psyches with histories that then exert their own pressures back on the boundaries between out and in, back on what we take to be the social world around a self or person."[3] The problem is that temporality—at least as envisioned by Butler, as the compelled (re)iteration of norms—cannot account for this phenomenon. These "bodies and psyches with histories" would seem to constitute the "entanglement of organism/psyche/sociality" that Martin is at pains to explain, but the joinder between history and sociality, between temporality and structuralism remains unspecified, elided in the parallel phrasing of her terms. Quite reasonably, then, Martin "worr[ies] about the degree to which normalization serves as an explanation of how power operates": temporality conceived through formalist narrative theory and sociality imagined as structuralist constraints are useful and illuminating models, but insufficient to account for the entanglements that Martin identifies. This is because these abstractions provide no point of intersection. It is in this context, then, that a specifically Peircean pragmatism may be seen to offer a particularly promising "renewed approach" to the questions that confront queer theory.

Girls, Visions and Everything puts this theory into practice. In the opening lines, we learn that "Lila Futuransky always knew she was an outlaw, but she could never figure out which one. She wanted to be free but couldn't decide what that meant" (3). In this sense, queer theory is a lot like Lila—characterized "less by consistent methodology than by its mobile oppositionality"; as Annamarie Jagose explains, "Its definitional indeterminancy, its elasticity, is one of its constituent characteristics."[4] Like Lila, queer theory embraces an outlaw attitude, but remains indecisive about long-term objectives. Like Lila, queer theory is "still young" and "alternately entertaining and antagonizing" (3). But while the fictional Lila sticks out the summer of '84 on the Lower East Side, rooted in her sweaty body, rent-controlled apartment, and familiar few blocks of the gentrification-threatened neighborhood, queer theory tends to rely on a notion of performativity strangely abstracted from material context.

Of course, Lila Futuransky is only a fictional character, the hero of a hilarious, complicated novel that offers, among other things, a scathing critique of Reagan's America, an extended rumination on the lesbian boyhood, and an ironized revision of Jack Kerouac's classic, *On the Road* (1957). But Lila is no anomaly. The lesbian perspective that she represents, a subjectivity developed alongside and within a pragmatic semiotic, still resonates within contemporary U.S. mass culture. Although neither semiotic sensibilities nor understandings of female homosexuality are simple, singular, or stable, some trace of pragmatism seems to have persisted within lesbian subcultures and self-representations through a century of contestation—and Schulman's social realist novel captures this connection. Despite the insistent dichotomization historically directed at lesbian experience, lesbians have persisted in a subtle subcultural understanding that refuses to invalidate our hard-won sense of *lesbian agency* by the negation of either of its terms, insisting instead that it is neither inauthentic (not really lesbian) nor inevitable (not really agency). This is the truth that Schulman's novel affirms, and the perspective from which it is narrated. Fittingly, it is a contingent truth, self-evident only from its own pragmatic perspective. As its protagonist struggles to reconcile freedom and attachment in her personal life, *Girls, Visions and Everything* constructs a realistic fictional universe in which the exercise of agency is reconciled with an understanding of its constraints. By revisiting the irreducibly material circumstances of Lila's reality, the novel reworks contested notions of community, coherence, spatiality, and temporality, reinventing Pragmatism in and for a self-consciously multicultural and postmodern United States—and potentially reinvigorating queer theory in the process.

Out of the Loop: "the identity of difference"

The anthology *Inside/Out* was among the founding texts of U.S. academic queer theory, and its editor, Diana Fuss, among the first to insist that "new (and old) sexual possibilities are no longer thinkable in terms of a simple inside/outside dialectic." But her introduction to that groundbreaking 1991 collection nevertheless maintains that "the figure inside/outside" is "an indispensable model for helping us to understand the complicated workings of semiosis" and "the very figure for signification and the mechanisms of meaning production." Accordingly, she imagines "the contortions and convolutions of . . . sexual identity formation" as something like a "figure-eight knot or four knot"—a sutured loop that might conceivably be turned "inside-out," but not undone. This figure evokes a structuralist understanding of meaning as relational, but cannot, of itself, accommodate or account for change over time in the patterns that structure meaning. The challenge, as Fuss recognizes, lies in our experience of a complex and changing reality unassimilable to that apparently indispensable model, inside/out. As Fuss suggests, we need to rethink the terms in which we theorize sexual possibilities. The time has come to think about *how we think about* sex.[5]

To begin with, the "inside/outside dialectic" is of course not simple at all. The "problem of the 'outside'" in such formulations is at the crux of a contemporary philosophical crisis extending far beyond the arguments between queer theorists and lesbian historians. Cary Wolfe calls it "the 'Gordian knot' of the realism/idealism debate," explaining that "all observations are based on a constitutive distinction (between figure and ground, say, or legal and illegal) that is paradoxical because it posits the identity of difference."[6] That is, any foundational distinction between "inside" and "out" is itself inescapably "in"—and hence not a foundational distinction at all, but a more or less arbitrary one. There is no ontologically secure "outside" to representation, however persistently we posit one. Judith Butler's account of subject formation employs a similar logic: "the subject is constituted through the force of exclusion and abjection, one which produces a constitutive outside to the subject, an abjected outside, which is, after all, 'inside' the subject as its own founding repudiation."[7]

The question, then, is why reality so obstinately appears *less* rather than *more* arbitrary; what is it that constrains representation if not a non-negotiable outside? Wolfe proposes that the only way to cut this knot is "to follow through to its conclusion the problem of contingency, to assert that 'everything that is said is said by someone,' and to *then* remember that all such assertions are based on a 'blind spot' of paradoxical distinction that not the observer in question, but only *other* observers, can disclose."[8] Following the insights of systems theory, he identifies an "incipient pluralism" within the process of meaning production.

Queer theory has typically followed a more Foucauldian route (apparently sharing Tom Cohen's understanding of genealogy as "critical narration . . . *designed to undo a historical knot in the present*").[9] Butler, for example, invokes Foucault as a corrective to presentist conceits[10] and insists that "construction not only takes place in time, but is itself a temporal process."[11] ("It is not simply that discourses are located in histories, but that they have their own historical character.")[12] For Butler, this temporal dimension inheres in performativity, specifically in its citational quality.

By situating acts of constitutive distinction in space and time, respectively, Wolfe and Butler point the way toward an understanding of constructivism in which meanings are constrained, but not permanently fixed. But the problem of materiality persists. Wolfe bemoans the tendency of both systems theory and the so-called neo-pragmatism to devolve into "an ideology of liberalism that, in its Rortyan version, declares out of the picture from the outset those social others whose very otherness or difference might lead to the critical reassessment of the beliefs of the liberal ethos."[13] And although Butler works toward precisely such critical reassessment of "heterosexual hegemony," she stakes her theory of temporality on an understanding of discursive performativity that has similarly sometimes been taken to obscure sociopolitical realities.

Martha C. Nussbaum, for example, criticizes Butler's brand of feminist theory for its "lofty obscurity and disdainful abstractness," arguing that it represents an irresponsible "turning from the material side of life[, from] the real situation of real women."[14] Ironically, *Bodies That Matter* is ostensibly devoted specifically to the question of materiality, to clarifying the connections between gender's performativity and the body's materiality—and in it Butler certainly comes closer than most to providing a workable understanding of the ways in which the symbolic, the social, the psychic, and the physical come together to produce what we perceive as actual. Why, then, do these criticisms persist? More to the point, why are they so persuasive? Butler herself touches on one reason: the tenacity of *born or made?*-type oppositions and the related tendency of putatively constructivist theories to ground themselves in or collapse back into foundationalist assumptions. In *Bodies That Matter*, she identifies three conventional trajectories of devolution. If in rejecting essentialism "[constructivist] theory cannot take account of sex as the site or surface on which it acts, then it ends up presuming sex as the unconstructed, and so concedes the limits of linguistic constructivism, inadvertently circumscribing that which remains unaccountable within the terms of construction." But if sex is taken into account as "a postulation, a construction, offered within language, as that which is prior to language, prior to construction," then constructivism collapses into either linguistic monism or essentialist humanism. The former "presumes that construction operates deterministically, making a mockery of human agency," while the latter "understands constructivism as presupposing a voluntarist subject who makes its [own] gender through instrumental action." Essentialism, determinism, liberal humanism—without sacrificing a great deal of philosophical specificity, we might term these three positions the *born*, *made*, and *chosen* schools of thought.

Bodies That Matter is devoted to developing a genuinely alternative understanding, one which "is no longer constructivism, but neither is it essentialism."

> For there is an "outside" to what is constructed by discourse, but this is not an absolute "outside," an ontological thereness that exceeds or counters the boundaries of discourse; as a constitutive "outside," it is that which can only be thought—when it can—in relation to that discourse, at and as its most tenuous borders. The debate between constructivism and essentialism thus misses the point of deconstruction altogether, for the point has never been that "everything is discursively constructed"; that point, when and where it is made, belongs to a kind of discursive monism or linguisticism that refuses the constitutive force of exclusion, erasure, violent foreclosure, abjection and its disruptive return within the very terms of discursive legitimacy.[15]

It is this "outside," in Butler's view, that drives materialization, sustains subjectivity, and secures the democratic promise of futurity.

In its first and paradigmatic figuration, this "outside" appears as "abjection." Because Butler is concerned specifically with "the materialization of bodies," and because she understands this process as indissociable from the process of subjectivization, abjection appears indissociable from materiality. As the "constitutive outside" of subjectivity (understood here as process, not product or ground), not its opposite ("for oppositions are, after all, part of intelligibility"), abjection emerges as "the excluded and illegible," "unthinkable" and "unlivable" domain of impossibility ineluctably produced in the very moment and self-same action as "intelligible bodies" are made to appear: "The forming of a subject requires an identification with the normative phantasm of 'sex,' and this identification takes place through a repudiation which produces a domain of abjection, a repudiation without which the subject cannot emerge." For Butler, "bodies that matter" are bodies endowed with subjectivity, "legitimate" bodies authorized within the scheme of social recognition. About bodies that don't matter—or don't "matter in the same way"—she asserts that "it will be important" to inquire into "how bodies which fail to materialize provide the necessary 'outside,' if not the necessary support, for the bodies which, in materializing the norm, qualify as bodies that matter."[16]

Precisely because the effects of signification are not and can never be fully fixed—they are haunted always by the abject domain that secures and threatens their borders—materiality must be understood as "a reiterated acting," as not merely coincidentally but constitutionally *temporal*. But because the mechanisms that secure this temporality are themselves characterized by simultaneity (by difference on the structuralist model, inside/out), the potentially productive "instabilities" ensured by this arrangement can assert themselves only as "gaps" or "fissures" in the repetition that they themselves compel. The continued production of such gaps is presumably ensured by the contemporaneous "acting" of diverse interpellations. Although she focuses on the (historical) function of heteronormativity in securing subjectivity, Butler is clear in her rejection of any "claim that there is a singular matrix that acts in a singular and deterministic way to produce a subject as its effect"—and in fact insists that the constitutive instability of subjectivity is "a function of the complexity and historicity of a social field that can never be [fully or adequately or conclusively] summarized by any given description, and that, for democratic reasons, ought never to be."[17]

Despite Butler's efforts to "think of the symbolic as the temporalized regulation of signification," however, the notion of "discourse" that grounds *Bodies That Matter* is easily—and perhaps not inappropriately—mistaken for "a quasi-permanent structure."[18] On the one hand, "the 'I' *neither precedes nor follows* the process of this gendering" ("where gendering is, among other things, the differentiating relations by which speaking subjects come into being").[19] On the other hand, however:

> Where there is an "I" who utters or speaks and thereby produces an effect in discourse, there is *first* a discourse which precedes and enables that "I" and forms in language the constraining trajectory of its will. Thus there is no "I" who stands behind discourse and executes its volition or will through discourse. On the contrary, the "I" only comes into being through being called, named, interpellated, to use the Althusserian term, and this discursive constitution takes place *prior to* the "I."[20]

Subjectivity and the materiality of sex emerge as effects here, continually re(per)formed through compulsory citation. But "discourse" remains an abstraction; the mechanisms of its own historicity remain opaque.

Butler emphasizes that gender "is not necessarily constructed by an 'I' or a 'we' who stands before that construction in any spatial or temporal sense of 'before,'" but this insistence obviates an important aspect of her turn to speech act theory: the materiality of speech and the indexicality through which it acts. In the founding gesture of structuralist linguistics, Saussure delimited his object of study by *distinguishing* it from speech—first removing it from space, and then separating it from time.[21] Like Saussure's *langue*, Butler's "discourse" can only be a theoretical fiction, an abstract approximation. The "discourse" described as appearing always and only *before* the "I" is specifically a *structuralist* abstraction; its quasi-permanence is a direct effect of its ideality.[22] This effect cannot be wished away by mere assertion, but a pragmatic perspective on the physical parameters of reference can reveal a constitutive temporality. Discourse *is* relatively more stable than speech or its referents, but discourse is also an effect of its uses.

If materiality has proven the lavender herring of queer theory, perhaps that's because we've persisted in posing it as the question instead of looking to it for answers. "Discourse" may precede and inform "subjectivity," but discourse only lives through the specific speech acts of actual subjects situated in time and space. An "I" (and, by implication, a "you" and a "they") does *stand before* each citation of discourse in precisely these senses of priority and alterity, even as it and the discourse that sustains it are continually reformulated through these acts of citation. Despite Butler's interest in temporality, her focus on an abstract "discourse," and on the "outside"/"inside" dynamic that defines it, may be seen to spatialize and distort relations of precedence. The difference is not so much that a trace of the past persists in the present (called memory, or expectation, or *habit*[23])—Butler would hold that a trace (marked absence) of the outside persists on the inside[24]—but that the mechanism of that persistence differs: the outside shapes the in by what it's not (its modes are absence, difference, and disjuncture); the past shapes the present by what it is (its modes are substance, similarity, and continuity). And here a pragmatic perspective can be especially helpful. Essentialists point to the body as though the materiality of sex were evidence of its extradiscursive, uninflected, eternal, universal, *elemental* nature. Seeking to complicate this notion, Butler insists that discourse always precedes the subject, that bodies come to "matter" always and only through a discourse antecedent to the materiality of their sex. Pragmatically speaking, however, it is precisely physicality that renders reality perspectival, mediated, and relentlessly indexical. Matter is constitutionally temporal, situated, relational. Abstractions may be imagined discrete, disconnected, self-identical, and self-contained, but matter is matter because it incorporates (however imperfectly) duration and situatedness. That is to say, whatever and however else it may "be," matter "is" in time *and* space.[25] Hence materiality is not merely the vehicle of citation, but the guarantor of discourse's temporality.

This implication of materiality within semiosis, via the indexical function, guarantees both complexity and historicity. The promise of democratic futurity, however, depends on our political responses to this reality.

Out on the Street: Lesbian Pragmatism

Girls, Visions and Everything is, among other things, a critique of an "America" that fails to pursue this promise. It is also good evidence that the mediating specification of "lesbian" and "cultural" in Laura Doan's formulation of "postmodern theory" offers more than faddish particularization.[26] In a era in which "postmodern" and "politics" are sometimes assumed antithetical, Schulman's novel dramatizes the pragmatic ways in which "a lesbian postmodern might enable an interventionist or transformative politics,"[27] exemplifying a postmodern lesbian cultural praxis in which the middle terms can be seen not to narrow the reach of the project, but precisely *through their specification* to enable and extend it. In Lila's world, lesbian culture self-consciously defines a contingent foundation from which agency, action, and accountability can emerge. Indeed, the dykes in *Girls, Visions and Everything* can be seen to represent what John Stuhr calls pragmatism's "challenge" to postmodernism: "to become political, to situate and localize wills to oppositionalities in social practices of resistance, transformation, and reconstruction, and to create space within experience for the possibility of those practices, as well as their contestation."[28] Read as a theory of representation, as well as critical commentary on the state of the nation, *Girls, Visions and Everything* bears a telling resemblance to pragmatism—and provides a plausible alternative to the theoretical stalemate currently stymieing lesbian studies.

Some of the same qualities that make *Girls, Visions and Everything* worth talking about also make it an especially difficult book to summarize: it's both unconventional and complicated, offering nuanced explorations of diverse interrelated themes and relying extensively on intra- and extratextual allusions. Lesbian giant Naiad Press reportedly declined to publish it because it "had no plot."[29] But it's not a difficult read. The book combines an "unrelentingly parodic perspective" with dead-on realism. Although some critics contend that Schulman's style is intentionally alienating, "almost jerking the reader into some consciousness of her activity of creating imaginative space,"[30] the novel is also enormously accessible, perhaps especially to lesbians. Along with everything else it does, *Girls, Visions and Everything* offers realistic representations of regular dykes. It may not have a conventional plot, but it does focus on particular subjects and follow their development over time. One story it tells is about Lila's progressive disenchantment with certain inherited understandings of personal and artistic freedom; another trajectory documents "the creepy, crawling invasion of gentrification into the neighborhood" (19) around Tompkins Square Park. Depending, perhaps, on one's personal degree of cynicism, the novel can also be read either as a love story or, as Sally Munt puts it, as "anti-romance."[31] Either way, it tells the story of Lila Futuransky's developing relationship with Emily Harrison, beginning with a casual encounter, elaborating a growing attraction and increasing intimacy, and concluding with Lila's declaration of commitment. This progression is impeded by Lila's attachment to notions of freedom and spontaneity she associates with the Jack Kerouac of *On the Road*; by the opacity of Emily's own motivations, desires, and forms of expression; and by the nonexistence of any inherited narrative structure suitable to propel it. The resolution, if it can be called one, is undercut by Lila's clear understanding that this love "mean(s) making compromises, giving up things" (177). The narrative, like Lila, wanders around a lot—in this, as elsewhere, the book recalls Whitman. But whereas Whitman simultaneously overwhelms with irreducible particularity and subsumes the specific and superficial into an ultimately harmonious whole, in *Girls, Visions and Everything* any semblance of epistemological coherence is clearly the tenuous and temporary result of socially-negotiated tensions. In place of the transcendental unity assumed and evoked by Whitman, Schulman installs history, language, and material circumstance as the "contingent foundations" of her fictional world.

Like Whitman, Schulman was a working journalist before turning (increasingly, but not exclusively) to other forms of expression; her novels, like his poetry, are infused by a documentary sensibility. Local reviews laud their authenticity: "Schulman *writes* New York, the New York we really live in."[32] *Girls, Visions and Everything* is especially attentive to geography, situating its story within precise physical boundaries, mostly a few square blocks smack in the middle of the Lower East Side. Schulman's "constant references to crisscrossing streets remind the reader of the systematic patterns of neighborhood and community."[33] But like Lila herself, these physical markers serve as points of reference whose formal stability is considerably complicated by specific histories. And Schulman is similarly documentary in her descriptions of such transformations. There's the "former Country-Western bar turned punk bar on First Avenue," for instance: "The new owners changed the name to *Beirut* and decorated it with barbed wire[;] they hadn't gotten around to the juke box though." Lila and her friends play *Ode to Billy Joe*, the Temptations and Santana (120). A little later in the novel, Lila and her friend Sal drop by "the Polish Country-Western bar turned Beirut turned gay men's fuck bar called The Manhole." Fortunately, "the place still had a good juke box" (142).

Changes have also come to the public library up on Forty-Second Street.

> The Jewish Room, being on the first floor of the giant main library building, had easy access and so became a resting place for those homeless men and women who were the inmates of the open wards of the city. Usually this room was noisy, smelled bad and was inhabited by a combination of religious Jews reading ancient texts and bag-ladies tearing up copies of *The New York Post*. Both sat there, rocking back and forth and talking to themselves. In the summer, it was hot and the windows were wide open, letting in the roar of the center city hustle outside. Two men collected money for a Black Museum that existed only in their dreams. Drug dealers promised Thai sticks, when it was only Mexican Cocoa-Cola buds. The Unification Church Missionaries, known as Moonies, drew diagrams explaining life and God with red and blue magic markers on portable boards. A bad saxophone player repeated over and over the theme song from *The Odd Couple* and then the theme song from *The Pink Panther*. All of this drifted into the Jewish Room. (138)

For all this sounds like an updated Whitman ("Always a knit of identity, always distinction, always a breed of life"), it is clearly a timebound collection of images. Many of Schulman's details index in a general way the widening wealth gap spurred by Reagan's economic policies. Many more—the homeless encampment in Tompkins Square Park (84), the burned-out buildings between Avenues B and C (101), the boarded-up

Orchidia (formerly "the world's only Ukranian-Italian restaurant" [173]), the growing police presence in Lila's neighborhood (118), including even "policemen on horseback" (31)—specifically signal the movements of capital that supported early-1980s efforts to gentrify the East Village. Historically, reinvestment flowed from west to east here, as developers sought to expand the profitable rental markets of Greenwich Village, Soho, and Tribeca into the East Side—displacing longtime residents of the traditionally low-income area in the process. Redevelopment was uneven, however. New School sociologist Janet Abu-Lughod points out that while "in general, the western blocks are in better condition than the eastern ones," the Lower East Side's unique social geography combined with the incursion of real estate interests to "create distinct microzones that can change block by block in unpredictable fashion."[34] Lila notices the same thing:

> Things were so bad that even Avenue A was unlivable. The Good Humor man had been replaced by tofutti-selling teenaged boys in teased Mohawks. Polish and Puerto Rican mom and pop soda fountains featuring Breyer's ice cream, vanilla or chocolate, bowed to the pressure of imported ices. Tanned Europeans in skimpy t-shirts sold one dollar and fifty cents scoops-du-jour. But, over by Avenue B, there was still life on Sixth Street. Lila passed an old Irish bar with a pool table, a few bodegas and the combination Jesse Jackson for President campaign headquarters and thrift shop. (19)

Sociologist Christopher Mele confirms that "reinvestment eventually priced out existing small-scale 'mom and pop' owners while encouraging large real estate development companies to enter the local market." Many lower-income residents were similarly priced out—of their homes. Those in rent-controlled units, however, had to be displaced by other means. When a friend of a friend warns Lila, "You better watch your ass. . . . They gonna be turning off the heat, robbing your apartment, refusing to make repairs" (100), he's only describing an all-too-realistic scenario. According to Mele, "illegal means [of driving out tenants], including turning off the heat and hot water in the winter, renting to drug pushers who terrorize tenants, or torching emptied units, have frequently been used by the more notorious landlords in the East Village."[35] (Unfortunately for Lila, her own landlord is "a notorious scum" [101]).

This collision of gentrification with rent-control regulations made for a period of widely disparate rents in the area, sometimes within the same building, in real life as in the novel. But when Lila wonders, "what kind of rich person would want to spend twelve hundred dollars a month to live here, with us?" the answer she gets is ominous: "There ain't gonna be no *us* by the time they move in" (100). And, indeed, retrospective demographic data shows telling changes in the neighborhood's "population composition": significant declines in African American and Latino populations, a "marked drop" in the number of children, displacement of "older and poorer residents."[36] As Lila notes, "developers liked to tear out six apartments filled with kids and put in one luxury duplex for some kind of rich artist" (31). Although Lila marvels that "the speculation going on around here is unreal" (99), Schulman's fictional figures are actually pretty much on the money: maybe Lila's landlord is a little optimistic in his hopes to turn over a $60,000 investment for $700,000 in two years' time; then again, the *average* sale price for buildings in some areas of the East Village increased almost tenfold between 1982 and 1985. In the midst of the early to mid-1980s "speculative frenzy" investors could indeed turn impressive profits with remarkable speed.[37]

This sort of documentary accuracy contributes to the sense of realism that the novel sustains, but I want to argue that it does something more, as well. This attention to particularity helps to establish an authorial sensibility attuned to the difference that difference makes. Consider Lila's impressions of an event she attends at a "local lesbian clubhouse known informally as the Kitsch-Inn" (4):

> Lila sat in the back row to get a good view of the real show, the usual assortment of local lesbians who made up the audiences at places like this.
>
> Whenever she was in a room full of lesbians, Lila fluctuated between two points of view. First she would have a sentimental rush of feeling, overwhelmed by the beauty and the courage of all these women who had gone through fire and ice just to find each other. *Every meeting place, tradition or ritual was built with nothing but their own determination, which kept everything vaguely together.* But, a split second later, Lila looked more distantly and the scene would be transformed into a roomful of victims. This one had her child taken away, that one got locked up by her parents, that one's girlfriend got queerbashed in front of her and there wasn't a thing she could do about it. (59, emphasis added)

Here the necessary and inevitable coexistence of competing perspectives is grounded in the reality of different social locations. Only when

Lila looks "more distantly" does she share the dominant view: "Nobody, *outside* of lesbians, had bought the line that they were strong, determined survivors. To everyone else they were invisible or pitiful and most straight people were plain glad they weren't queer" (59, emphasis added). As this remark implies, one thing *Girls, Visions and Everything* does is bring the "outside" *in*. Early on, Lila realizes that the trick to enjoying *On The Road* is "to identify with Jack instead of with the women he fucks along the way" (17). The trick to reading *Girls, Visions and Everything* is to identify with the lesbians.

By presenting Lila's point of view as *author*itative, rendering it legitimate, Schulman sets the stage for a pragmatic response to Judith Butler's question, "How is it that the abjected come to make their claim through and against the discourses that have sought their repudiation?"[38] Within Butler's binary schema of construction via exclusion, materiality emerges as an (always imperfect and impermanent) effect, but not a ground or cause. Because it is an effect constituted and sustained through a reiterated acting, change is inevitable: iteration is necessarily imperfect. Coherence comes, to the extent that it does, only by force of memory, expectation, or habit. Because these temporalized effects don't figure *back into* the ongoing process of construction, however, subversion can be imagined only as resistance—i.e., disruption or interruption, a refusal to act (or to act as expected), a negative intervention enacted from an abject or foreclosed space. But to figure resistance in this way—as always and only inaction, non-compliance, withholding participation—is to adopt the dominant perspective. From Lila's lesbian point of view, things look a little different.

In the tradition of Marilyn Frye, *Girls, Visions and Everything* offers a theatrical metaphor for the mechanisms of abjection:

> Once Lila and Isabel went to an off-Broadway theatre to see what shows were like when you paid twenty-five dollars for a ticket. . . . The lesbian characters kissed each other and hit each other. The gay male characters made jokes about the sizes of each other's penises. The Black characters ran around with afro-picks in their pockets and occasionally stopped combing their hair long enough to play three-card monte while saying "motha-fucka" a lot and grabbing their own crotches. All of this provided an appropriately colorful background for the white heterosexual characters to expose their deeply complex emotional lives.

Lila's friend Isabel dubs the genre "fake social realism" (18).

By foregrounding this background, authorizing the conventionally abjected, Schulman's novel upsets the familiar dynamic. But the difference is not a simple reversal. The book also points out that "there is always more to a person than what somebody else does to them" (168)—even more, I would argue, than what *everyone* else does to them. There is also material substance and subjective presence, the sedimentation of the subject's own past.

Unfortunately, this element of Schulman's vision is easily obscured by queer theory's predilection for prioritizing discursive foundations. Munt's conclusion that in *Girls, Visions and Everything* Schulman "inhibits the sense-making process (or narrative hermeneutic) by constantly invoking and corrupting the conventional literary topology"[39] makes sense only from the perspective conventionally authorized in American literature; like Judith Roof, it sees "the possibility of intervention" only at narrative's "points of failure."[40] Schulman's unconventional heroines provide a different point of view. "Everybody runs around complaining that New Yorkers control the world," Isabel observes. "But it's not the people who really live here. It's the ones who came from somewhere else, you know, like Americans."

> Then after they're here awhile, they write these plays and books and songs about what it was like coming here from somewhere else. As if this was a city full of golden angels getting off the Greyhound bus with a suitcase full of dreams battling their way past the local slugs until they get to their righteously deserved pot of gold. (18)

The ambiguity of Isabel's explanatory tag—"you know, like Americans"—only underscores the ubiquity of this national hermeneutic. Equally example and analogy, "Americans" are understood to be self-promoting opportunists who come from someplace else to appropriate indigenous resources—and to rationalize their exploitation with a self-serving myth as old as Manifest Destiny and as vigorous as the economic interests driving gentrification.

Within both popular culture and the scholarly literature, zones ripe for reinvestment are frequently imagined as "urban frontiers,"[41] but audiences are generally encouraged to identify with the cowboys, not the Indians. As William Sites explains, "A typical scenario attributes gentrification to the large cohort of baby-boom professionals who, rejecting suburban living, became urban pioneers and saved moribund inner-city neighborhoods." Sites argues that "such interpretations are doubly problematic" in that they "demean long-term inner-city residents, whose often-thriving communities are uprooted" and also "imply . . . a kind of consumer sovereignity on the part of 'gentrifiers,' or a free-market inevitability that operates without any political dynamic."[42] Schulman was not the only East Village artist to challenge this logic in the mid-1980s. The Political Art Documentation/Distribution Project against Displacement, for example, produced graphic critiques of the "invasion." Nancy Sullivan's PAD/D poster employed a strategy very similar to Schulman's, satirically enjoining "Area Natives" to "Make Your Reservation Now"—with Old West iconography and the parenthetical caveat "treaties non-negotiable" clearly conferring double meanings on the words "native" and "reservation."[43] In Frederick Jackson Turner's model, U.S. democracy was forged on a frontier that necessitated cooperation, but nurtured individualism—and the quintessential American was the rough and ready pioneer remade at that "meeting place of savagery and civilization," the one "who came from somewhere else" to triumph over native adversity. "According to Lila," however, "artists were supposed to show that there were other ways of seeing." In her view, art is for reaching out to people "because you had something to tell them, and that something, thought Lila, should not be the same old thing" (65). *Girls, Visions and Everything* denaturalizes the national narrative by providing a different perspective on familiar events.

Thus, although Munt is on target with her observation that Lila "reinvents New York from her position as 'other' as a heterotopia of cultural intertextuality," she seems a little off base in the insistence that "she *is* Jack Kerouac—the character, not the author—claiming, even as a Jewish lesbian, that 'the road is the only image of freedom that an American can understand.'"[44] This assessment overlooks the novel's frequent jabs at the kind of "freedom" supposedly celebrated by *On the Road*, as well as Lila's own increasing ambivalence about her romantic identification with "Jack." It also fails to incorporate the protagonists' oppositional relation to the term "America." When Lila and her friend Vicki take a trip to New Jersey, "two Van Halen fans . . . in a dirty white Chevy" shout racist insults. "'You take one step into America and look what happens,'" Vicki says. "'At least that's one way of looking at it'" (97).[45] When some guy in a bar queer-baits her pal Sal Paradise, Lila dismisses him as "a typical American asshole" (142). And it's obviously "Americans," by Isabel's definition, behind the new neighborhood group organizing on Lila's street:

> Usually block associations were good, helping everyone get to know each other, planting trees, getting a new street light. But this one had a bad feeling about it. First they put up posters of a young white couple walking fearfully down a city street filled with menacing jungle animals, like baboons. The caption read 'Clean Up Our Street.' It hadn't taken Lila very long to recognize that any group of people who wanted to clean up another group of people were usually bad news. (30)[46]

"I hate the Fourth of July," Vicki announces. "Between the bombs and the flags, it's too American for me. Even uptown it sounds like there's a war going on. I'm going camping this year, to get away from that red, blue and *white*" (97). By the time Isabel (not Lila) observes (in chapter 39) that "the road is the only image of freedom an American can understand," the protagonists' ambivalence about identifying with "America" has been well established.

The novel's ironicized relation to *On the Road* is further emphasized by Isabel's admission that "there's something weird about [the Kerouac book], like it has a magic power." "Even though I hated the main guy," she says, "by page three I wanted to be him" (163). But the critical distance comes across most clearly in descriptions of Lila's own increasing ambivalence:

> Lila had been reading and rereading *On The Road*, she was almost through. But the closer she got to those final pages, the more doubts creepy crawled into her mind. She shared Jack's vision of women as sexual treasures and mystical beings who come in and out of your life[,] but there were still questions that Jack never touched on. Like what do you do once you get to know them? He never stayed around long enough for that.

Lila spends much of the book thinking that "she needed to take a trip like Jack's," but she comes to wonder if "maybe it would be different for a woman. Maybe it didn't require a road at all" (137).

Munt reads *Girls, Visions and Everything* as "anti-romance" because she assumes that, in the end, "Lila resorts to Emily . . . knowing it is the wrong decision and nostalgically lamenting the end of the road of selfhood." And certainly *Girls* is not a happily-ever-after, Naiad kind of novel. But neither is it so pessimistic as Munt might have us believe; Lila's "disillusionment" should not be confused with "resignation."[47] In rejecting "Jack's" dream of the open road, Lila rejects the exclusionary illusions on which that dream is predicated, and opens the door to a selfhood experienced as material rather than transcendent, relational rather than absolute; precarious, mutable, vulnerable, accountable.

This is precisely the understanding of self that James Hoopes locates at the core of his pragmatic corrective to Rorty's exclusionary liberalism. Hoopes argues that "Peirce, alone among the pragmatists, explains [how] communicative, interpretive, semiotic relations are at the heart of being."[48] It is also consistent with Lila's characterization throughout the novel. Whereas Lila's sometimes-lover Muriel emerges as a self-involved individualist, Lila refuses opportunities for self-expression predicated on the abjection of others.

> There were good things to Muriel and bad things to Muriel and this was one of the worst. She was completely undependable. Lila, on the other hand, if she promised one girl a cup of coffee and another offered her a weekend on a yacht, you know you would find her in the coffee shop, smiling through the grease. *Why should the rich and glamorous get everything?* she asked herself repeatedly in a combination of defiance and sheer wonder. (49)

Muriel's understanding of artistic freedom is grounded in a studied "American" ignorance of the effects its exercise may have on others. She describes one frustrated attempt at self-expression to Lila:

> I was performing a series of experimental dances, using haphazard movement without form. In the first piece I thought that Roberta and I were going to go into a slow contact, like a tango, and then we started dancing. But, she said *too slow*, so I moved out of the dance. Later, when I asked her why, she said I wasn't dancing *with* her, I was dancing *on* her, but I know that if my dance is refused during the improvisation, I just lose all my concentration. (47)

Muriel "always make[s her] decisions based on what is best for [Muriel]," ignoring Lila's insistent reminders: "Sometimes there are other people involved too, you know" (68).

So while Muriel abandons her friends and responsibilities, jetting off to glamorous locales, Lila considers taking off only for "a Jack Kerouac-second" before declaring, "No goddammit . . . , I'm committed to here" (50). She finds in Emily a "compatible imagination" (153) without losing sight of the fact that "she and Emily saw identical situations with completely different eyes" (92). Listening to her friend Lacy contend with an interviewer's unselfconscious preconceptions, Lila observes that "everyone she knew or encountered had their own particular reality but what they all shared was a common difficulty in keeping to it in the face of mounting adversity" (98). In *Girls, Visions and Everything*, that adversity generally goes by the name "America." But in elaborating Lila's specifically lesbian perspective, Schulman resuscitates a different "American" tradition, the pragmatic semiotic entwined with lesbian subjects since the late nineteenth century.

Lila "tell[s] it like it is from [her] perspective"—which is, as the friendly drug dealer Ray recognizes, "the only way that you can tell it" (25)—but she relies on others' viewpoints to fill in the blind spots and keep things interesting. (Even Muriel's: "Dance wasn't Lila's way of seeing, but it was a way, and she was glad to know it was there" [46].) Hence, although Lila is in ways encumbered by her connection to Emily, she is also freed: "Lila perceived and felt daily occurrences with an insight beyond her own capability. When she was confronted by a more complex place of understanding, she knew it was not her interpretation alone but that of she and Emily together" (153–54). Lila's worldview is not a "gap" or "fissure" in "the sense-making process"; it *is* a sense-making process—a pragmatic semiotic organized around her own lesbian perspective. Summing up Peirce's position on the inevitability of interpretive mediation, Sandra Rosenthal concludes that "worldly truth is thus perspectival, and other perspectives are always possible. Truth involves convergence, but convergence within a common world that we have partially made and continue to remake."[49] The institutions, rituals, and relationships that Lila and her friends daily reconstruct function as linchpins of a self-sustaining reality, keeping everything "vaguely together" (59) in its service. Reminiscing about gay days past, Lila finds herself "thinking about all these crazy images and how they came together into one thing that actually made sense, which was their community, and realize[s] the nuances [are] only identifiable from the inside out" (109). By making Lila's "inside" her book's narrative center, Schulman makes visible nuances conventionally obscured. But because this inside is more than simply the dominant culture's abjected outside, *Girls, Visions and Everything* effects something more than a simple reversal of terms.

Like Diana Fuss, Schulman seems to recognize that "the figure inside/outside" offers insight into an aspect of semiosis without telling the whole story; like Judith Butler, she apparently understands that "story" may be the operative term, that discourse must somehow incorporate temporality.

But of course structuralist abstractions like "inside/out" can't *incorporate* anything. More clearly than either theorist, Schulman documents the semiosic relations by which abstractions are predicated on material contexts made sensible by abstract frames of reference (themselves drawn from specific material circumstances, and so on, *"ad infinitum"*). *Bodies That Matter* offers the very pragmatic observation that "to take up the political signifier . . . is to be taken into a chain of prior usages, to be installed in the midst of significations that cannot be situated in terms of clear origins or ultimate goals"[50]; for all practical purposes, we can only "begin" *in medias res*. Important as this is, it perhaps underemphasizes the pragmatic implications of Maxine Wolfe's observation that "people can only be where they are at"[51]—that the *links* in this chain are inescapably *material* indices. Butler's efforts to think the temporality of discourse are impeded by her inattention to its implication within actual, as opposed to figurative, space. As Sally Munt observes, "abstraction has its costs."[52] In overlooking the ubiquity of indexicality, Butler ignores the most obvious and democratic example of linguistic contingency and historicity—the dimension of semiosis that situates epistemological observations within the lived experience of material limits and contested meanings. This is the experience that Sarah Schulman calls up in her realistic portrayals of average lesbians and the little things they know and care about.[53] Schulman's fiction anticipates Butler's interest in "the reworking of abjection into political agency," while recognizing the necessity of locating that effort within the material interactions of everyday life.

Peirce tells us that "a *Sign* is a First which stands in such a genuine triadic relation to a Second, called its *Object*, as to be capable of determining a Third, called its *Interpretant*, to assume the same triadic relation to its Object in which it stands itself to the same Object."[54] But like Butler, Peirce provides for the possibility that "the same object" is not in fact self-identical over time. Because it incorporates relationality, the object is always already imbued by the social, by the practice of signification:

> The triadic relation is *genuine*, that is its three members are bound together by it in a way that does not consist in any complexus of dyadic relations. That is the reason the Interpretant, or Third, cannot stand in mere dyadic relation to the object, but must stand in such a relation to it as the Representamen itself does. Nor can the triadic relation in which the Third stands be merely similar to that in which the first stands, for this would make the relation of the

> Third to the First a degenerate Secondness merely. The Third must indeed stand in such a relation, and thus must be capable of determining a Third of its own; *but besides that, it must have a second triadic relation in which the Representamen, or rather the relation thereof to its Object, shall be its own (the Third's) Object, and must be capable of determining a Third to this relation. All this must equally be true of the Third's Third and so on endlessly. . . .*[55]

I propose that this passage is important because it suggests another way of thinking about the concept of "rigid designation" that Butler derides.[56] Mapping out the actual mechanisms of performativity over time and in space, Peirce provides for the incessant interpenetration of representation, interpretation, and objective reality.

In Schulman's novel, these relations are grounded in the unexceptional occurrences of everyday lesbian life.

> Lila cruised First Avenue between Seventh Street and Tenth Street quite often in the course of her daily life and every time she ran into three men: Ray, Tony, and Solomon. Each one had their own personal story but they were also part of the same old story of men hanging out, just hanging out. (23)

Like Peirce's objects, these men are both generic and specific; they serve as points of reference within Lila's reality, but each has his own reality, his own perspective, as well.[57] *What do you do once you get to know them?* As we might expect, Lila does stick around long enough to find out, and what she works out is a democratic logic not unlike that which Butler purports to seek.

Arriving at a protest against U.S. involvement in Central America, for example, Lila is "faced with the usual dilemma of having to decide which contingent to march with."

> In other words, which part of her complex identity would be the base from which to express her opposition to the latest outrage? Ideally, she would have loved to find a sign proclaiming "Girls Against War." However, the only banner relating in any way to anyone female came from a small left party that always had signs proclaiming "Women for Somebody Else." There was also a "Lesbians and Gays for Jesse Jackson" placard, but that seemed a little too specific, although she would definitely have carried one saying "Jesse Jackson for Lesbians and Gays." She tried the New Jewish Agenda Brooklyn Chapter, but after half a block decided,

> in all good conscience, she couldn't march with a group from Brooklyn. As always, she finally ended up with an ad-hoc collection of vaguely associated dykes, all without places to march. (81–82)

The passage literalizes Butler's question about "the possibilities of politicizing *dis*identification, this experience of *misrecognition*, this uneasy sense of standing under a sign to which one does not [fully] belong," setting the theoretical query in motion within specific, realistic circumstances. So maybe "Women For Somebody Else" isn't the kind of sign Butler is talking about, but Lila's solution seems not terribly far removed from Butler's conclusion that "it may be that affirmation of that slippage, that failure of identification is itself the point of departure for a more democratizing affirmation of internal difference."[58]

Lila also has some experience with *misrecognition*. The first time she's mistaken for a prostitute, Lila decides it's "an honest mistake." ("Why else would a woman be walking down the street wearing a shoulder bag?") Then it happens again. Then she gets mistaken for a racist. "People don't look closely enough," Lila concludes. "They see tits and assume they're for sale. They see white skin and assume they're among friends." Then she is mistaken for straight: "The bar sitter flapped his wrists expecting, of course, that swish-baiting was just fine with everyone" (141–2). These examples are outrageous, but in parodying such "slippage" they suggest not only its inevitably, but also the promise of pragmatic efforts to effect "a more democratizing affirmation of internal difference." Tony, Solomon, and Ray can't finally be contained by any one understanding of "men hanging out," although each one's personal story is imbued by that generic convention. Lila can't find a sign that fully expresses her complex identity, but she goes to the march anyway. In her eyes, the impossibility of achieving ideal representation is fully compatible with the idea of participatory democracy, an idea she takes very seriously despite her observation that "in the U.S. people are allowed to be political as long as they don't actually have an effect on anything" (81).

The group of otherwise unaffiliated lesbians that Lila winds up walking with offers a fair approximation of pragmatic community—ad hoc, vague, shifting—a microcosm perhaps of the "new type of neighborhood" that Abu-Lughod and her colleagues observe in the Lower East Side.[59] Unlike traditional "urban villages" characterized by homogeneity and "bound together by preexistent 'primordial' ties," the "social space of the East Village is fragmented, subgroup by subgroup, differentiated by age, ethnicity, income, values, and lifestyle."[60] According to Abu-Lughod, "conventional sociological categories cannot capture the true level of diversity in the neighborhood," nor explain why these circumstances do not "yield a classic case of the anomie and social disorganization that standard urban sociological theories predict."[61] She suggests that "mutual tolerance and careful attention to social, physical, and temporal boundaries" may have something to do with the relative harmony, and notes that "what unanimity and organization are achieved must be hammered out in a complex process of conflict and negotiation."[62] Because the continued functioning of such community depends on recognition of the inevitable slippage between the generic and the specific, the expected and the actual, it requires participants to pay the kind of close attention that Lila does to nuances perceptible only from the inside out. Only a sensibility accepting of fallibility and cognizant of the inevitability of "blind spots"—i.e., a pragmatic sensibility—can even come close to supporting James Hoopes' vision of "a discourse in which all could participate with the possibility of genuine communication."[63] At the beginning of this chapter, I asked the question, "What is it that constrains representation if not a non-negotiable outside?" Pragmatism answers, "a negotiated one." And *Girls, Visions and Everything* suggests that democracy is about redefining the circumstances of those negotiations.

To that end, Schulman effects a specificity that is not atomistic. Like Lila, she is an advocate of "looking closely," of "paying attention." "I like it when you watch me eating you out," Emily tells Lila. "I know it sounds strange, but I like that you're absolutely sure of who is making you feel that way" (122). Lila looks at a travel display in a store window and muses "that since the time of maps, people have been able to look at other countries as empty pink and green shapes." This is an apt metaphor for the sort of atomistic essentialism advanced by *Rubyfruit Jungle*'s Molly Bolt; racial difference remains a compelling analogy for her own expression of sexual difference because even once she supposedly "gets to know" Calvin and Holly, she can't imagine that their identities have any "actual" or "dynamic" relation to her own. "We're different people and it has nothing to do with . . . color or any of that shit," she says. "That's that."[64] Lila, on the other hand, observes that "each country's maps projected different interpretations of size, boundary and centrality," and that maps in general seem to presume that "the most important division in life [is] geographical" (38). Whereas Molly is adept at seeing others as "empty . . . shapes" unriven by internal complexities, Lila, because she values different ways of seeing and respects the different histories that inform these perspectives, is unable to ignore this diversity, unable to dismiss conflicts as fundamental, inexplicable, and non-negotiable.

In Munt's reading of *Girls, Visions and Everything*, "the final chapter sees Lila torn between the 'masculine' trajectory of *On the Road* individualism, the expression of the urban street-poem, and the 'feminine' stability of emotion and relationship commitment, which is depicted as static."[65] But I would argue that these are not the only options. Just as dyke culture has developed alternatives to conventionally binary gender, the tradition of lesbian pragmatism provides Schulman with a semiotic alternative to the essentialist /(post)structuralist stalemate. I think Lila cries at the end because that all-too-American dream of unfettered freedom is finally lost to her forever, replaced by a much more complicated vision of political responsibility. Pure creativity, pure self-expression is no longer a tenable goal, as abstractions (even philosophical ones) are shattered by particularity, as much as by personal connection. (*What* do *you do once you get to know them?)* What holds, for the time being, is commitment, community, diversity, fallibility—the *importance of paying attention* to the histories and perspectives of those diverse others who constitute the ad hoc collection of participants in a democratic, pragmatic community. In this view, the documentary specificity with which Lila's world is rendered is not incidental to Schulman's achievement, but an integral aspect of the pragmatic sensibility that permeates her project and informs her lesbian perspective. And it stands in stark relief to the ahistoricized abstractions associated with academic queer theory conceived "in the shadow of Saussure's tree."[66]

Butler insists that "it would be a mistake . . . to claim that all conceptual language or philosophical language is 'presentist,' a claim which would be tantamount to prescribing that all philosophy become history." But from a lesbian pragmatist's perspective, historicizing philosophy seems not such a bad idea. This is, after all, the sense in which Cornel West's characterization of pragmatism as an "evasion of philosophy" seems most salient: pragmatism is "anti-philosophical" in its embrace of historical specificity.[67] By insisting on the indexical dimension of signification, pragmatism situates the *relation* between object and sign inexorably *in history*; indexicality is characterized by actual, material connection—and materiality is inextricable from space and time. Rosenthal tells us that "for Peirce, the epistemic import of such a logic of language lies in the fact that it incorporates the dynamics of lived experience at the most rudimentary level, a dynamics that in turn reflects a semiotic structure operative at its most fundamental level."[68] Contrary to any essentialist understanding, then, pragmatism's "most rudimentary" and "most fundamental" categories are always already contingent. But as Rosenthal points out, "this is not a vicious circle but an exemplification of the cumulative process involved in the pragmatic, experimental interplay between meanings and experience."[69] Peirce, like Lila, "understood the phenomenon of process" (3).

To the degree that philosophical language represents an effort to come to terms with "rudimentary" or "fundamental" logic, I suggest, it must become historical. And part of becoming historical is taking into account "the dynamics of lived experience"; in *Girls, Visions and Everything*, Schulman reminds us that this requires *paying attention* "to how real inequality in the economic and social sphere complicates and compromises" the promise of pluralism.[70]

Afterword

How is it that identities take hold? How can subversively variant representations get traction in the actual world of physical things and material relations? Judith Roof must be right that the psychic leap of identification is one way in which this happens, but this seems at best a partial explanation for the real changes in human possibility observable over time.[1] And as Judith Butler's detractors have argued, it is not at all clear that "repetition with a difference" can exert sufficient conceptual force to actually transform relations of power and politics.[2] The survey of influential fictions assembled here, however, suggests that, as suspected, representations are not irrelevant, that they have over the course of the past century occasionally found purchase beyond their own pages and beyond the individual psyches of susceptible readers; in fact, they have sometimes engaged the spirit of their age to transform the very conditions of possibility in which we live. On other occasions, of course, they have not. How can we begin to explain the relative efficacy of certain "repetitions" in comparison to the apparent irrelevance of others? The question is important in that it may offer insight useful in formulating more productive strategies of engagement for political projects aimed at effecting socio-cultural transformation.

One thing that the examples assembled here indicate, I think, is that the "radical and irreducible incoherence"[3] between minoritizing and universalizing accounts, between synchronic structuralism and narrative theory, between materialism and poststructuralism, essentialism and constructivism, "history" and "theory" may be semiosically productive precisely because it does not directly engage and cannot finally comprehend the everyday evidence of spatialization and temporality unproblematically united in physical bodies: people and things. But when those material elements are taken up indexically in the performative aspect of signification, they become part of the nexus of meaning that will inform future understandings as well as future acts of representation; they become part of history, but also of the present and of future possibilities. *Which* material elements are taken up, and *how*, can be influenced but not fully guaranteed in context of the always ongoing process of semiosis.

A provocative pairing of essays in the Winter 2000 issue of *Hypatia* seems to me suggestive in this regard. The first, by Fiona Webster, revisits the *Feminist Contentions* debate between Judith Butler and Seyla Benhabib to frame the "trouble" that poststructuralist theorizing has presumably brought to political projects such as feminism.[4] The second, by Shannon Sullivan, revisits John Dewey's pragmatic conception of "habit" in connection with Butler's *Gender Trouble* in the interest of mutual illumination.[5] Briefly, Webster contends that Benhabib's fears of "debilitating consequences" engendered by Butler's theory are exaggerated, but remains finally unsatisfied by Butler's account of agency, as well. Webster allows that "Butler cannot be accused of *disallowing* agency," but concludes that her theory of performativity is "*inadequate* to explain or to provide an account of the actual practice of freedom by subjects or groups of subjects in the political arena."[6]

Sullivan, however, begins to bridge this gap between theory and practice by pointing out the consonance of Dewey's conception of "habit"—as "the effect of sedimentation in our lives[,] grooves that are part of ourselves and can run very deep"—with Butler's theory of performativity.[7] The notion of "habit" at issue in Sullivan's essay is not as finely tuned nor so fully elaborated as the account that Teresa de Lauretis provides[8]—presumably at least in part because de Lauretis' understanding is derived from Peirce, while Sullivan adopts Dewey's more imagistic and less nuanced description. What Dewey offers that Peirce does not, however—besides more felicitous prose—is a clear programmatic vision for cultural and political change. On the understanding that habits are "structures of stability and identity," but also dynamic, capable of growth and change, rather than fixed," Sullivan follows Dewey in advocating the development of educational institutions that would work "to enable people to develop firm habits that support flexible, fluid modes of being."[9] Curiously, however, this essay locates the capacity for change (in individuals or institutions) in the "conflict," "friction," and "complexity" configured in the intersections among habits.[10] Indeed, it recalls Butler's proposal that the contradictory discourses comprising the conditions of performativity portend the production of "gaps," "fissures," and "inconsistencies" conducive to subversion, resistance, or "repetition with a difference." Thus, although Sullivan's emphasis on collective efforts and institution-building seems promising, Webster's desire "for a stronger account of agency" is understandable.[11] The implication that change—individual or institutional—comes (only) from "complexity," contradiction, or dissonance seems both descriptively inaccurate and theoretically problematic. On the one hand, this formulation ignores the direct *dependence* of the status quo on specific instances of "radical incoherence."[12] And on the other, although it's certainly true that this is one way to leverage political/institutional change, the theoretical implications of this model, taken in isolation, appear ultimately counter-democratic. If change is motivated by a drive *toward* consistency and homogeneity, in other words, what happens when we get there? How is this grounding complexity guaranteed against a dynamic apparently devoted to its eventual obsolescence?

In this context, I find it suggestive that whereas Webster discounts the fear that "Butler's theory goes *too far* in its explanation of subject constitution, insofar as it tends toward attributing too much power to culture (/society/discourse) as a constitutive force," she herself is concerned that "*too little* attention is paid by theorists such as Butler to two issues: first to identifying the relation between the individual and the processes through which they are constructed; and, second, to locating points of intervention in those processes."[13] Indeed, we might consider that Butler's theory appears politically "inadequate" precisely to the extent that *it does not go far enough* in elaborating performativity's inevitable material implications and engagements. By enriching Butler's description of "the relation between the individual and the processes through which they are constructed," I contend, a pragmatic account of indexicality also aids in specifying possible points—and means—of intervention.

There's no advantage in rehashing the theoretical overview of this idea advanced in Chapter 6, so I will instead conclude by offering a very modest example of the kind of insight that I think a perspective informed by lesbian pragmatism might provide. Let me start by juxtaposing a couple of contemporary phenomena. One is the by-now-familiar but still underattended-to difficulty that lesbian and queer theories have had in articulating an adequate or even useful "conception of racialized sexualities."[14] The other is the bizarre propensity of novels about white lesbians to metaphorically associate their protagonists' sexual difference with projections of racial "otherness," figured most typically in evocations of African American or American Indian identity. As described at length in Chapter 5, Rita Mae Brown's *Rubyfruit Jungle* offers an especially salient and familiar example, but it is not at all atypical. Mary McCarthy's Elinor Eastlake, discussed in Chapter 4, is set apart by her "Indian blood" and the "queer dark-blue rim around the iris of her green eyes." More recently, Dorothy Allison's brilliant National Book Award nominee *Bastard out of Carolina* makes repeated reference to its heroine's "Cherokee eyes"; when the heroine's cousin calls her "all black-headed and strange," he associates it with what he calls the "man-type part" of her. And in *Stone Butch Blues*, Leslie Feinberg's protagonist experiences an almost mystical identification with the Native American women who care for her in her infancy, and an ongoing fascination with Native American traditions and myths—including cultural traditions that transcend gender binaries. Nor does recourse to such associations appear restricted entirely to depictions of Anglo-American protagonists; Arden Benbow, in Sheila Ortiz Taylor's *Faultline* and *Southbound*, for example, regularly associates the lesbian in her with her "Indian self."[15] Gloria Anzaldúa's explorations of lesbian identity in the context of "mestiza consciousness"—sometimes carefully historicized and physically situated, sometimes more metaphorical—may be seen as an ambivalent engagement with this tradition.[16]

In any case, contemporary manifestations of this phenomenon confront Evelynn Hammonds' contention that "white feminists must refigure (white) female sexualities so that they are not theoretically dependent upon an absent yet-ever-present pathologized black female sexuality."[17] While I would want to extend the injunction to include pathologized images of American Indians and other nondominant groups, I recognize that Hammonds' intervention is both crucial and overdue. But I would suggest that the dynamic she identifies is not simply a theoretical problem (whatever that means) but an historical one: coming to terms with these images and exclusions requires a turn to historical analysis, and refiguring these sexualities will require more than a theoretical solution.

It seems to me that if the intersection of European sexology with the particular evolutionisms popular in the United States at the turn of the last century produced a lesbian subjectivity strongly imbued with assumptions about race, representation, and progress that continue to inform popular conceptions and possibly self-understandings today, then theorizing the relays by which this implantation occurred and continues to be affirmed requires a self-conscious turn towards history—not simply the history of those images and their evolution, but the history of semiosis itself, or, if it's the best we can do for the moment, of semiotic theory.

To take up Hammonds' challenge, in other words, requires taking seriously Butler's injunction to "think the symbolic as the temporalized regulation of signification." As I argued in Chapter 6, however, queer theory—including in particular Butler's theory of performativity—still struggles at times to escape the presentism implicit in the structuralist tradition, as well as the universalisms and individuation to which psychoanalysis is prone. But I think that Butler's turn to speech act theory also portends—without explicitly elaborating—attention to the materiality of speech and the indexicality through which it acts. It is precisely this need for pragmatic attention to location, relation, and historicity that motivates Teresa de Lauretis' turn to the semiotic theories of C.S. Peirce. In "The Technology of Gender," de Lauretis argues that subjectivity is produced "in the process of assuming, taking on, identifying with the *positionalities* and *meaning effects* specified by a particular society's gender system."[18] Significantly, those positionalities and meaning effects are not always and only discursive abstractions; to the contrary, they crucially engage and accrue in actual material relations and bodies. In somewhat different ways, then, both de Lauretis and Butler suggest a turn towards history, towards situating "discourses" within specific material and temporal contexts—despite the tendency of much of their work (Butler's on discursive systems abstracted from actual fact and de Lauretis' on "intrapsychic" as opposed to "institutional mechanisms") to direct attention away from the historical specificity that they advocate.

In this context, Hammonds' contention that "public discourse on the sexuality of particular racial and ethnic groups is shaped by processes that pathologize those groups" seems self-evident. But the persistent implication of racist evolutionary theories implicit and explicit in the conception of lesbian subjectivity that developed over the course of the twentieth century in the United States also offers convincing support for her claim that "lesbian and gay theory [too often] fails to acknowledge that these very processes are connected to the construction of the sexualities of whites, historically and contemporaneously."[19] I have argued that this failure is itself implicit in a more general difficulty in coming to terms with historical process. But just as "[Judith] Butler cannot be accused," as Webster so graciously acknowledges, "of wholly undermining the basis for feminist political action," a better *theory* cannot, of itself, solve the problem at the heart of Hammonds' critique.[20] The rough genealogy of the lesbian index sketched in this volume suggests that a disturbingly *actual* dependence upon "absent yet-ever-present pathologized" images of black and American Indian subjectivities has *in fact* become an integral part of certain lesbian subjectivities in the United States at least over the course of the twentieth century—a "habit" of being, as Sullivan (and presumably Peirce, Dewey, and de Lauretis) would have it, that threatens to persist well into the twenty-first century as well, if the popular texts mentioned above are any indication.

Any useful response will necessarily involve a conscious effort to avoid engaging these discourses in lesbian (self)representations—but of course habit cannot be divested so easily and is not simply a matter of individual choice or control. The capacity of "discourse" and "culture" to reappropriate or recuperate determinedly subversive variations has been convincingly established both theoretically and empirically. And identification appears too weak a mechanism of joinder to effectively lever the individual against the social; this is because the problematic racializations upon which certain enactments of implicitly white lesbian subjectivity have come to rely are themselves predicated on relations both discursive *and material*. Notably, these modes of relation are conjoined in part precisely through their indexical invocation in the ongoing sedimentation of contemporary lesbian subjectivities. If lesbians cannot—simply, willfully—separate our selves from this, we can however work to change the *this* on which the problematic aspects of those selves depend.

Let me give an example from close to home. Certainly, it is incumbent upon queer theory at least to attend to its own contexts of production within increasingly corporatized colleges and universities. The most egregious recent reminder of this process at the institution where I work has been the reassignment of many custodial workers from an early morning to graveyard shift. The administration's motivating objective is presumably efficiency; their strategy, apparently, is to inconvenience some of the worst-paid and supposedly most expendable workers in order to keep them out of the way of consumers (students) and management during the hours when the campus is most heavily in use. For the affected workers, the majority of whom are African American women, the effects are specific, immediate, and mostly injurious—sleep deprivation, transportation difficulties, disrupted relations, conflicting second jobs, compromised personal safety (both on the job, as the risk of accident increases, and in traveling to and from work at unsafe hours), child care crises. For the faculty and administrators (the majority of whom are white men) and for the students (overwhelmingly white, although a slight majority are women), the putative benefits of such a move are not clear (and have, to the credit of these groups, been much contested). One other effect of the proposed change, however, seems both obvious and inevitable: the shift would make this necessary labor invisible to the vast majority of those who directly benefit from it. To ignore this fact is to risk giving rise to the self-congratulatory illusion that scholarship "suddenly appears from some protean slime" instead of slowly emerging from contexts conditioned by the generally unacknowledged labor of many, many people. In this sense, the strategy brings to mind those foundationalist theories that refuse to historicize their own premises; it works to reify the divide between meaning and materiality that impedes our ability to engage proactively with each other and the world.

In the context of such circumstances, in the context of its history and current configurations, lesbian scholarship must actively resist association with racist conceptualizations *and lesbian scholars must also work to change the material conditions on which those concepts depend.* Until and unless the contexts of our performative engagements can be made to accommodate the more democratic arrangements necessary to sustain substantially subversive variation, "repetition with a difference" won't make much difference at all.

Notes

Introduction

1. Joan W. Scott, "The Evidence of Experience," *Critical Inquiry* 17 (summer 1991): 773–797; reprinted in Henry Abelove, Michèle Aina Barale, and David M. Halperin, eds., *The Lesbian and Gay Studies Reader* (New York: Routledge, 1993), 397–414, to which subsequent citations refer. (An abbreviated version appeared under the title "Experience" in Judith Butler and Joan W. Scott, eds., *Feminists Theorize the Political* [New York: Routledge, 1992], 22–40.)

2. Scott, 399.

3. Sue-Ellen Case, "Making Butch: An Historical Memoir of the 1970s," in *butch/femme: Inside Lesbian Gender,* Sally R. Munt, ed., (London: Cassell, 1998), 37–45; 40.

4. Butler and Scott, eds., *Feminists Theorize the Political*, xiv.

5. Scott, 402–403.

6. Teresa de Lauretis, "Habit Changes," *differences* 6, no. 2–3 (summer-fall 1994): 296–313; 301.

7. Scott, 402. Teresa de Lauretis, *Alice Doesn't: Feminism, Semiotics, Cinema* (Bloomington: Indiana University Press, 1984), 19.

8. Scott, 412.

9. Who writes, "Experience is that determination of belief and cognition generally which the course of life has forced upon a man" within the general context of perception conditioned by signs (C. S. Peirce, *Collected Papers of Charles Sanders Peirce*, ed. Charles Hartshorne and Paul Weiss [vols. 1–6] and Arthur Burks [vols. 7–8], [Cambridge, MA: Harvard University Press, 1931–58], 2.138).

10. James Hoopes, introduction to *Peirce on Signs,* James Hoopes, ed., (Chapel Hill: University of North Carolina Press, 1991), 1–13; 11.

11. I borrow the phrase from de Lauretis, who points out that Saussurean structuralism posits "an essential discontinuity between the orders of the symbolic and the real" (Teresa de Lauretis, *Technologies of Gender* [Bloomington: Indiana University Press, 1987], 39).

12. David M. Halperin, "Is There a History of Sexuality?" *History and Theory* 28 (1989): 257–274; reprinted in Abelove, et al, eds., 416–431. David M. Halperin, "How to Do the History of Male Homosexuality," *GLQ* 6, no. 1 (2000): 87–124; 87.

13. i.e., an understanding of "sexuality itself as a semiosic process in which the contingencies of both a personal and a social history produce the subject as their shifting point of intersection" (de Lauretis, *The Practice of Love: Lesbian Sexuality and Perverse Desire* [Bloomington: Indiana University Press, 1994], 303); or, as she would later clarify, "by *sexual structuring* I want to designate the constructedness of sex, as well as of the sexual subject, its being a process, an accumulation of effects that do not rest on an originary materiality of the body, that do not modify or attach to an essence, matter or form—whether corporeal or existential—prior to the process itself" ("Habit Changes," 301).

14. Peirce, *Collected Papers*, 2.283; 2.305; 2.287; 2.298.

15. As Peirce explains, "the action of indices depends on association by contiguity, and not upon association by resemblance or upon intellectual operations" (2.306).

16. Scott, 412.

17. Although pragmatism is of course accepted as a fitting subject for historical accounts of the sort that Scott decries, its relevance to historical methodology has been underappreciated; James Livingston's *Pragmatism and the Political Economy of Cultural Revolution, 1850–1940* (Chapel Hill: University of North Carolina Press, 1994) is an ambitious exception.

18. Including by Scott herself; see Lisa Duggan, "The Discipline Problem: Queer Theory Meets Lesbian and Gay History," *GLQ* 2 (1994); reprinted in *Sex Wars: Sexual Dissent and Political Culture,* Lisa Duggan and Nan D. Hunter, eds., (New York: Routledge, 1995), 194–206 (see especially 202).

19. Marilyn Frye, "To Be and Be Seen: The Politics of Reality," in *The Politics of Reality: Essays in Feminist Theory* (Trumansburg, NY: The Crossing Press, 1983), 152–174. For a welcome exception, see Wendy Lee-Lampshire, "Spilling All Over the 'Wide Fields of Our Passions': Frye, Butler, Wittgenstein and the Context(s) of Attention, Intention and Identity (Or: From Arm Wrestling Duck to Abject Being to Lesbian Feminist)," *Hypatia* 14, no.3 (summer 1999): 1–16.

20. Frye, 170.

21. Duggan, 203; from Scott, 400. (Duggan's italics.)

22. Duggan 203, Duggan's italics.

23. Frye, 171. Indeed, this exclusion could be interpreted as additional evidence for Frye's position that culturally dominant conceptual schemes cannot countenance lesbian subjectivity.

24. Peirce proposes to define "habit" as "some general principle working in a man's nature to determine how he will act" (2.170); Teresa de Lauretis clarifies that it denotes "a somatic disposition at once abstract and concrete, the crystallized form of past muscular/mental effort"—and hence "is powerfully suggestive of a subject touched by the practice of signs, a subject physically implicated or bodily engaged in the production of meaning, representation, and self-representation" (*Alice Doesn't*, 183).

25. Judith Halberstam, *Female Masculinity* (Durham: Duke University Press, 1998), 51.

26. De Lauretis describes her interest in Peirce as motivated by a desire "to find a linkage between Freud's privatized view of the sexual subject and Foucault's eminently social view of sexuality"—this in a work "more concerned," as she clearly states, "with intrapsychic than with institutional mechanisms" ("Habit Changes," 307, 303). The project I pursue here is deeply indebted to de Lauretis' insights, and I hope that this study, with its more explicitly historical concerns, may be seen to complement her groundbreaking theoretical work.

27. Eve Kosofsky Sedgwick, *Epistemology of the Closet* (Berkeley: University of California Press, 1990), 85.

28. Biddy Martin, "Sexualities without Genders and Other Queer Utopias," *Diacritics*, 1994; reprinted in *Femininity Played Straight: The Significance of Being Lesbian* by Biddy Martin, (New York: Routledge, 1996), 71–94; 92.

29. Perhaps too obvious—as Lisa Duggan warns, "The emphasis in much academically privileged work on the analysis of canonized literary and artistic texts or widely circulated pop culture texts implicitly aligns the critic with privilege or popularity," while "the relative neglect of studies of ghettoized or stigmatized populations and texts keeps the associated denigration and humiliation at a distance" and "the hierarchy which has endowed the academic author with greater institutional resources and cultural privilege is reinforced" (197). Although my turn to Schulman in Chapter 6 might be seen to mitigate this tendency in *The Lesbian Index*, it is arguably an inadequate response to the dynamic that Duggan describes.

30. Laura Doan, ed., *The Lesbian Postmodern* (New York: Columbia University Press, 1994), xi.

31. Judith Butler, *Bodies That Matter: On the Discursive Limits of "Sex"* (New York: Routledge, 1993).

32. Scott, 411.

33. Sarah Schulman, *Shimmer* (New York: Avon Books, 1998), 146.

Chapter 1

1. *Collected Papers of Charles Sanders Peirce*, ed. Charles Hartshorne and Paul Weiss (vols. 1–6) and Arthur Burks (vols. 7–8), (Cambridge, MA: Harvard

University Press, 1931–58), 5.416.

2. "Within this schema, the butch–femme couple inhabit the subject position together. . . . These are not split subjects, suffering the torments of dominant ideology. They are coupled ones that do not impale themselves on the poles of sexual difference or metaphysical values, but constantly seduce the sign system, through flirtation and inconstancy into the light fondle of artifice, replacing the Lacanian slash with a lesbian bar." (Sue-Ellen Case, "Toward a Butch–Femme Aesthetic," *Discourse* 2, no. 1 (1988–89): 55-73; reprinted in *Making a Spectacle*, ed. Lynda Hart [Ann Arbor: University of Michigan Press, 1989], 283.)

Case's bar was the celebrated Maud's, on Cole Street in San Francisco; mine was a place called Bullwinkle's, located in the basement of a former Moose Lodge, kitty–corner from the Monroe County Jail in downtown Bloomington, Indiana.

3. "Even after constructionists claim to have won the debate, and essentialists claim to have exposed the bad scholarship produced by it, and everyone else claimed to be sick and tired of it, the basic question about the historicity of sexuality remained" (David Halperin, "How to Do the History of Male Homosexuality," *GLQ* 6, no. 1 [2000]: 87–124).

4. Case, "The Apparitional Community," *American Quarterly* 48, no. 1 (March 1996): 164.

5. Laura Doan, ed., *The Lesbian Postmodern* (New York: Columbia University Press, 1994), ix.

6. Lisa Duggan and Nan D. Hunter, *Sex Wars: Sexual Dissent and Political Culture* (New York: Routledge, 1995), 196.

7. Marilyn Farwell, *Heterosexual Plots and Lesbian Narratives* (New York: New York University Press, 1996), 4; quoting Bonnie Zimmerman, "What Has Never Been: An Overview of Lesbian Feminist Criticism," *Feminist Studies* 7, no. 3 (1981): 456, and Paulina Palmer, "Contemporary Lesbian Feminist Fiction: Texts for Everywoman" in *Plotting Change: Contemporary Women's Fiction*, ed. Linda Anderson (London: Edward Arnold, 1990), 60.

8. Suzanna Danuta Walters, "From Here to Queer: Radical Feminism, Postmodernism, and the Lesbian Menace (Or, Why Can't a Woman Be More Like a Fag?)," *SIGNS* 21, no. 4 (Summer 1996): 830–869; 841–842 (emphasis added).

9. In *Female Masculinity*, for example, Judith Halberstam defines her "queer methodology" against "those presentist models espoused by critics, such as Castle, who actually seek to find only what they think they already know." ("It is my contention," she explains, "that many contemporary lesbian historians cannot extricate themselves from contemporary understandings of lesbian identities long enough to interpret the vagaries of early same–sex desire. Accordingly, we have any number of analyses claiming to find lesbians or protolesbians in any number of different historical periods without proper consideration of the sexual and gender forms in question.") Halberstam, *Female*

Masculinity (Durham: Duke University Press, 1998), 10, 54, 50.

10. Walters, 836, 855.

11. Duggan and Hunter, 197.

12. Case, 164.

13. Halperin's observation that "current work in the history of sexuality still appears to be poised in its emphasis between the two poles of identity ["the aspects of sexual life that seem to persist through time"] and difference [i.e., "the dramatic differences between historically documented forms of sexual experience"]"—which he contends "represent merely reformulated versions of the old essentialist and constructivist positions"—indicates that this is not an issue specific to lesbian studies. The particular intervention that I pursue in these pages, however, is. (David Halperin, "How to Do the History of Male Homosexuality," *GLQ* 6, no. 4 [2000]: 87–123; 88).

14. Judith Butler, "Imitation and Gender Insubordination" in *Inside/Out: Lesbian Theories/Gay Theories*, ed. Diana Fuss (New York: Routledge, 1991), 15.

15. Terry Castle, *The Apparitional Lesbian: Female Homosexuality and Modern Culture* (New York: Columbia University Press, 1993), 13–14.

16. Castle, 14.

17. Judith Roof, *A Lure of Knowledge: Lesbian Sexuality and Theory* (New York: Columbia University Press, 1991), 5.

18. Castle, 5.

19. Castle, 4.

20. Castle, 7–8.

21. Judith Butler, *Bodies That Matter: On the Discursive Limits of "Sex"* (New York: Routledge, 1993), 3.

22. Eve Kosofsky Sedgwick, "Queer Performativity: Henry James's *The Art of the Novel*," *GLQ* 1, no. 1 (1993): 1-16.

23. Quoted in Teresa de Lauretis, *The Practice of Love: Lesbian Sexuality and Perverse Desire* (Bloomington: Indiana University Press, 1994), 83; Jean Laplanche and Jean–Bertrand Pontalis, "Fantasy and the Origins of Sexuality" in *Formations of Fantasy*, ed. Victor Burgin, James Donald, and Cora Kaplan (London: Methuen, 1986), 18.

24. Walters, 851.

25. John J. Stuhr, *Genealogical Pragmatism* (Albany: State University of New York Press, 1997), 92.

26. Butler, 15.

27. Saskia E. Wieringa and Evelyn Blackwood, eds., *Female Desires: Same-Sex Relations and Transgender Practices across Cultures* (New York: Columbia, 1999), 14.

28. As, of course, does Butler; see especially her chapter entitled "Arguing with the Real" (*Bodies That Matter* 187–222), in which she explains "that there is an 'outside' to the socially intelligible, and that this 'outside' will always be that which negatively defines the social," but also emphasizes that "to delimit

that outside through the invocation of a preideological 'law,' a prediscursive 'law' that works invariably throughout all history, and further, to make that law function to secure a sexual differential that ontologizes subordination, is an 'ideological' move in a more ancient sense" (206). The assertion of historicity, however, is not the point of the distinction I hope to draw here.

29. de Lauretis, 308 (emphasis added).

30. de Lauretis, 82–83.

31. de Lauretis, 309, 303.

32. Stuhr, 92. As Walters complains of Butler's work, "provisos (as in 'performance is never simply voluntaristic action') do little when the performances remain removed from a social and cultural context that either enables or disenables their radical enactment" (855).

33. Case, "Toward a Butch–Feminist Retro Future," in Heller, *Cross–Purposes*, 210.

34. Cary Wolfe, *Critical Environments: Postmodern Theory and the Pragmatics of the "Outside"* (Minneapolis: University of Minnesota Press, 1998), 1.

35. Stuhr, 110.

36. Wolfe, 18, 1, 22 (Wolfe's italics).

37. Butler, *Bodies That Matter*, 30.

38. James Hoopes, *Community Denied: The Wrong Turn of Pragmatic Liberalism* (Ithaca: Cornell University Press, 1998), 2, 17–18.

39. H.O. Mounce, *The Two Pragmatisms: From Peirce to Rorty* (London: Routledge, 1997).

40. Peirce, *Collected Papers*, iii.

41. Peirce, *Collected Papers*, 5.253; Hoopes, 184.

42. Peirce settled on the name, he explains, because "the most striking feature of the new theory was its recognition of an inseparable connection between rational cognition and rational purpose" (*Collected Papers*, 5.412, Peirce's italics).

43. Hoopes, 5; Tom Cohen, "The 'Genealogies' of Pragmatism," in *Rhetoric, Sophistry, Pragmatism,* ed. Steven Mailloux (Cambridge: Cambridge University Press, 1995), 94–104; 94.

44. "If there is an American 'pragmatism' that foregrounds these issues of linguistic materiality—and there is, it is called American Literature—it might be objectionable from certain perspectives in [Cornel] West's program for appearing at points frankly 'post–modern'" (Cohen, 108). I will suggest in Chapter 6 that Sarah Schulman's *Girls, Visions and Everything* might be considered an example of this tendency towards postmodern pragmatism in American literature, although not of the specifically nihilistic inclinations that Cohen also mentions.

In her exploration of ways in which "flesh transforms theory" in considerations of butch lesbianism, Ann Cvetkovich also turns to American literature, and concludes that the texts she discusses offer "a density of detail and affective power that confounds not only stereotypes but abstractions" (169). Significantly, Cvetkovich's interest in butch emotional styles portends a conceptualization of interiority that does not depend on liberal humanist abstractions. (Ann Cvetkovich, "Untouchability and Vulnerability: Stone Butchness as Emotional Style," in *butch/femme: Inside Lesbian Gender*, ed. Sally R. Munt (London: Cassell, 1998), 159–169; 169.

45. The phrase is Vincent Colapietro's; see Colapietro, "The Vanishing Subject of Contemporary Discourse: A Pragmatic Response," *Journal of Philosophy* 87, no.11 (1990): 644–55; Vincent Colapietro, *Peirce's Approach to the Self: A Semiotic Perspective on Human Subjectivity* (State University of New York Press, 1989). Stuhr also invokes this phrase to make this argument, see especially p. 92.

46. Consider Peirce on the scientific, experimentalist set of mind that constitutes the pragmatic perspective: "When you have found, or ideally constructed upon a basis of observation, the ideal experimentalist, you will find that whatever assertion you make to him, he will either understand as meaning that if a given prescription for an experiment ever can be and ever is carried out in act, an experience of a given description will result, or else he will see no sense at all in what you say. If you talk to him as Mr. Balfour talked not long ago to the British Association [for the Advancement of Science, on August 17, 1904] saying that 'the physicist . . . seeks for something deeper than the laws connecting possible objects of experience,' that 'his object is physical reality' unrevealed in experiments, and the existence of such non–experiential reality 'is the unalterable faith of science,' to all such ontological meaning you will find the experimentalist to be colorblind" (*Collected Papers* 5.411).

47. Stuhr, 92.

48. Cornel West, *The American Evasion of Philosophy: A Geneaology of Pragmatism* (Madison: University of Wisconsin Press, 1989), 5, 45.

49. Butler, "Contingent Foundations," in *Feminist Contentions: A Philosophical Exchange*, by Seyla Benhabib, Judith Butler, Drucilla Cornell, and Nancy Fraser (New York: Routledge, 1995), 47.

50. For further discussion, see Chapter 2.

51. Peirce, *Collected Papers*, 2.242.

52. Peirce, *Collected Papers*, 2.228.

53. Cohen, 104.

54. Peirce, *Collected Papers*, 2.231.

55. Cohen, 104.

56. "Peirce goes very far in the direction that I have called the deconstruction of the transcendental signified, which, at one time or another, would place a reassuring end to the reference from sign to sign" (Jacques Derrida, *Of Grammatology* [Baltimore: Johns Hopkins University Press, 1976], 49).

57. *Collected Papers*, 2.303.

58. Roof, 108. Roof's specifically psychoanalytic observation is discussed in greater depth and detail in Chapter 4.

59. Quoted in Irene Costera Meijer and Baukje Prins, "How Bodies Come to Matter: An Interview with Judith Butler," *SIGNS* 23, no. 2 (winter 1998): 275–286; 278.

60. Butler, *Bodies That Matter*, 10.

61. Martin, 92.

Chapter 2

1. Judith Halberstam, *Female Masculinity* (Durham: Duke University Press, 1998), 87.

2. F.E. Daniel, "Castration of Sexual Perverts," *Texas Medical Journal* (Austin), August 1893, 255-71; excerpted in Jonathan Ned Katz, *Gay American History* (revised edition; New York: Meridan, 1992), 135-37. C.S. Peirce, "The Architecture of Theories," the *Monist* 1 (January 1891): 161-76; "The Doctrine of Necessity Examined," the *Monist* 2 (April 1892): 321-37; "The Law of Mind," the *Monist* 2 (July 1892): 533-59; "Man's Glassy Essence," the *Monist* 3 (October 1892): 1-22; and "Evolutionary Love," the *Monist* 3 (January 1893): 176-200. Alice Mitchell, quoted in "Jealousy the Motive: A Strange Story Told By The Memphis Girl Murderer," the *New York Times,* 29 January 1892, page 1, col. 3; excerpted in Jonathan Ned Katz, *Gay/Lesbian Almanac* (New York: Harper and Row, 1983), 224. Siobhan B. Somerville, *Queering the Color Line: Race and the Invention of Homosexuality in American Culture* (Durham: Duke University Press, 2000), 4.

3. Henry Nash Smith, *Virgin Land: The American West as Symbol and Myth* (New York: Vintage, 1957), 90–119.

4. For an historical overview of these and other medical approaches, see Jonathan Ned Katz, *Gay American History: Lesbians and Gay Men in the U.S.A.* (1976; revised edition, New York: Meridian, 1992), 129–51. For discussion of adaptation and appropriation of turn–of–the–century medical discourses on female homosexuality by the popular press, see Lisa Duggan, "The Trial of Alice Mitchell: Sensationalism, Sexology, and the Lesbian Subject in Turn–of–the–Century America," *Signs* 18, no. 4 (summer 1993): 791–814.

5. Indeed, until "experts" were summoned to the second trial, "no suggestion was ever made in any quarter, official, semi–official, or otherwise, that seemed an adequate, or even tolerable explanation of Norma's strange conduct, except the theory of insanity." J[ohn] W[esley] Carhart, *Norma Trist; or Pure Carbon: a Story of the Inversion of the Sexes* (Austin, TX: Boeckmann, 1895), 184. Subsequent references to the novel will be cited parenthetically within the text.

6. The terms "determinism" and "degeneration" are borrowed from Mark Seltzer, *Bodies and Machines* (New York: Routledge, 1992). Seltzer's study of machine culture and the late nineteenth–century novel characterizes the subject of the realist novel as "the internal genesis and evolution of character in society,"

explaining that "the realist novel, through techniques of narrative surveillance, organic continuity, and deterministic progress, secures the intelligibility and supervision of individuals in an evolutionary and genetic narration." The naturalist novel, in contrast, "involves a mutation in these techniques that consists also in a systematic and totalizing intensification of their effects." Thus, "far from resisting the realist premises of genesis and generation, the naturalist aesthetic doctrines of determinism and degeneration systematically render explicit and reinforce these premises and the power–effects inscribed in them" (43).

7. Asa Gray, "Fertilization of Orchids through the Agency of Insects," *American Journal of Science* 84 (1862): 420–29. Notably, Gray even "admitted to a vein of 'petite malice' in doing so because he knew that Darwin did not accept this view." (Edward Pfeiffer, "The United States," in *The Comparative Reception of Darwinism*, ed. Thomas F. Glick [Austin, Texas: University of Texas Press, 1974], 185.)

8. Cynthia Eagle Russett, *Darwin in America: The Intellectual Response 1865–1912* (San Francisco: Freeman, 1976), 1–10. Indeed, Gray went so far as to include a chapter entitled "Evolutionary Teleology" in his collection *Darwiniana* (New York, 1876. [Reprint. Cambridge, MA: Harvard University Press, 1963]).

9. Glick, 175.

10. Peter J. Bowler, *The Eclipse of Darwinism: Anti–Darwinian Evolution Theories in the Decades around 1900* (Baltimore, MD: Johns Hopkins University Press, 1983), 119.

11. Bowler, 120.

12. Somerville, 22.

13. Spencer's essay "The Development Hypothesis" was published in 1852 (see also Russett, 7).

14. Paul F. Boller, *American Thought in Transition: The Impact of Evolutionary Naturalism, 1865–1900* (Chicago: Rand McNally, 1969), 49.

15. This unlikely alliance of determinism and human agency seems uniquely amenable to U.S. thought—perhaps imaginable only as part of the peculiar legacy of Puritan predestination.

16. Evolutionary stages analogous to infancy and old age were assumed to resemble each other (as they presumably did in human development).

17. Herbert Spencer, *Study of Sociology* (New York: D. Appleton, 1884), 345. Sociological applications and appropriations of Spencerian neo–Lamarckism are discussed in detail in Boller, 199–226.

18. In a study based on the 1890 census, for example, Frederick L. Hoffman, a statistician for Prudential Insurance Company, attributed to African Americans an "inherited organic weakness," carefully clarifying that

> It is not in the *conditions of life* but in *the race traits and tendencies* that we find the causes of the [Negro's] excessive mortality. So long as these tendencies are persisted in, so long as immorality and

> vice are a habit of life of the vast majority of the colored population, the effect will be to increase the mortality by the hereditary transmission of weak constitutions, and to lower still further the rate of natural increase, until the births fall below the deaths, and gradually extinction results.

In accordance with this odd amalgamation of belief in both inborn "race traits and tendencies" and the inheritance of acquired characteristics, Hoffman concluded that African Americans were not only an inferior race, but also a poor insurance risk (*Race Traits and Tendencies of the American Negro* [n.p., 1896]; quoted in Boller, 209).

19. Josiah Strong, D.D., *Our Country: Its Possible Future and Its Present Crisis*, rev. ed. (New York: American Home Missionary Society, c. 1885). Fiske's essay and Strong's book are both excerpted in Boller, 212–14.

20. Seltzer, 43. See also John J. Conder, *Naturalism in American Fiction: The Classic Phase* (Lexington: University Press of Kentucky, 1984); Donald Pizer, *Twentieth–Century American Literary Naturalism: An Interpretation* (Carbondale: Southern Illinois University Press, 1982).

21. Peirce, *The Essential Peirce*, ed. Nathan Houser and Christian Kloesel (Bloomington: Indiana University Press, 1992), 1:289–90 (emphasis added).

22. Frederick Jackson Turner, *The Frontier in American History* (New York: Holt, 1920), 2–3.

23. Turner, 10–11.

24. To be fair, Turner himself cannot be held individually responsible for this particular interpretation. Indeed, he does not celebrate Anglo–Saxon purity, but credits the frontier for promoting "the formation of a composite nationality for the American people." "The coast was predominantly English," he explains, "[and] later tides of continental immigration flowed across to the free lands." Interestingly, however, only "the Scotch–Irish and the Palatine Germans" are singled out for explicit mention (22).

25. Prentiss Ingraham, *Buffalo Bill, from Boyhood to Manhood: Deeds of Daring, Scenes of Thrilling Peril, and Romantic Incidents in the Early Life of W. F. Cody, the Monarch of Bordermen* (Beadle's Boys' Library of Sport, Story, and Adventure, no. 2, 1884), 2. For an excellent overview of the genre, see Bill Brown, ed., *Reading the West: An Anthology of Dime Westerns* (Boston: Bedford, 1997).

26. Henry Nash Smith, *Virgin Land: The American West as Symbol and Myth* (New York: Vintage, 1957), 111.

27. David Montejano, *Anglos and Mexicans in the Making of Texas, 1836–1986* (Austin: University of Texas Press, 1987), 1–74, especially 8–9, 34–37, 70–74.

28. Perhaps predictably, then, Marie seems to have retained her predilection for romantic friendship:

> It is pertinent to our story to remark that, after the expiration of the term of office of Captain Rodriquez, he and his beautiful bride

> returned to the City of Mexico, where he became a cabinet officer of President Diaz, and his beautiful and accomplished wife has ever remained the warm and near friend of Mrs. Diaz, who esteems her for her courtly beauty, but even more because of her noble qualities of heart and mind. (Carhart, 189).

29. F.E. Daniel, "Castration of Sexual Perverts," *Texas Medical Journal* 9 (December 1893): 255–71.

30. Strictly speaking, of course, no cattle were "native" to the Americas. Those that were introduced at the time of the Spanish Conquest, however, were colloquially considered "American" breeds by the late nineteenth century.

31. The identity of carbon, curiously, became a point of focus during the famous Boston debates on Darwinism between Louis Agassiz and William Barton Rogers. In response to Rogers' assertion that paleontologists in general accepted, as Agassiz did not, that identical forms occur in rocks of different geological periods, Agassiz sought to demonstrate that scientific opinions often change. As Thomas Glick reports:

> [Agassiz asserted] that opinions change similarly in chemistry; chemists once did not distinguish platinum from silver. This was an unfortunate analogy for Agassiz to draw, because Rogers at once pointed out that chemistry had also reduced to one many supposedly different mineral species, for instance, diamond, plumbago, and carbon [—thus suggesting the existence of a common origin and supporting a theory of evolution]. (Glick, 179).

Carhart's use of the term in his title seems to draw on similar associations; "pure carbon" figures as pure possibility, the undifferentiated life force, its individuation dependent upon experience and environment.

32. The term is taken from the title of an 1893 article by Dr. C.H. Hughes, editor of the journal *Alienist and Neurologist.* Excerpts from this essay, "Erotophobia—Morbid Eroticism," appear in Jonathan Ned Katz, *Gay/Lesbian Almanac* (New York: Harper Colophon, 1983), 245–47.

33. The school president is aptly named. I wish to argue that it is their refusal to accept a theory of random variation which renders "Spencerian" thinkers unable to imagine the existence of an individual such as Norma.

34. Philadelphia publisher F.A. Davis brought out this authorized English translation of the seventh, enlarged and revised, German edition of Richard von Krafft–Ebing's *Psychopathia Sexualis* just as Peirce was developing a pragmatist theory of signs which, with its emphasis on effects as opposed to essences, would challenge the determinism of Philosophical Naturalism even as the increasingly accessible texts of European sexologists attributed more and more of the observable world to the influence of an individual's essential nature. Schrenk–Notzing's *Therapeutic Suggestion in Psychopathia Sexualis* (which advocated hypnosis as a treatment for homosexuality) appeared in an English–language American edition in 1895, the same year that the U.S. journal *Alienist and Neurologist* published Havelock Ellis's "Sexual Inversion in Women"—

and the same year that *Norma Trist* came out. Clearly, the close of the nineteenth century marked a juncture at which ideas about inversion, identity, and the making of meaning were peculiarly open to debate.

35. Richard von Krafft–Ebing, *Psychopathia Sexualis: A Medico–Forensic Study*, trans. Harry E. Wedeck (from the 12th German ed. [Vienna, 1903]), (New York: Putnam, 1965), 331–33.

36. ibid., 332.

37. ibid., 336.

38. ibid., 357.

39. ibid., 367–372.

40. ibid., 364.

41. ibid., 370.

42. Katz, *History*, 53–58, 576. For further discussion of the significance of Mitchell's trial in the context of sexological discourses, see Duggan (n. 4 above).

43. Quoted in Katz, *Almanac*, 246, 232.

44. Krafft–Ebing employed the phrase as well. In "Perversion of the Sexual Instinct" (*Alienist and Neurologist*, October 1888), for example, he characterizes "the sexual predilections of an individual for those of his or her own sex, with an aversion for sexual intimacy with those of the opposite sex" as "a strange freak of nature" (quoted in Katz, *Almanac*, 205).

45. A helpful introduction to the historical contexts of Peirce's philosophy is available in Christopher Hookway, *Peirce* (Boston: Routledge and Kegan Paul, 1985), especially 3–12.

46. Peirce, *Semiotic and Significs: The Correspondence between Charles S. Peirce and Victoria Lady Welby*, ed. Charles S. Hardwick (Bloomington: Indiana University Press, 1977), 24.

47. Butler, "Contingent Foundations," 47; see also Chapter 1 of this volume, especially pp. 32–34.

48. *Semiotic and Significs*, 24–25 (final emphasis added).

49. Even in speaking of "the quality itself" independent of perception or memory, Peirce is careful to clarify for his reader that, "I do not mean that you are to imagine that you *do not* perceive or remember it." Instead, he instructs us to "drop out of account that which may be attached to it in perceiving or remembering, *but which does not belong to the quality*" (emphasis added) — thus leaving open the possibility for inclusion in our conception of "the quality itself" those aspects attached to it through perception and memory which *do* "belong to the quality." He is similarly careful in discussing the specific example, explaining that "the quality of red *is not thought of* as belonging to you, or as attached to liveries" (emphasis added). *The mental act of abstraction itself exiles ideas to the realm of firstness.* What matters is not the extent to which the idea of red is *in fact* influenced—or even effected—by material conditions or human action, but whether we *think of it* as isolable from our experience of it. Thus the category of firstness may be construed as being comprised of *mental* entities unavailable to direct experience or examination. This does not, however,

mean that such entities are in fact independent from experience—on the contrary, each may be seen to owe its particular existence to the incessant interaction of experience and such abstraction as makes experience interpretable. Nor, however, are these immaterial entities entirely passive—instead, they "act" on experience and interpretation in return. Interpretation assumes involvement with the category of "Thirdness," the terrain where materiality and abstraction come together to effect the making of meaning. Representation *per se* inheres in the act of relation definitive of this terrain: "Thirdness is the mode of being" of language, of signs, of all "that which is such as it is, in bringing a second and a third into relation to each other." And Peirce is careful to clarify that

> [A] Sign can only represent the Object and tell about it. It cannot furnish acquaintance with or recognition of that object; for that is what is meant . . . by the Object of a Sign; namely, that with which it presupposes an acquaintance in order to convey some further information concerning it. (*Collected Papers* 2.230)

Thus the object presupposed—perhaps a quality in the mode of firstness, such as "the scarlet of [the English] royal liveries" or the lesbianism of Carhart's Norma Trist—grounds even those acts of representation by which experience is constituted and its own particular existence is informed.

50. Stephen Gordon is the protagonist of Radclyffe Hall's *The Well of Loneliness* (1928. [Reprint. New York: Anchor, 1990]), a text central to the discursive construction of modern lesbian identity in the United States (see Chapter 3).

51. Although his initial examples are perhaps misleading, Peirce proceeds to define indexicality more inclusively as he discusses it more specifically:

> [An index is] a sign, or representation, which refers to its object not so much because of any similarity or analogy with it, nor because it is associated with general characters which that object happens to possess, as because it is in dynamical (including spatial) connection both with the individual object, on the one hand, and with the senses or memory of the person for whom it serves as a sign, on the other hand.

He defines demonstrative and personal pronouns, as ordinarily used, as "genuine indices," but emphasizes that "it would be difficult, if not impossible, to instance an absolutely pure index, or to find any sign absolutely devoid of the indexical quality." Ultimately, he writes, "psychologically, the action of indices depends upon association by contiguity, and not upon association by resemblance [as do icons] or upon intellectual operations [as do symbols]." Indexicality thus exists in the function of dynamical connection between both the object and the sign itself and between the sign itself and the person intrepreting it as such. "Anything which startles us is an index," Peirce says, "insofar as it marks the junction between two portions of experience." More specifically, Peirce explains, when signs refer "to a situation relative to the observed, or assumed to be experientially known, place and attitude of the speaker relatively to that of the hearer, then the indexical element is the dominant element." The above examples regarding "signs" of inversion crucially involve this aspect of indexicality, as well. (*Collected Papers*, 2.285–306. Also see Justus Buchler, *Charles Peirce's Empiricism* [New York: Octagon, 1966], 105–111).

52. Krafft–Ebing, 361.

53. ibid., 361.

54. ibid., 364.

55. ibid., 335.

56. Katz, *Almanac*, 277.

57. It is worth remarking that even to the end, the Alphonso/Norma opposition remains effectively unresolved. Alphonso "wins" Marie only in Norma's absence; indeed, the apparent interchangeability in Marie's eyes of the story's two most androgynous actors underscores their essential equivalence.

58. Peirce, *Collected Papers*, 6.287–317; 6.299.

59. *The Monist*, vol. 1 (1891), 161–176; *Collected Papers*, 6.7–34.

60. *Collected Papers*, 6.295; 6.302; 6.304.

61. Or, for that matter, as Trist, the surname of the diplomat (Nicholas Trist) who negotiated the Treaty of Guadalupe–Hidalgo on behalf of the United States—ending the U.S./Mexican War on much more favorable terms for Mexico, apparently, than he had been authorized to accept.

Chapter 3

1. Leigh Gilmore, "Obscenity, Modernity, Identity: Legalizing *The Well of Loneliness* and *Nightwood*," *Journal of the History of Sexuality* 4, no. 4 (1993): 603–623.

2. Radclyffe Hall, *The Well of Loneliness* (1928; New York: Anchor, 1990), 20, 22, 25.

3. Teresa de Lauretis, *The Practice of Love* (Bloomington: Indiana University Press, 1994), 204, 212.

4. Judith Halberstam, *Female Masculinity* (Durham: Duke University Press, 1998), 96, 83, 85.

5. Catharine R. Stimpson, "Zero Degree Deviancy: The Lesbian Novel in English," *Writing and Sexual Difference.*, ed. Elizabeth Abel (Chicago: University of Chicago Press, 1982), 249.

6. Esther Newton, "The Mythic Mannish Lesbian: Radclyffe Hall and the New Woman," *The Lesbian Issue: Essays from SIGNS*, ed. Estelle Freedman, et al. (Chicago: University of Chicago Press, 1985), 10. (Reprinted from *Signs* 9, no. 4 [summer 1984]).

7. Halberstam, *Female Masculinity*, 96.

8. Jane Rule, *Lesbian Images* (Trumansburg, NY: Crossing Press, 1975), 50.

9. Blanche Wiesen Cook, "'Women Alone Stir My Imagination': Lesbianism and the Cultural Tradition," *Signs* 4, no. 4 (summer 1979): 718.

10. "A ridiculous book, trite, superficial" (Romaine Brooks, quoted in Lillian Faderman, *Surpassing the Love of Men: Romantic Friendship and Love between Women from the Renaissance to the Present* [New York: William Morrow, 1981], 322); "a meritorious, dull book" (Virginia Woolf, as recounted in Rule, 53); "As a novel, written in a language which is unfalteringly clear, sometimes beautiful and often irritatingly Biblical, it is unduly long and overburdened with detail frequently irrelevant to the story's progress" (Vera Brittain, *Radclyffe Hall: A Case of Obscenity?* [New York: A.S. Barnes, 1969], 48–49 [first published in London, by Femina Books, 1968]); "melodramatic" (Cyril Connolly, *The New Statesman*, 25 August 1928); "Inflated and sentimental and diffuse as it is, one cannot deny the earnestness" (L.P. Hartley, *Saturday Review*, 28 July 1928).

11. Or as Cook puts it, "most of us lesbians in the 1950s grew up knowing nothing about lesbianism except Stephen Gordon's swagger, Stephen Gordon's breeches, and Stephen Gordon's wonderful way with horses" (719).

12. Gilmore, 604.

13. L.P. Hartley in the *Saturday Review*, July 28, 1928; Ida Wylie in the *Sunday Times*, August 5, 1928; Leonard Woolf in the *Nation and Athenaeum*, August 4, 1928. For further discussion of early English reviews, see Michael Baker, *Our Three Selves: The Life of Radclyffe Hall* (New York: Morrow, 1985), 220–29.

14. Woolf, 593.

15. James Douglas, "A Book That Must Be Suppressed," *Sunday Express*, 19 August 1928.

16. Baker, 223–28; 239–45.

17. *New York Times*, October 6, 1928 (p. 6, col. 4).

18. A.A. Knopf to Radclyffe Hall, July 19, 1928 (Knopf Collection, Harry Ransom Humanities Research Center, the University of Texas, Austin, Texas).

19. The office of A.A. Knopf to Radclyffe Hall, September 25, 1928 (Knopf Collection, HRHRC).

20. Among friends, Radclyffe Hall was customarily called "John."

21. Blanche Knopf to Radclyffe Hall, September 20, 1928 (Knopf Collection, HRHRC).

22. According to Edward de Grazia, Friede took this action because he "wished to avoid the situation in which some defenseless clerk in a bookstore would be arrested and perhaps frightened into a guilty plea or led to make an inadequate defense." Moreover, de Grazia notes, "provoking a successful test case would also build up sales." (Edward de Grazia, *Girls Lean Back Everywhere: The Law of Obscenity and the Assault on Genius* [New York: Random House, 1992], 198).

23. Roscoe Pound, "Liberty of Contract," *Yale Law Journal* XVIII (1909): 464.

24. Benjamin Cardozo, *The Nature of the Judicial Process* (New Haven: Yale University Press, 1921), 102.

25. Nor were such tendencies restricted to the realm of legal theory—by 1905, Peirce was so put off by the "abuse" of his increasingly popular term "pragmatism" (especially by literary critics!) that he renamed his own position "pragmaticism," a term he hoped "ugly enough to be safe from kidnappers." (Peirce, "What Pragmatism Is," *The Monist* 15 (1905): 161–181; *Collected Papers* 5.414) I invoke the term here to mark Peirce's dissatisfaction with the ways in which his ideas were sometimes taken up in the early decades of the twentieth century, but will generally rely on his original "pragmatist" and insist on a more Peircean interpretation than it is sometimes accorded.

26. *New York Miscellaneous Reports* 133: 612–13.

27. *Regina* v. *Hicklin*, L.R. 3 Q.B. 360; quoted in defense memorandum. "Memorandum submitted on behalf of the defendants," *People* v. *Friede* (HRHRC, Radclyffe Hall collection), n.p.

28. *New York Miscellaneous Reports* 133: 612–613.

29. *New York Miscellaneous Reports* 133: 615, 613.

30. Gilmore, 606.

31. C.S. Peirce, *The Collected Papers of Charles Sanders Peirce*, ed. Charles Hartshorne and Paul Weiss, 2nd ed., (Cambridge, MA: Harvard University Press, 1963), 5.422. (Original publication: "What Pragmatism Is," *The Monist* 15 [1905]: 161–181.)

32. "When Nicola Sacco and Bartolomeo Vanzetti were electrocuted on August 23, 1927, a tremor of seismic proportions rolled around the world." Herbert B. Ehrmann, *The Case That Will Not Die* (Boston: Little, Brown, 1969), *x*.

33. Felix Frankfurter, *The Case of Sacco and Vanzetti* (Boston: Little, Brown, 1927), 38–40.

34. Louis F. Post, *The Deportations Delirium of 1920* (Chicago: Kerr, 1923).

35. G. Louis Joughin and Edmund M. Morgan, *The Legacy of Sacco and Vanzetti* (New York: Harcourt, Brace, 1948), 213; Osmond Fraenkel, *The Sacco–Vanzetti Case* (London: George Routledge & Sons, 1931), 5.

36. Ehrmann, 58, 477–79, 325.

37. Quoted in John Dewey, "Psychology and Justice," *Characters and Events* (New York: H. Holt, 1929), 2:527. (Originally published in *The New Republic*, 23 November 1927).

38. Dewey, 528–29.

39. Baker, 217–18.

40. Anna Elisabet Weirauch, *Der Skorpion* (1919); *The Scorpion*, trans. Whittaker Chambers (New York: Greenberg, 1932).

41. Terry Castle, *The Apparitional Lesbian: Female Homosexuality and Modern Culture* (New York: Columbia University Press, 1993), 142–44, 179.

42. Richard von Krafft–Ebing, *Psychopathia Sexualis: A Medico–Forensic*

Study, trans. Harry E. Wedeck (New York: Putnam, 1965), 358.

43. Hall, 13.

44. For an interesting Oedipal reading of the novel, see Newton (especially 21–22).

45. Radclyffe Hall, *The Well of Loneliness* (New York: Anchor, 1990 [1928]), 18. Subsequent citations will be provided parenthetically within the text.

46. See Gilmore for more detailed discussion of the English obscenity trial.

47. *New York Miscellaneous Reports* 133: 613.

48. Baker, 220.

49. See, for example, Havelock Ellis, *Studies in the Psychology of Sex*, vol. 2, *Sexual Inversion* (3d ed.), (Philadelphia: F.A. Davis, 1915).

50. de Lauretis, 213.

51. See Hall, 204–5, 293.

52. "O God, Thou All–pitying, Almighty One! Thou seest my distress; Thou knowest how I suffer. Incline Thyself to me; extend Thy helping hand to me, deserted by all the world." (Quoted by Krafft–Ebing, 361).

53. Blanche McCrary Boyd, afterword to *The Well of Loneliness*, by Radclyffe Hall (New York: Anchor, 1990), 439.

54. Castle, 50–52.

55. de Lauretis, 211.

56. Quoted in "'Well of Loneliness' Cleared in Court Here," *New York Times*, 20 April 1929, p. 20, col. 2.

57. Morris L. Ernst and Alan U. Schwartz, *Censorship: The Search for the Obscene* (New York: Macmillan, 1964), 79.

58. See, for example, Halberstam, *Female Masculinity*, 93, 96.

59. Eve Kosofsky Sedgwick, *Epistemology of the Closet* (Berkeley: University of California Press, 1990), 85.

Chapter 4

1. Bonnie Zimmerman, *The Safe Sea of Women: Lesbian Fiction 1969–1989* (Boston: Beacon, 1990), 7.

2. Mary McCarthy, *The Group* (New York: Harcourt, 1963; New York: Avon, 1980). Parenthetical citations refer to the Avon reprint.

3. Stanley Kauffmann, "Miss McCarthy's Era," *New Republic*, 31 August 1963, 26.

4. In sexological taxonomies, "inverts" were often classed as a "third sex." By McCarthy's time, the phrase had become a kind of colloquialism for homosexuality. (Indeed, a book entitled *The Third Sex*, edited by Isadore Rubin, was published in 1961.)

5. See Elizabeth Lapovsky Kennedy and Madeline Davis, *Boots of Leather, Slippers of Gold: The History of a Lesbian Community* (New York: Routledge,

1993); Lillian Faderman, *Odd Girls and Twilight Lovers: A History of Lesbian Life in Twentieth–Century America* (New York: Columbia University Press, 1991).

6. Eve Kosofsky Sedgwick, *Epistemology of the Closet* (Berkeley: University of California Press, 1990), 82.

7. In "Lesbian Culture and the Lesbian Novel," Bonnie Zimmerman points out that "more lesbian novels were published in the United States during the 1950s and early 1960s than at any other time in history"—and claims that "the written word was crucial to sustaining and promoting lesbian identity" (Zimmerman, *The Safe Sea of Women*, 9).

Also see Kate Adams, "Making the World Safe for the Missionary Position: Images of the Lesbian in Post–World War II America," in *Lesbian Texts and Contexts*, ed. Karla Jay and Joanne Glasgow (New York: NYU Press, 1990).

8. McCarthy's own relationship to lesbian possibility is difficult to read; her life and the body of work it produced appear to embody ambivalence similar to that described in *The Group*. But in this work, at least, her writer's eye and keen intelligence reveal certain cultural truths which the author herself may have been unable or unwilling to acknowledge.

9. A ninth, Norine, is an outsider peripheral to "the group" although often involved in the action in *The Group*.

10. McCarthy's appeal to racial difference as a means of marking and exoticizing undefined sexual difference plays off a familiar paradigm. See, for example, Kathryn Hinojosa Baker, "Delinquent Desire: Race, Sex, and Ritual in Reform Schools for Girls," *Discourse* 15, no. 1; Lisa Moore, "Something More Tender Still Than Friendship: Romantic Friendship in Early–Nineteenth–Century England," *Feminist Studies* 18, no. 3, especially 513–17.

11. Kauffmann, 27.

12. Robert Kiely, "The New Wayfarers," *The Nation*, 21 September 1963, 164–5.

13. William Abrahams, "After the Daisy Chain," *Partisan Review* (January/February 1964), 109–110.

14. Kauffmann, 26–7.

15. Granville Hicks, "What to Be After Poughkeepsie," *Saturday Review*, 31 August 1963, 19.

16. Hicks, 30; Kiely, 163; Norman Mailer, "The Mary McCarthy Case," *New York Review of Books,* 17 October 1963, 3; Kauffmann, 25.

17. Although Norman Mailer also notes the "atrocious anachronism" of the novel's 1950s "consciousness" (3), he attributes it to oversight or inconsistency on McCarthy's part, never considering that it might be intended.

18. Abrahams, 108. Interestingly, Abrahams also identifies in the novel an emotional depth that other reviewers generally do not see. "A sense of anti–climax, of accommodation," he says, "haunts *The Group* and gives its often hilarious comedy a depth and pathos" (109). Hicks also notes the novel's "compassion," remarking that this is "a quality that one has not come

to expect from this particular author" (30).

19. Podhoretz is quoted in Mailer (1). "As an admirer"(?!), Kauffmann imposes on the book the imperative to "illuminate and preserve in art a journey through our time as experienced with female brains, intuitions, glands, genitals" (28). Meanwhile, without mentioning gender, Kiely laments that "the section of society Miss McCarthy has chosen to cut through obviously limits her field," while praising the author for recognizing her limitations: "one of the virtues of *The Group* is that it is an unassuming and economically constructed novel which displays a brilliance for the particular, rather than symbolic" (163). Characteristically, Mailer manfully shoulders the burden of making explicit tensions not generally acknowledged in mixed company: *The Group*, he says, is not just any "lady–book" (1), but "the best novel the editors of the women's magazines ever conceived in their secret ambitions" (3).

20. Hicks, 19. Nor has this bias been blunted by the passage of time; while representing itself as a retrospective, Frances Kiernan's 1993 *New Yorker* essay is in this respect almost indistinguishable from Hicks' 1963 review:

> At least four of the eight girls in the novel fare badly—at the hands of a husband or lover or at the hands of their implacable creator. If Polly Andrews or Helena Davison are in many respects admirable characters, they are a little too nice to stick in a reader's mind. It is Kay Strong with her transparent pretensions, or Dottie Renfrew, with her failed love affair, whom you remember. A couple of the girls—Libby MacAusland, a would–be book editor, and Pokey Prothero, flying her private plane to Cornell to study veterinary medicine—seem downright silly. The most glamorous of the lot, Elinor Eastlake, or Lakey, turns out to be a lesbian.

(Frances Kiernan, "Group Encounter," *The New Yorker*, 7 June 1993, 58).

21. Kauffmann, 26, 28 (emphasis added).

22. Kiely, 165.

23. Even Kay, who had looked up to them both, had by the time of her death begun to see through Harald's pretensions.

24. Frederick J. Newmeyer, *The Politics of Linguistics* (Chicago: University of Chicago Press, 1986), 51–56. (Graves, comments in the session "Meeting the Government's Need in Languages," *Report on the Second Annual Round Table Meeting on Linguistics and Language Teaching*, ed. J. De Francis [Washington, D.C.: Georgetown University Press, 1951], 1; quoted in Newmeyer, 56).

This emphasis on language teaching and practical applicability combined with linguists' interest in representing their discipline as the only truly scientific approach to language (at a time when the physical sciences themselves were overwhelmingly empiricist in orientation) to shape the developing discipline around an almost exclusively empiricist approach. Simply stated, the research that found funding was research that focused on collection and quantification of extensive primary data. Thus those professionals who developed the study of language on its own terms into a viable—and visible—intellectual pursuit were, like Mary McCarthy, attentive in the extreme to the inexhaustible resource of everyday speech.

25. Noam Chomsky, *Syntactic Structures* (The Hague: Mouton, 1957).

26. See John Searle, "Chomsky's Revolution in Linguistics," *New York Review of Books*, 29 June 1972, 16–24; Frederick Newmeyer, "The Chomskyan Revolution," *Linguistic Theory in America: The First Quarter–Century of Transformational Grammar* (New York: Academic Press, 1980), 19–59; John Lyons, *Noam Chomsky* (New York: Viking, 1970). Although this characterization is now contested, at the time, as Newmeyer argues, most "commentators took it for granted that the publication in 1957 of *Syntactic Structures* by Noam Chomsky ushered in an intellectual and sociological revolution in the field" (Newmeyer, *Generative Linguistics: A Historical Perspective* [New York: Routledge, 1996], 23). This assessment of the book's reception is affirmed by Dell Hymes and John Fought, who themselves argue for a more inclusive and continuous interpretation of the structuralist tradition (Dell Hymes and John Fought, *American Structuralism* [The Hague: Mouton, 1981], 18 and passim). Even revisionist historians Geoffrey J. Huck and John A. Goldsmith agree that "virtually everyone active in the American linguistics community in the late 1950s and early 1960s was at least aware that something very different and exciting was being put together by Chomsky" (*Ideology and Linguistic Theory: Noam Chomsky and the Deep Structure Debates* [New York: Routledge, 1995], 14). Chomsky, *Syntactic Structures*, 5.

27. Chomsky, 50.

28. Chomsky, 45–46.

29. Newmeyer, *Linguistic Theory in America*, 86.

30. J. Edgar Hoover, *Masters of Deceit: The Story of Communism in America and How to Fight It* (New York: Holt, 1958), v.

31. Hoover, 97–105.

32. However, Chapter 2 of this volume proposes that the threat certain homosexualities sometimes pose to foundationalist epistemology may be a factor. See also John D'Emilio, "The Homosexual Menace: The Politics of Sexuality in Cold War America," in *Making Trouble*, by John D'Emilio (New York: Routledge, 1992); Lee Edelman, "Tearooms and Sympathy, or, The Epistemology of the Water Closet," in *Nationalisms and Sexualities*, ed. Andrew Parker (New York: Routledge, 1992).

33. Mary McCarthy, "Greenwich Village at Night," *New York Post*, 20 February 1950, 7.

34. Hoover, 105–6.

35. Hoover, 86.

36. Paul Welch, "A Secret World Grows Open and Bolder," with photos by William Eppridge (66–74); Ernest Havermann, "Scientists Search for Some Answers" (76–80), *Life*, 26 June 1964, 66–80; 66. (Also quoted in Edelman, 267).

37. Hoover, 5.

38. Judith Roof, *Come as You Are: Sexuality and Narrative* (New York: Columbia University Press, 1996), xxxiv–xxxv.

39. Catharine R. Stimpson, "Zero Degree Deviancy: The Lesbian Novel in English," in *Writing and Sexual Difference*, ed. Elizabeth Abel (Chicago: University of Chicago Press, 1982), 253.

40. According to Freud, "The [male] has only one principle sexual zone—only one sex organ—whereas the [female] has two: the vagina, *the true female organ*, and the clitoris, which is analogous to the male organ" (197, emphasis added). For the female, achieving sexual maturity depends on moving beyond the clitoral sexuality associated with childhood in order to embrace the "specifically feminine" sexuality centered in vaginal satisfaction. "Parallel with this," Freud explains, is a necessary shift in "object–choice[:] At the end of a girl's development it is the man—the father—who must come to be the new love–object; i.e. as she changes in sex, so must the sex of her love–object change" (from "Female Sexuality" [1931], as excerpted in Sigmund Freud, *Sexuality and the Psychology of Love*, ed. Philip Rieff [New York: Macmillan, 1963]).

41. Lest readers miss the implication, McCarthy follows up with a description of Dottie's fear that she "had wanted to be 'relieved' of her virginity and *was using Dick simply as an instrument*" (50, emphasis added).

42. The observation of another character that "Dottie, with her poor health and Boston heritage, was terrified of becoming an old maid" (188) helps to clarify the significance of Dick's nickname for her—this allusion to "Boston marriages" once again invokes without acknowledging the underlying lesbian threat. (I am indebted to Kathryn Baker for this observation.)

43. A subsequent chapter further satirizes psychoanalysis by suggesting its immobilizing effect on "one of the most normal men [Polly Andrews] had ever met, at least to the naked eye, which was all she had to judge with" (265). Gus, Polly's lover, is finally too involved in analyzing his life to get around to living it. "A curious thing," concludes Polly, this "treating yourself as if you were a dense, opaque object. Or as if you were not you but someone else, whose motives you could only guess at" (269). This raises the inevitable question: "Was this strange, flat objectivity what was the matter with Gus or was it an effect of the treatment?" (269).

44. The similarly feminine—but supposedly sexually ambivalent—central love interest of protagonist Stephen Gordon in Radclyffe Hall's *The Well of Loneliness*.

45. I am indebted to Kate Adams' essay "Making the World Safe for the Missionary Position" (note 7 above), in which an analogous argument is made, for suggesting this insight.

46. McCarthy, "Greenwich Village at Night," *New York Post*, 20 February–3 March 1950.

47. Kennedy and Davis, 69.

48. McCarthy, "Greenwich Village at Night," *New York Post*, 22 February 1950, 35.

49. McCarthy, "Greenwich Village at Night" *New York Post*, 23 February 1950.

50. Extending this set of equivalences to make clear the Freudian symbolism available in the group's "South Tower" affiliation, McCarthy specifies that "Harald had come to figure in Norine's mind as an 'erect phallus' just out of her reach, *like the Tower group*" (141, emphasis added).

51. Sedgwick, 86.

52. Noam Chomsky, *The Logical Structure of Linguistic Theory* (1955–56; Chicago: University of Chicago Press, 1975), 57; *Syntactic Structures*, 17.

53. Newmeyer, *Generative Linguistics*, 135.

54. Newmeyer, *Linguistic Theory in America*, 138.

55. Randy A. Harris, "The Origin and Development of Generative Semantics," *Historiographia Linguistica* 20 (1993): 399–440; 409–410.

56. Huck and Goldsmith, 2–3, ix; Newmeyer, *Generative Linguistics*, 137.

57. Newmeyer, *Linguistic Theory in America*, 31.

58. Huck and Goldsmith, 136.

59. The phrase is taken from Randy A. Harris, *The Linguistic Wars* (Oxford: Oxford University Press, 1993), another account of the "deep structure debates" between Chomskyites and the generative semanticists.

60. Sedgwick, 85.

61. Mailer, 2–3.

62. Roof, *Come As You Are*, 59–60.

63. For other discussions of lesbian possibility imagined through narrative, see Carolyn Allen, *Following Djuna: Women Lovers and the Erotics of Loss* (Bloomington: Indiana University Press, 1996); Julie Abraham, *Are Girls Necessary? Lesbian Writing and Modern Histories* (New York: Routledge, 1996); Marilyn R. Farwell, *Heterosexual Plots and Lesbian Narratives* (New York: New York University Press, 1996).

64. Huck and Goldsmith, 15.

65. Indeed, Newmeyer attributes the significance of the Chomskyan revolution to "the recognition that a linguistic theory is a formal model of a speaker's abstract linguistic competence," and contends that "it is this scientific idealization more than any specific proposal about transformational rules, deep structures, or semantic representations that has enabled linguistics to break free from the grip of taxonomy and anecdotality" (Newmeyer, *Linguistic Theory in America*, 250).

66. Roof, *Come As You Are*, 187.

67. Even back in her 1947 essay "Tyranny of the Orgasm," McCarthy's own "clear intellect" and sharp observations clearly are not dulled by heterosexist constraints. Attacking the assumptions of *Modern Woman, The Lost Sex*—in which authors Marynia Farnham and Ferdinand Lundberg conclude that since American women's capacity for orgasm seems to diminish as their level of

education increases, women should not be educated—McCarthy hones right in on suspicious data. Dispassionately observing that "the unsexed career woman may be frigid with men and amorous with women," she asks: "Is the lesbian orgasm not certified by these authorities?" (Mary McCarthy, *On the Contrary* [New York: Farrar, 1961], 172).

Chapter 5

1. Rita Mae Brown, *Rubyfruit Jungle* (Plainfield, VT: Daughters, 1973; New York: Bantam, 1977).

2. Lyndall MacCowan, "Re–collecting History, Renaming Lives: Femme Stigma and the Feminist Seventies and Eighties," in *The Persistent Desire: A Femme–Butch Reader*, ed. Joan Nestle (Boston: Alyson, 1992), 299–328; 311.

3. Siobhan B. Somerville, *Queering the Color Line: Race and the Invention of Homosexuality in American Culture* (Durham: Duke University Press, 2000), 21.

4. Carol M. Ward, *Rita Mae Brown* (New York: Twayne Publishers, 1993), 41.

5. Mark D. Uehling with Nikki Finke Greenberg, "Life Without Martina," *Newsweek*, 19 August 1985, 9.

6. Patricia Holt, "Rita Mae Brown," *Publishers Weekly*, 2 October 1978, 16–17; Carole Horn, "Rita Mae Brown: For Her, Being Different Really Isn't So Different Any More," *Washington Post*, 2 October 1978, C1, C13 and Lenore Fleischer, "Lenore Fleischer Talks with Rita Mae Brown," *Washington Post Book World*, 15 October 1978, E2; Dolores Alexander, "Rita Mae Brown: 'The Issue for the Future Is Power,'" *Ms.*, September 1974, 110–113. "Impish" and "gutsy" are from the inside cover copy of the Bantam edition, seventh printing.

7. Rita Mae Brown, *Plain Brown Rapper* (Oakland, CA: Diana Press, 1976), 140–41.

8. Brown, *Plain Brown Rapper*, 68.

9. Leslie Fishbein, "Rubyfruit Jungle: Lesbianism, Feminism, and Narcissism," *International Journal of Women's Studies*, March–April 1984, 155–59, 157. Quoted in Ward, 47.

10. Quoted in Ward, 42.

11. Bonnie Zimmerman, *The Safe Sea of Women: Lesbian Fiction 1969–1989* (Boston: Beacon, 1990), 250.

12. Seventh printing; Bantam copyrighted a new cover design in 1988.

13. Alice Echols, *Daring to Be Bad: Radical Feminism in America, 1967–1975* (Minneapolis: University of Minnesota Press, 1989), especially 203–286.

14. Peirce's understanding of this relation is discussed more fully in Chapter 6.

15. "The Self Affirms Herself" (1966) is the title of a poem included in Rita

Mae Brown, *The Hand That Cradles the Rock* (New York: New York University Press, 1971).

16. Ward, 46.

17. Hall opens her novel with an evocation of place, effectively prioritizing not the individual per se, but the particularity and the importance of context. This description of Stephen's ancestral homestead is inflected with a sense of history and followed by the story of her parents' first meeting, their courtship, and their early life together. The temporal and spatial coordinates of Stephen's existence are thus clearly set from the start; the meaning of the life Hall constructs will evolve within this carefully established frame (Radclyffe Hall, *The Well of Loneliness* [1928; New York: Anchor, 1990], 11–13).

18. The one lesbian literary antecedent it mentions by name, interestingly, is Virginia Woolf's more respectable *Orlando*, originally published in the same year (1928) as *The Well of Loneliness*. (Brown, *Rubyfruit Jungle*, 95–96.)

19. In the introduction to *Plain Brown Rapper,* Brown recalls her desire to "gather the lights about me as did Gertrude in Paris in the 1920's" and observes that "New York City is America's Paris" (Brown, *Plain Brown Rapper*, 10).

20. Hall, 437.

21. Zimmerman, *Safe Sea of Women*, 46–47.

22. Hall, 72, 75.

23. Hall, 77.

24. Hall, 152.

25. See, for example, Judith Halberstam's discussion of Stephen's "masculine identity expressed through a female self" in "'A Writer of Misfits': John Radclyffe Hall and the Discourse of Inversion" (Judith Halberstam, *Female Masculinity* [Durham: Duke University Press, 1998], 75–110), especially 95–107. Against attempts to excuse, recuperate, or reject *The Well* within conventionally gendered terms, Halberstam proposes we "take seriously Hall's representation of female masculinity as part of an ongoing transformation of gender binarism" (97).

26. Shane Phelan, "Lesbian Identity and Politics," *SIGNS* 18, no. 4 (summer 1993): 765–790.

27. For a succinct biographical sketch, see Ward, 1–10. Brown provides autobiographical accounts in *Starting from Scratch, a Different Kind of Writer's Manual* (New York: Bantam, 1988), 3–21; and in *Rita Will.*

28. Somerville, 13.

29. Somerville, 32.

30. The most readily evident example must be Dorothy Allison's brilliant *Bastard Out of Carolina* (New York: Dutton, 1992), although metaphorically orphaned protagonists such as Vincent in Jo Sinclair's *The Changelings* (New York: McGraw–Hill, 1955; New York: The Feminist Press, 1985) are arguably part of this tradition, as well. For more detailed exploration of this phenomenon, see Judith Roof, "'This Is Not for You': The Sexuality of Mothering" in *A Lure*

of Knowledge: Lesbian Sexuality and Theory (New York: Columbia University Press, 1991), 90–118, and the Afterword to this volume.

31. Hall, 105.

32. Hall, 365.

33. For an interesting discussion, see W.T. Lhamon Jr., *Raising Cain: Blackface Performance from Jim Crow to Hip Hop* (Cambridge, MA: Harvard University Press, 1998).

34. Biddy Martin, *Femininity Played Straight: The Significance of Being Lesbian* (New York: Routledge, 1996), 86–87.

35. See Lisa Walker, "How to Recognize a Lesbian: The Cultural Politics of Looking Like What You Are," *SIGNS* 18, no. 4 (summer 1993): 866–890, for a particularly interesting discussion of "how issues of visibility and invisibility or passing resonate between the identities 'lesbian' and 'woman of color.'" Particularly germane to my argument here is her observation that "in theory by white critics, racial difference repeatedly underpins constructions of butch identity" (869).

36. Roof, "1970s Lesbian Feminism Meets 1990s Butch–Femme," in *butch/femme: Inside Lesbian Gender*, ed. Sally R. Munt (London: Cassell, 1998), 27–35; 32.

37. The symbolic importance of this supposed uncertainty is suggested by the fact that Molly *does* now know who her birth mother is, at least—and Carl knows both birth parents, but dismisses the possibility of African American heritage without reference to this knowledge: "It'd show, Molly. Who knows what you are, you're a mongrel, that's all" (59).

38. Enmeshed in an explicitly "unprejudiced" text, this recurrent impulse results in occasional incongruities. It is plausible, for example, that *The Well*'s Stephen Gordon must leave both the country estate of her birth and even more cosmopolitan London before directly experiencing any significant interaction with African American individuals (in Paris, of course). It is rather remarkable, in contrast, that Molly Bolt manages to make it from rural Pennsylvania to southern Florida to Gainesville and finally to New York without, apparently, having met a single African American in the course of her U.S. childhood and adolescence. (I'm grateful to Lora Romero for this observation).

39. Anonymous, "SNCC Position Paper: Women in the Movement" (1964); reprinted in Sara Evans, *Personal Politics: The Roots of Women's Liberation in the Civil Rights Movement and the New Left* (New York: Knopf, 1979), 234.

40. Quoted in Evans, 236.

41. Roof, "1970s Lesbian Feminism," 30.

42. Judith Butler, *Bodies That Matter: On the Discursive Limits of "Sex"* (New York: Routledge, 1993), 18. See also, Roof, "All Analogies Are Faulty," in *A Lure of Knowledge*, 216–236; Yvonne Yarbro–Bejarano, "Expanding the Categories of Race and Sexuality in Lesbian and Gay Studies," in *Professions of Desire: Lesbian and Gay Studies in Literature*, ed. George E. Haggerty and Bonnie Zimmerman (New York: Modern Language Association, 1995), 124–135.

43. Somerville, 7.

44. Roof, "1970s Lesbian Feminism," 30.

45. MacCowan, 311.

46. Rita Mae Brown, *Rita Will: Memoir of a Literary Rabble Rouser* (New York: Bantam, 1997), 204–5.

47. Ward, 4.

48. James Anthony Schnur, "Cold Warriors in the Hot Sunshine: The Johns Committee's Assault on Civil Liberties in Florida, 1956–1965" (M.A. thesis, University of South Florida, 1995), 184.

49. Brown, *Rita Will*, 183.

50. Brown, *Plain Brown Rapper*, 81–84; *Rita Will*, 181–87; see also: Ward, 3; Brown, *Starting from Scratch*, 11.

51. A driving force in the Committee's creation, Johns served as its chair from 1957 until 1963; in Florida today, the FLIC is generally referred to as "the Johns Committee."

52. For an excellent overview of the FLIC's history, see James Schnur, "Closet Crusaders: The Johns Committee and Homophobia, 1956–1965," in *Carryin' On in the Lesbian and Gay South*, ed. John Howard (New York: NYU Press, 1997), 132–63.

53. Schnur, "Cold Warriors," 114, 110.

54. Apparently an actual establishment; my thanks to Sarah Schulman for pointing this out to me.

55. Brown, *Rita Will*, 195.

56. Alice Echols, *Daring To Be Bad: Radical Feminism in America, 1967–1975* (Minneapolis: University of Minnesota Press, 1989), 243.

57. Echols, 8.

58. Echols, 240–43.

59. Brown, "It's All Dixie Cups to Me," in *Plain Brown Rapper*, 193–220.

60. Roof, *A Lure of Knowledge*, 90–118, especially 108–9.

61. ibid., 110.

62. ibid., 108.

63. See also Teresa de Lauretis, *The Practice of Love: Lesbian Sexuality and Desire* (Bloomington: Indiana University Press, 1994); and Butler, "Arguing with the Real," in *Bodies That Matter*, 187–222.

64. Brown, *Plain Brown Rapper*, 200.

65. Brown, *Plain Brown Rapper*, 121.

66. Brown, *Plain Brown Rapper*, 197.

Chapter 6

1. Lillian Faderman, afterword to *Cross–Purposes: Lesbians, Feminists, and the Limits of Alliance*, ed. Dana Heller (Indiana University Press, 1997), 221–229; 228.

2. Sarah Schulman, *Girls, Visions and Everything* (Seattle: Seal Press, 1986). Hereafter, page numbers will be provided parenthetically in the text.

3. Biddy Martin, *Femininity Played Straight: The Significance of Being Lesbian* (New York: Routledge, 1996), 93.

4. Annamarie Jagose, *Queer Theory: An Introduction* (New York: New York University Press, 1996), 1.

5. Gail Rubin's article "Thinking Sex: Notes for a Radical Theory of the Politics of Sexuality" opens with the pronouncement, "The time has come to think about sex." (Rubin, "Thinking Sex," in *Pleasure and Danger: Exploring Female Sexuality*, ed. Carole S. Vance [Boston: Routledge and Kegan Paul, 1984]; *The Lesbian and Gay Studies Reader*, ed. Henry Abelove, Michèle Aina Barale, and David Halperin [New York: Routledge, 1993], 3.)

6. Cary Wolfe, *Critical Environments: Postmodern Theory and the Pragmatics of the "Outside"* (Minneapolis: University of Minnesota Press, 1998), xviii.

7. Judith Butler, *Bodies That Matter: On the Discursive Limits of "Sex"* (New York: Routledge, 1993), 3.

8. Wolfe, 18.

9. Tom Cohen, "The 'Genealogies' of Pragmatism," in *Rhetoric, Sophistry, Pragmatism*, ed. Steven Mailloux (Cambridge: Cambridge University Press, 1995), 94–108, see 96 (emphasis added).

10. Butler, *Bodies That Matter*, 282 (note 8).

11. ibid., 10.

12. ibid., 282 (note 7).

13. Wolfe, xvii.

14. Martha C. Nussbaum, "The Professor of Parody," *The New Republic* (22 February 1999), 38. I want to be clear that my own engagement with Butler is motivated not by an objection to her sometimes difficult language or by an uneasiness with "theory" *per se*, but with a much more specific concern that vestiges of structuralist idealization can be seen to imbue her theorization of performativity to unfortunate effect.

15. Butler, 8.

16. Butler, 16. Throughout, Butler wisely maintains a "certain suspicion towards grammar" which she holds necessary "to reconceive the matter in a different light" (7). And, indeed, grammar might seem to fail us here. If it is in any case difficult to conceive of "bodies which fail to materialize," it is next to impossible to reconcile this figuration of the abject as "bodies" devoid of materiality with Butler's insistence that "the abject designates [a domain] *densely populated* by those who do not enjoy the status of the subject, but whose living under the sign of the 'unlivable' is required to circumscribe the domain of the subject" (3). By seeming to conflate (rather than connect) legitimacy with materiality, "bodies that matter" threatens to dissolve into meaningless metaphor instead of signalling the complex interrelation between authority and existence it is intended to convey.

In a 1998 interview, however, Butler invites us to reconceive this dilemma in the context of "a different kind of question, namely, How is it that the domain of ontology is itself circumscribed by power?" The "whole domain of ontology," she argues, "is profoundly tainted from the start." In this context, the idea of "abject bodies" is reconceived as a "performative contradiction" intended to "endow ontology to precisely that which has been systematically deprived of the privilege of ontology," to "confound the conceptually proper philosopher," and to "pose a question about the secondary and derivative status of ontology" (Irene Costera and Baukje Prins, "How Bodies Come to Matter: An Interview with Judith Butler," *SIGNS* 23, no. 2 (Winter 1998): 275–286; 280. Although I would argue that pragmatism similarly complicates the "conceptually proper" division between ontology and epistemology, I remain somewhat less sanguine about the capacity of assertions to "endow ontology." Butler proposes that her project is "to roundly inaugurate an ontological domain[;] it is discursively to institute one" (280–281).

17. Butler, 8, 221. This is a vision of poststructuralism that resembles multiple structuralisms, each sutured into its own reality, collectively destined to continual conflict and mutual misapprehension. Within the framework of such understandings, change can be explained only as an effect of internal inconsistency, either inherent (a decidely determinist model) or (on the linguistic model) instigated by contagion or conquest. Either way, the tendency would appear to be towards greater homogeneity, away from multiplicity. Clearly, this is not what Butler has in mind when she speaks of "the kind of variation and rearticulation required for an anti–essentialist radical democratic project" (211).

18. ibid., 22.

19. ibid., 7 (emphasis added).

20. ibid., 225 (emphasis added).

21. In the founding gesture of structuralist linguistics, Saussure divides language into two distinct spheres, *langue* (the abstract system of language) and *parole* (actual speech), and asserts that the domain of linguistic science is properly restricted to the former. He further divides the study of (abstract systems of) language into two distinct branches, synchronic ("static") and diachronic ("evolutionary") linguistics, and focuses the lectures that would become his famous *Course in General Linguistics* on the former. In other words, Saussurean structuralism delimits its object of study by first removing it from space, and then separating it from time. Saussure insists it is "absolutely impossible to study simultaneously relations in time and relations within the system"; structuralism is the study of relations within the system. (Ferdinand de Saussure, *Course in General Linguistics*, ed. Charles Bally and Albert Sechehaye, in collaboration with Albert Riedlinger, trans. Wade Baskin [The Philosophical Library, 1959; McGraw–Hill paperback edition, 1966], see especially 98, 81.)

22. Saussure's lectures state plainly that "the linguistic sign unites, not a thing and a name, but a concept and a sound–image," which Saussure terms "signified" and "signifier." If the notes seem somewhat inconsistent regarding the nature of the latter term, they at least make quite clear that the signifier "is

not the material sound, a purely physical thing." To the contrary, both signifier and signified "are psychological and are united in the brain by an associative bond[;] this point must be emphasized" (Saussure, *Course*, 65–67).

23. By Peirce, for example. See also Teresa de Lauretis, "Habit Changes," *Differences* 6, no. 2–3 (summer–fall 1994): 296–313.

24. "The subject is constituted through the force of exclusion and abjection, one which produces a constitutive outside to the subject, an abjected outside, which is, after all, 'inside' the subject as its own founding repudiation" (Butler, *Bodies That Matte*r, 3).

25. This is not to say that it escapes the conceptual, but exactly the opposite—situation and duration are suffused by the social.

26. Laura Doan, ed., *The Lesbian Postmodern* (New York: Columbia, 1994), xi.

27. ibid., x.

28. John Stuhr, *Genealogical Pragmatism: Philosophy, Experience, and Community* (Albany, NY: State University of New York Press, 1997), 108.

29. Naiad is the oldest and largest lesbian press active in the United States. Sarah Schulman, *My American History: Lesbian and Gay Life During the Reagan/Bush Years* (New York: Routledge, 1994), xvii.

30. Sally Munt, "'*Somewhere over the rainbow . . .*' Postmodernism and the Fiction of Sarah Schulman," in *New Lesbian Criticism: Literary and Cultural Readings*, ed. Sally Munt (New York: Columbia University Press, 1992), 42. An abbreviated, but not substantially revised version of this reading is incorporated in Sally R. Munt, *Heroic Desire: Lesbian Identity and Cultural Space* (New York: New York University Press, 1998), 45–47.

31. Munt, *Heroic Desire*, 47.

32. *Midnight Notes*; quoted on back cover of *Girls, Visions and Everything* (Seattle: Seal Press, 1986).

33. Munt, "'*Somewhere Over the Rainbow*,'" 40; see also *Heroic Desire*, 46.

34. Janet L. Abu–Lughod, ed., *From Urban Village to East Village: The Battle for New York's Lower East Side* (Cambridge, MA: Blackwell, 1994), 28.

35. Christopher Mele, "The Process of Gentrification in Alphabet City," in Abu–Lughod, 181.

36. Abu–Lughod, 33, 34; Mele, 170.

37. Mele, 172–174.

38. Butler, 224.

39. Munt, "'*Somewhere Over the Rainbow*,'" 42.

40. Roof, *Come As You Are*, 179.

41. Neil Smith, Betsey Duncan, and Laura Reid, "From Disinvestment to Reinvestment: Mapping the Urban 'Frontier' in the Lower East Side," in Abu–Lughod, 149.

42. William Sites, "Public Action: New York City Policy and the Gentrification of the Lower East Side," in Abu–Lughod, 189.

43. Nancy Sullivan, Political Art Documentation/Distribution Project against Displacement poster, 1984. Reproduced in *Arts in America* 72, no. 6 (summer 1984): 163.

44. Munt, "'*Somewhere Over the Rainbow*,'" 42; *Heroic Desire*, 47. *Girls, Visions and Everything*, 164.

45. Interestingly, the incident interrupts an interlude of identification between Lila and Vicki grounded not in a shared relation to contemporary popular culture, but in their somewhat similar family histories.

> [Driving back to the city, T]hey sang along with the radio for awhile, but they didn't know any of the same songs, so then they started talking about their grandmothers. Vicki's had worked the land in Louisiana, Lila's worked the land in Lithuania. Both of their moms used to take them to the library to read books. Both of their moms freaked out when they got new ideas from the books they read. Both had inherited remnants of poverty that they were the first generation to avoid. (96)

Schulman refuses to allow her characters' similar experiences or chosen affiliation to erase the particularities of their personal histories or obscure the specificity of their in(ter)dependent situations. Vicki's grandmother saved scraps of aluminum foil; Lila has one grandmother who always "added rice to stretch her chopped meat," but another who "always had cream in her coffee" (96). Their crucially different relation to intransigent American racism is a salient dimension of their distinct experiences and knowledges—a difference that Schulman, like America, won't let us forget—but it's not the whole story.

46. Apparently, another true–to–life detail: Abu–Lughod notes that "'cleaning up the park' became central to the city's and developers' strategy of 'cleaning up the city'" in the 1980s (7).

47. Munt, "'*Somewhere Over the Rainbow*,'" 42; *Heroic Desire*, 47.

48. James Hoopes, *Community Denied: The Wrong Turn of Pragmatic Liberalism* (Ithaca: Cornell University Press, 1998), 184. See also Vincent M. Colapietro, *Peirce's Approach to the Self: A Semiotic Perspective on Human Subjectivity* (Albany, NY: State University of New York Press, 1989).

49. Sandra B. Rosenthal, *Charles Peirce's Pragmatic Pluralism* (Albany, NY: State University of New York Press, 1994), 11. And in light of Peirce's clear disinterest in "clear origins and ultimate goals," Rosenthal's conclusion that "it is the foundation for such a pluralistic community, rather than the drive toward unanimity in final knowledge, that lies at the heart of Peirce's pragmatic position" makes sense (20).

50. Butler, 219.

51. Paraphrased in Schulman, *My American History*, 6.

52. Munt, *Heroic Desire*, 47.

53. In *Girls, Visions and Everything*, Isabel's plays are described as "tales of average lesbians and the little things they knew and cared about" (17).

54. C.S. Peirce, *Collected Papers of Charles Sanders Peirce*, ed. Charles

Hartshorne and Paul Weiss (vols. 1–6) and Arthur Burks (vols. 7–8) (Cambridge, MA: Harvard University Press, 1931–58), 2.274 (Peirce's italics).

55. Peirce, 2.274, emphasis added.

56. "To the extent that a term is performative, it does not merely refer, but acts in some way to constitute that which it enunciates. The 'referent' of a performative is a kind of *action* which the performative itself calls for and participates in. Rigid designation, on the other hand, presumes the alterity of the referent, and the transparency of its own indexical function." (Butler, 217, Butler's emphasis)

57. And each of these perspectives is similarly grounded in shifting points of reference, and so on, *ad infinitum*.

58. Butler, 219.

59. Abu-Lughod, 28

60. ibid., 36, 28.

61. ibid., 36.

62. ibid., 28.

63. Hoopes, 184.

64. Rita Mae Brown, *Rubyfruit Jungle* (1973; New York: Bantam, 1977), 172.

65. Munt, "'*Somewhere Over the Rainbow*,'" 41. (In 1998, she revises these terms to "the 'masculine' trajectory of *On The Road* individualism and the 'feminine' circularity and disruption of affective liaisons" [*Heroic Desire*, 46].)

66. Brian Massumi, *A User's Guide to Capitalism and Schizophrenia: Deviations from Deleuze and Guattari* (Cambridge, MA: MIT Press, 1992), 178 (note 73); quoted in Wolfe, 87–88.

67. Cornel West, *The American Evasion of Philosophy: A Genealogy of Pragmatism* (Madison: University of Wisconsin Press, 1989).

68. Rosenthal, 27.

69. Rosenthal, 84.

70. Wolfe, 129.

Afterword

1. Roof acknowledges that it is a problematic and precarious foundation for engendering social change:

> Identification is the mode of joinder that brings narrative and life together. While narrative's transformations may appear to be internal to any specific story, social benefits come from the assumption that narrative's content will effect, reinforce, and shift social behavior. The mechanism for such affect is not simply narrative's irresistible offer of mastery but also some form of imitation that initiates the story's reproduction elsewhere. Imitation is understood in terms of identification, a more psychically

> specific mechanism whose assumed site in the person (instead of in culture or in the story) presumably accounts for how narratives get from culture to the individual, from example to praxis.

If narrative is understood to "provide the possibility of social transformation," Roof acknowledges, "the mechanism upon which all of this depends is identification, which, as a narrative process itself, may be more a heteroideological fiction than a useful assumption of praxis" (*Come As You Are*, 152–53).

2. For particularly responsible and astute engagements, see Suzanna Danuta Walters, "From Here to Queer," *SIGNS* 21, no. 4 (summer 1996): 830–869; Shane Phelan, "(Be)Coming Out: Lesbian Identity and Politics," *SIGNS* 18, no. 4 (summer 1993): 765–790; Biddy Martin, "Sexualities Without Genders and Other Queer Utopias," *Diacritics*, 1994; reprinted in Martin, *Femininity Played Straight* (New York: Routledge, 1996), 71–94.

3. Eve Sedgwick, *Epistemology of the Closet* (Berkeley: University of California Press, 1990), 85.

4. Fiona Webster, "The Politics of Sex and Gender: Benhabib and Butler Debate Subjectivity," *Hypatia: A Journal of Feminist Philosophy* 15, no. 1 (winter, 2000): 1–22.

5. Shannon Sullivan, "Reconfiguring Gender with John Dewey: Habits, Bodies, and Cultural Change," *Hypatia: A Journal of Feminist Philosophy* 15, no. 1 (winter, 2000): 23–42.

6. Webster, 12, 18.

7. Indeed, she observes, and I would agree, that Butler is on occasion "very pragmatist–sounding" (Sullivan, 26, 33).

8. In *Alice Doesn't*, 158–186, and *Technologies of Gender*, 38–42, as well as in *The Practice of Love*, 298–312.

9. Sullivan, 34. She also quotes Dewey on this point: "What is necessary is that habits be formed which are more intelligent, more sensitively percipient, more informed with foresight, more aware of what they are about, more direct and sincere, more flexibly responsible than those now current."

10. "The lack of agreement between the various habits that we are undercuts any final, stable, unified identity that we might think our habits, as constitutive of ourselves, might provide" (35); or, more directly, "Because of the complexity and criss–crossing of the lines of cultural power that penetrate the body via its habits, gender (as well as other) habits can cut against one another to break up both their own fixity and the fixity of cultural gender constructs" (24).

11. Sullivan, 37–39; Webster, 18.

12. As discussed, for example, in Chapter 4.

13. Webster, 18 (emphasis added).

14. Evelynn Hammonds, "Black (W)holes and the Geometry of Black Female Sexuality" *differences* 6, no. 2–3 (summer–fall 1994): 126–145; 131.

15. Rita Mae Brown, *Rubyfruit Jungle* (Plainfield, VT: Daughters, 1973; New York: Bantam, 1977); Mary McCarthy, *The Group* (New York: Harcourt, 1963); Dorothy Allison, *Bastard out of Carolina* (New York: Dutton, 1992);

Leslie Feinberg, *Stone Butch Blues* (Ithaca: Firebrand, 1993); Sheila Ortiz Taylor, *Faultline* (Tallahassee: Naiad, 1982).

16. Gloria Anzaldúa, *Borderlands/La Frontera: The New Mestiza* (San Francisco: Spinsters/Aunt Lute, 1987).

17. Hammonds, 131.

18. Teresa de Lauretis, "The Technology of Gender," *Technologies of Gender: Essays on Theory, Film, and Fiction* (Bloomington: Indiana University Press, 1987), 1–30.

19. Hammonds, 128.

20. Webster, 18. (Needless to say, this would require a performative power well beyond what Butler herself appears ready to claim.)

Index